Legal Issues in
Counselling &
Psychotherapy

Ethics in Practice Series

Ethics in Practice edited by Tim Bond is a series of short, practical guides to ethical issues which confront counsellors, psychotherapists and other professionals everyday. Suitable for both students and practitioners, the books are designed to give a clearer understanding of issues which are often considered complex and contentious.

Books in the series:

Therapy with Children
Debbie Daniels and Peter Jenkins

Pastoral Care & Counselling
Gordon Lynch

Legal Issues in Counselling & Psychotherapy

Edited by
Peter Jenkins

SAGE Publications
London • Thousand Oaks • New Delhi

First published 2002

 SAGE Publications Ltd
6 Bonhill Street
London EC2A 4PU

SAGE Publications Inc
2455 Teller Road
Thousand Oaks, California 91320

SAGE Publications India Pvt Ltd
32, M-Block Market
Greater Kailash - I
New Delhi 110 048

British Library Cataloguing in Publication data

A catalogue record for this book is available
from the British Library

ISBN 0 7619 5480 5
ISBN 0 7619 5481 3 (pbk)

Library of Congress Control Number: 2001132959

Typeset by C&M Digitals (P) Ltd., Chennai, India
Printed in Great Britain by TJ International Ltd, Padstow, Cornwall

Contents

List of Contributors   vii

Acknowledgements   x

Introduction   1
Peter Jenkins

Part I: The Legal Context of Therapeutic Practice   13

1   Confidentiality: A case study   15
    Stephen Palmer

2   Psychoanalyst subpoenaed   21
    Anne Hayman

3   Legal pitfalls in counselling and psychotherapy practice,
    and how to avoid them   24
    Gideon Cristofoli

4   Taking legal action against a therapist
    for professional negligence   34
    Inge Power

5   Transparent recording: Therapists and
    the Data Protection Act 1998   45
    Peter Jenkins

6   Preparing reports and presenting evidence in court:
    A guide for counsellors and psychotherapists   57
    Philip Pollecoff

Part II: Legal Challenges for Therapy   73

7   Regulating counselling and psychotherapy:
    Lessons from complementary medicine   75
    Julie Stone

8 Legal Issues in therapeutic work with adult survivors
   of sexual abuse   88
   Annabell Bell-Boulé and *Très Roche*

9 Counselling in legal settings: Provision for jury
   members, vulnerable witnesses and victims of crime   105
   Brian Williams

10 The law of confidentiality – a solution or part
   of the problem?   123
   Tim Bond

11 False memories or recovered memories? Legal and
   ethical implications for therapists   144
   Peter Jenkins

12 The implications of the Human Rights Act 1998 for
   counsellors and psychotherapists   165
   Vincent Keter

   Appendix 1 The Academy of Experts: Model
   form of Expert's Report   173

   Appendix 2 Therapy notes and the law   176
   Stephen Jakobi and *Duncan Pratt*

   Appendix 3 Relevant organisations   183

   References   188

   Table of Cases   188

   Table of Statutes   189

   Index   190

List of Contributors

Annabell Bell-Boulé is a UKCP Registered Psychotherapist and Senior Lecturer in Law at Nottingham Trent University. She is a trainer in law and ethics for counsellors and psychotherapists, and is the author of 'Psychotherapy and the law', *International Journal of Psychotherapy* (1999), Vol 4, No 2.

Tim Bond (PhD, FBACP) is Reader in Counselling and Professional Ethics at the University of Bristol. He is a former chairman of the British Association for Counselling (1994-6). He researches and writes about ethical, legal and professional issues for counselling and the caring professions, and is the author of *Standards and Ethics for Counselling in Action* (Sage, 2000).

Gideon Cristofoli is a partner in the legal firm of Bookers and Bolton Solicitors, in Hampshire. He has regularly advised the United Kingdom Council for Psychotherapy, and has a niche practice, advising therapy and psychotherapy institutions and individuals in contentious and non-contentious law.

Anne Hayman retired in 1998 after more than forty years' practice as a psychoanalyst of adults and children, being much involved latterly in teaching as training analyst of the British Psychoanalytical Society. Inter alia she was council member, secretary of Education committee and chair of Scientific Committee. Publications include various psychoanalytic scientific papers.

Stephen Jakobi was formerly a solicitor to the Psychologists Protection Society. He is currently a human rights lawyer, and Director of Fair Trials Abroad, a legal charity.

Peter Jenkins is Lecturer in Counselling at the University of Manchester and a member of BACPs Professional Conduct Committee. He has written widely on aspects of the law and therapy, and is the author of *Counselling, Psychotherapy and the Law* (Sage, 1997), and is co-author, with Debbie Daniels, of *Therapy with Children* (Sage, 2000).

Vincent Keter holds a law degree from Birkbeck College, and has since qualified as a barrister. He has acted in a number of key legal cases concerning therapists and their professional associations, such as the UKCP and BPS. He represents clients and psychotherapists in disciplinary tribunals, complaints proceedings and judicial review. Vincent is currently completing a PhD in Law and Psychoanalysis at Birkbeck.

Stephen Palmer (PhD, FBACP) is Director of the Centre for Stress Management, London, Honorary Professor of Psychology at City University, and Visiting Professor of Work Based Learning and Stress Management at the National Centre for Work Based Learning Partnerships at Middlesex University. He is a Chartered Psychologist and UKCP Registered Psychotherapist. He has written or edited over 25 books.

Philip Pollecoff is a solicitor and senior partner in a firm franchised to undertake legal aid work in family, crime, matrimonial and housing law. He provides training for organisations on legal issues and counselling.

Inge Power is a pseudonym.

Duncan Pratt is a barrister in specialist healthcare law chambers. He has conducted clinical negligence claims involving most medical specialties. Other areas of practice include substantial personal injury claims, solicitors' negligence, product liability, employment and disciplinary tribunals.

Très Roche is a BACP Registered Counsellor. She is the co-ordinator of the Sexual Abuse Project, which offers group therapy to adult women survivors of childhood sexual abuse. She is a counsellor and supervisor based in Nottingham.

Julie Stone was, at the time of writing, Visiting Scholar, Department of Political Science, University of Hawaii. A lawyer and long time lecturer in health care ethics and law, she has been a member of the Regulation and Education Working Groups of the Prince of Wales' Initiative, the Foundation for Integrated Medicine. She was a member of the North Thames Multi-Centre Research Ethics Committee, and the Management Committee of the Prevention of Professional Abuse Network (POPAN). She has recently published *An Ethical Framework for Complementary and Alternative Therapists* (Routledge, 2002) and co-authored *Complementary Medicine and the Law* (Oxford University Press, 1996).

Dr Brian Williams is Professor in the Community and Criminal Justice Division at De Montfort University, Leicester. He is the author of *Working with Victims of Crime* (Jessica Kingsley, 1999), and *Counselling in Criminal Justice* (Open University Press, 1996), as well as a number of articles. He worked for 13 years as a probation officer, and is a volunteer with a Victim Support project.

Acknowledgements

I would like to acknowledge the work that has gone into the production of this book from a wide range of people, including, not least, the contributors and those who have kindly agreed to the reprinting of their previously published material. Tim Bond, as Series Editor, enthusiastically oversaw the book from its initial inception to its eventual appearance. Staff at Sage, including Alison Poyner, Louise Wise, Joyce Lynch, and Rachel Burrows, have been unfailingly helpful, as always. My colleagues at the University of Central Lancashire, including Maureen Robinson, Jim Martin, Peter Cardew, Judith Warren, Angie Smith, Andrew Webb, John Dunn, Peter Glenn and other counselling colleagues have been a major source of support and encouragement. My wife, Jane, and my daughters, Rachel and Lisa, are also gratefully thanked for allowing me the space to work on this, in between the more pressing requirements of modern family life.

Acknowledgements are due to the following journals and organisations for kind permission to reprint material:

The Lancet for the article by Anne Hayman, first published as 'Psychoanalyst Subpoenaed' in *The Lancet*, October 16, 1965, pp. 785–6 © *The Lancet*.

Counselling and Psychotherapy Journal (British Association for Counselling and Psychotherapy) for the article by Peter Jenkins on data protection © BACP.

British Journal of Guidance and Counselling for the article by Peter Jenkins on false memory © Taylor & Francis. See www.tandf.co.uk

The Academy of Experts for the Model Form of Expert's Report reproduced as an Appendix.

The Psychologist (British Psychological Society) for the article by Stephen Jakobi and Duncan Pratt © *The Psychologist*, reproduced as an Appendix.

Disclaimer

Nothing in this book constitutes legal advice and the reader is cautioned against relying on any of the material in respect of any specific legal issue with which they are faced, since the material reflects only the opinion and commentary of the respective authors in general terms. These opinions may have changed since the publication of this book or the original publication of those articles which have been reprinted. Furthermore there may have been changes in the law since publication.

Introduction

Peter Jenkins

This book is aimed at a broad readership from the world of counselling, counselling psychology and psychotherapy, including students, trainees, practitioners, supervisors and service managers. It is a response to the need for up to date and often more specialised coverage of issues which increasingly present a challenge to therapists. (The terms 'therapist' and 'therapy' are used here in a generic sense.) From a (perhaps fantasised?) halcyon time when external constraints could largely be ignored, many therapists now express anxiety about, or face the uncomfortable reality of, the law intruding into the private space of their work with clients. This can take the form of court requests for notes, with such accounts of incidents featuring increasingly prominently in the professional press (Barnett 2001; Hudson Allez 2001). Changes in data protection law similarly represent a significant inroad into the prized concept of therapeutic privacy for therapist and client alike. Requests for the provision of court reports thrust the practitioner into an arena where their professional training and expertise may be limited or subject to abrupt and unsettling challenge by lawyers. Professional competence is an issue further at stake in the hostile context of litigation, where aggrieved clients may seek to achieve redress for real or imagined wrongs. Statutory regulation, once perceived as a major potential solution to the problems of monitoring and policing 'bad therapy', will itself, no doubt, encounter fresh difficulties, if the relevant experience of parallel groups such as complementary medicine is any guide. As therapists have engaged with major social concerns within their work, such as the effects of childhood sexual abuse, recovered and false memories of such abuse, and the needs of those caught up in the criminal legal system, the real complexity of their task has become more apparent. While case law on therapy has grown gradually (for reasons of major significance), recent changes in statute law present significant challenges to established therapeutic practices in the areas of data protection and human rights. These factors make an update on the state of therapy and the law an imperative rather than an option for hard-pressed practitioners, given the relative paucity of accessible material on this topic. And, it should be said, if there is a pressing need for therapists to get to grips with the legal dimensions of their practice, there is a corresponding, and still largely unrecognised, parallel need for *lawyers* to appreciate the therapeutic and emotional dimensions of their legal activities: hence this book.

The format of the book requires some introduction. There has gradually developed a resource base for practitioners of key articles on the subject of therapy and the law, of which Anne Hayman's article is probably the most striking example. These constitute essential points of reference, but are often hard to obtain for those without easy access to university or more specialised professional libraries. This book, therefore, includes several key articles already published, which fall into this category of invaluable, but hard-to-find, sources. These are supplemented by other more recently published material, dealing with topics of major importance for therapists currently concerned about the law, but, again, largely confined to the readership of the specialist or professional press. Finally, there are commissioned chapters dealing with areas of clear concern to therapists, such as the use of contracts, report writing, and confidentiality. In addition, there are chapters exploring areas of therapeutic practice with a significant legal loading, such as in victim and witness support, work with survivors of sexual abuse and the prospects for statutory regulation. A number of chapters are written by solicitors and barristers with particular knowledge of their areas, as well as by therapists, some legally qualified, on their respective areas of expertise. The book is unusual, and indeed privileged, to contain a personal account by a client detailing the difficulties experienced in therapy leading to successful litigation against her own therapist, in the face of the multiple obstacles presented by the legal system.

The book hints at the state of the present, somewhat uneasy, relationship of therapy to the law. The current state of play is seen in terms of *challenges* to counselling, psychotherapy and related fields, rather than in terms of more loaded language, which might depict it as a process of threat, intrusion, or even eclipse of the therapeutic enterprise. Critics of the unequal relationship of law and psychoanalysis such as Christopher Bollas and David Sundelson, for example, have railed passionately against the creeping process of the 'legalisation of therapy' (1995). However, the current state of play between therapy and the law still offers limited but real opportunities for therapy to influence apparently inflexible legal priorities, as in the vital area of provision of therapy for vulnerable child and adult victims of crime (CPS, 2001; Home Office, 2002; Palmer 2001). While there is clearly no cause for complacency about the potential and actual inroads into client and therapist confidentiality available to the courts, it is argued in these pages that this is a time for taking stock, rather than for admitting defeat.

Any exploration of the relationship of therapy to the law needs perhaps to state the obvious, that the law is not a unitary system in the United Kingdom and that there are significant differences between the three legal systems covering England and Wales, Scotland and Northern

Ireland. The focus of this book deals mainly with the law relating to England and Wales, unless otherwise stated. In addition, the actual application of the law may vary according to the *employment context* of the individual therapist, i.e. whether the therapist is working as self-employed or employed by an organisation, and according to *setting*, such as working for a statutory agency or in private practice. Client factors such as *age* may also have a direct bearing on the legal context of practice, as in determining the relative weight that can be given to the autonomous wishes of young people under sixteen, according to the *Gillick* principle (Daniels and Jenkins, 2000).

The structure of the book is based on first setting out the legal context of therapeutic practice, in terms of confidentiality, contract, data protection, court reports and litigation against therapists. The second part then explores specific areas of legal challenge to counselling and psychotherapy, such as statutory regulation, and the potential impact of human rights law. Related concerns include working within the criminal justice system, issues arising from therapy with adult survivors of sexual abuse, and the associated problematic issue of allegedly false memories of such abuse.

A different grouping of the book's material on a thematic basis could be made, as a way of drawing out some linking themes and ideas within the differing contributions. Law can be variously experienced by therapists as setting the legal context for practice, as authorising an unwelcome intrusion into therapeutic privacy, or, more positively, as offering opportunities for engagement and dialogue with the legal system. Many of the articles contain material which reflects more than one theme, so this basis would not be appropriate here as a rationale for the actual ordering of the sequence of contributions. Rather, it is offered as a way of linking some of the recurring concerns and motifs of the various contributions, and perhaps also providing some perspective on the state of the law's varying impact on therapeutic work.

Law as the context for therapy

The law provides the necessary social context for therapeutic practice in a number of respects, not least in providing a sanction for professional malpractice, via litigation or action for breach of contract. The barriers presented by the system of negligence law to effective client redress are taken up in the piece writtten under a pseudonym by Inge Power. She graphically describes her experience of 'falling for therapy' (cf Sands, 2000). Inge Power portrays the emotional and financial exploitation which her therapist wreaked upon her via a co-existing unethical set of dual relationships as therapist, mentor and business partner. She outlines also her radically changing perception of these overlapping relationships, ultimately coming to see her mentor-therapist as an unscrupulous charlatan, rather than as a gifted and charismatic practitioner. She recounts the devastating personal impact of repeated boundary violations, the confusion generated by the interaction of multiple roles, and the underlying and pervasive influence of transference in this situation. The key role of support organisations such as POPAN is made clear, particularly in helping a client to unpick those elements of close therapeutic relationships which are valued, and those which are abusive. Translating emotional distress into the unyielding categories of the law is not an easy or straightforward process, particularly when the relationship is clouded by ambivalence, by the real (and metaphorical) 'roses and thorns' invoked by the author. Not least, this contribution illustrates the difficulties involved in seeking to bring a successful legal action for negligence against a therapist. Even this case ended with a moral victory, in the form of an out of court settlement, rather than with a legal resolution taking the form of a decision of a judge or jury. The account also shows how crucial it can be to obtain sympathetic and well-informed legal assistance, when the numbers of solicitors conversant with the relevant case law, such as *Werner v Landau*, are still comparatively few in number.

Protecting vulnerable clients is a standard element in arguments for statutory regulation, and this is addressed by Julie Stone. She reviews the case for regulation of the psychological therapies, as the other side of the coin to the bitter experiences of Inge Power. Stone concurs in the view that 'to suggest that incompetent or abusive therapy cannot cause harm to a patient is ludicrous', in reviewing the lessons arising from the process of regulation in the field of complementary and alternative medicine. However, her conclusion is that state control, in enforcing professional standards, protecting vulnerable clients, and punishing incompetent practitioners, is ultimately of limited value. Statutory regulation is not a panacea, she warns. This is instructive, at a time when the therapeutic community has just concluded a second major cycle of lobbying for government intervention, following on from the original unsuccessful phase of 1970–81 (Jenkins, 1997: 279–300). The third, and possibly conclusive cycle will now apparently take the provisions of the Health Act 1999 as its main axis for change, promising a further round of concerted activity by the major professional organisations.

Controlling malpractice remains a major, but not the sole, justification for the introduction of statutory regulation of therapy. As a solicitor, Gideon Cristofoli offers an alternative, or complementary, measure of self-regulation, via his exposition of the value of using contracts as a basic tool within the therapeutic relationship. He argues for the preventative value of contracts in establishing clear expectations, boundaries and communication between therapist and client, particularly concerning potentially contentious issues such as consent to physical touch within the context of therapeutic work.

Tim Bond writes with widely recognised authority on the topic of confidentiality. He has played a major pro-active role in clarifying legal and ethical issues for practitioners, based on recourse to legal opinion in several key situations. He claims, with justification, that 'few issues produce as much concern and are a source of such difficulty' for current practitioners as the practical management of confidentiality. The concept of therapeutic confidentiality occupies a position as a boundary post, marking the contested frontier between the private sphere of therapy, and the public sphere delineated by the courts and the legal system. Therefore, therapy is inevitably inserted into a context of pre-existing legal relationships concerning the control, release and diffusion of personal information.

Common law defences of 'confidence', to use the lawyer's preferred term for once, have now been buttressed by statute. The editor's own chapter on the impact of data protection legislation takes the view that this represents a major change to the traditional practice of therapeutic recording. The adoption of a more open, European-based, perspective on the keeping of personal data will require a definite shift towards more transparent systems of recording. Data protection law presents a major cultural challenge to established forms of professional recording within therapy, namely the existence of a 'dual system'. The latter consists of factual, 'objective' and public forms of recording existing alongside a more associative, subjective and private form of recording. Whatever the perceived value of such personal forms of recording for training, personal reflection and professional development, the onus is now on the therapeutic community to adapt to a more open and shared style of record-keeping, as other professional groups in social work and medicine have had to undertake under pressure of earlier similar legislation.

The other major piece of legislation with significant implications for therapists is the Human Rights Act 1998. Vincent Keter, a barrister, writes from the vantage point of personal and professional experience of using the law to challenge decisions made by professional bodies in the world of therapy, such as the United Kingdom Council for Psychotherapy and the British Psychological Society. He claims, perhaps surprisingly in view of the generally received wisdom on this topic, that the human rights law actually strengthens the relative position of counsellors and therapists, rather than clients. He also explores the process of the increasing 'legalisation' of professional complaints procedures, and its relationship to the developing principles of human rights law.

Law as terrain for resolving social conflicts

The law exists as more than simply providing a context for therapeutic work, as in terms of contract, confidentiality and duty of care. The legal system also operates as the *terrain* for deciding and resolving contentious issues which directly impinge on the *content* of therapeutic work with clients. The most striking example of this has surely been the caustic debate on false memories as opposed to recovered memories of early childhood sexual abuse. This has been a powerful psychodrama in legal garb, played out in the courtroom as well as in the therapeutic workspace. The litigation associated with this phenomenon has arguably represented the most serious legal challenge to the integrity and scientific credibility of therapeutic culture in the past decade on both sides of the Atlantic. The editor's approach has been to explore this contentious and often confusing issue from the perspective of ethics as well as in terms of the law, and to try to tease out some of the conflicting loyalties and priorities that can be experienced by therapists in this demanding area of practice.

Ethical issues and legal duties may overlap or be in potential conflict here, as elsewhere in counselling and psychotherapy. As Tim Bond suggests in his own chapter, 'what is ethical may not be legal. What is legal may be unethical'. This chapter also uses a basic therapeutic model, the drama triangle drawn from Transactional Analysis, to help elucidate the legal roles and adversarial positions adopted in the false memory debate, with regard to the otherwise complex processes of litigation and counter-litigation on this issue.

Law as intrusion into therapeutic practice

The preceding chapters revolve around the theme of the law as providing a context for therapeutic work. A counterpoint to this theme is that of the law as constituting an unwelcome *intrusion* into the therapeutic space. This theme is strongly present in the chapter contributed by Stephen Palmer, a case study featuring the encroachment of the legal process into the fragile privacy of the therapeutic space. This is an expanded version of an article originally published in various forms in the professional press, presented here with updated client consent. The piece charts the progressive intrusion of the legal process into the written, and then audio, recordings of therapeutic work, culminating in the formal requirement for the therapist to act as a witness in court proceedings. This painful experience does more than underline the point made elsewhere about the lack of privilege for counsellors and psychotherapists in court proceedings: it powerfully illustrates the double disadvantage faced by clients involved in legal action, where court access to records of therapy has become a hotly contested issue. In the first place, the client cannot restrict or limit the disclosure of sensitive personal information, simply by picking and choosing what the court can have or not have access to in terms of records. This choice rests ultimately solely with the authority of the court itself. Second, the client may be pressured to release the broadest range of personal information, which is often much more sensitive and potentially damaging than first realised. Failure to do so may lead to a further disadvantage for the client, in the shape of threats to discontinue their civil case for compensation or the prosecution of an alleged offender without their full co-operation in disclosing potential evidence. The result is often the client and therapist having to balance a substantial erosion of personal and professional privacy, against the necessarily uncertain outcome of a court case. The court case, in any event, may possibly lead to the further exposure of client and therapist personal and professional vulnerability via the challenging process of examination-in-chief and cross-examination.

The motif of resistance to this diminution of the therapeutic space is strongly expressed in the classic article written by Anne Hayman, a psychoanalyst. This piece, originally written as an anonymous article for *The Lancet*, and republished here with a brief postscript, is frequently referred to in the literature on the subject of therapeutic privilege. It cogently describes her situation as a psychoanalyst, taking a principled stand against releasing *any* information, including even confirmation of the accused's status as her patient, as a breach of professional and therapeutic obligations, at the risk of being found in contempt of court. This commitment to clients, in terms of 'keeping their secrets under all circumstances' finds a contemporary echo in the impassioned rhetoric of Christopher Bollas (2001). There, the latter has argued fiercely for defending the 'freedom to free associate', without which serious therapeutic work becomes impoverished, and even eclipsed by dubious considerations of the public interest. Many practitioners would undoubtedly agree with Hayman's emphatic conclusion that 'Justice, as well as our ethic, is likely to be served best by silence'.

The 'Hayman case' as it is sometimes referred to, is often quoted and even more frequently misunderstood by therapists, who see it as establishing a defence of therapeutic privacy, which has, furthermore, been openly recognised by the courts. The truth is more prosaic than this, in that this represented an instance of *judicial discretion*, rather than the setting of a formal legal precedent. That is, unless it is thought that the precedent is for therapists to risk contempt of court, and a possible fine or jail sentence, in defiance of a witness summons to give evidence regarding a client. The other noteworthy point about this account is the sympathetic hearing obtained for the concept of transference in a court of law. This resonates with the crucial importance afforded the same concept in the main case of therapist negligence, *Werner v Landau* (Jenkins, 1997). This suggests that the courts are not entirely impervious or hostile to key therapeutic principles, capably translated to inform the workings of the law.

The legal basis of the lack of therapeutic 'privilege' is set out in the advice note produced by Stephen Jakobi and Duncan Pratt for the British Psychological Society, reprinted here with permission, as an appendix. This sets out very clearly the lack of legal protection for therapy records against an order for their disclosure by the courts. This is an issue with dramatically increasing immediacy and relevance for practitioners, given that the number of requests by solicitors for access, or the issuing of court orders for the release of documents, is becoming more routine. Solicitors appear to be enormously interested in the large amounts of 'soft' and often circumstantial information held on clients by therapists, either in their files, or in their memories. It seems increasingly to be standard practice for lawyers to enquire with legal clients whether they have received counselling for any condition in the past, when considering taking action in the courts. Alternatively, solicitors may suggest that their clients receive counselling, in order to provide additional evidence of a disputed condition, such as 'workplace stress'. This also provides access to an additional source of evidence or validation in the event of going to court.

Therapists are caught between a rock and a hard place on the issue of disclosure, as the experiences of Stephen Palmer and Anne Hayman can confirm. The threshold for disclosure has been an exacting one in the past. Under the quaintly referenced 'Peruvian Guano' case, there was formerly a duty for litigants to disclose the existence of documents 'even if they were of the most peripheral apparent relevance to the case' (Foster et al., 1996: 3). Yet there is a strong case to be made *against* the use of such fishing expeditions, trawling for therapeutic evidence of limited relevance to any legal case. Therapists were heartened by the view of one judge, Mr Justice Sedley, who forcefully argued at Crown Court that 'the grounds for production [of potential evidence] are limited to the possession or control of documents which are themselves admissible in evidence' (*R. v Hussain*, (1996)). This shift towards a much more proportionate and discriminating use of disclosure is strongly signalled in the recent *Civil Procedure Rules*, which confirm the overriding principle that 'disclosure should be restricted to what is necessary in the individual case' (CPR, 2001, 31.0.3). This would set a much higher and more appropriately exacting standard for limiting disclosure. Disclosure of therapeutic records would therefore be restricted to those essential to the proper hearing of a case, rather than those which were simply of more speculative interest.

Law as opportunity for engagement and dialogue

The final theme of contributions in this book concerns the potential for developing a partnership, or a more equal relationship, between therapy and the law. Annabell Bell-Boulé and Très Roche write with wide experience of working with adult survivors of sexual abuse, and apply key legal principles, such as duty of care and negligence, to this difficult area of practice. They pinpoint the relative lack of training in this field, and again stress the importance of working with solicitors who can understand the legal implications of abuse in a rounded and professional manner. While there is need for therapists to understand the broad contours of the law, there is no less a need for lawyers to come to terms with the complex relationship of therapy to legal processes. The pace of dialogue may be slow, but it is encouraging that the Crown Prosecution Service is now acknowledging the contribution to be made by therapeutic work with child and vulnerable adult victims of abuse, as noted previously.

The authors point to the complex dynamics of working with survivors, which can result in retraumatising the client in the process of seeking justice. There is often a strong and compelling need for survivors to regain their voice by telling their story, initially to a skilled and receptive therapist, and later, if need be, to a court of law. This can have powerful and unintended psychological consequences for the survivor him or herself, and also potentially for the therapist, which needs to be carefully considered.

This process is further explored by Brian Williams, writing from extensive experience of research and practice in the field of criminal justice. He writes about the process of secondary victimisation and revisiting of emotional trauma, as an often unavoidable requirement of the present legal system. The process of seeking justice can have damaging consequences for those caught up in it, such as witnesses, victims of crime, therapists, volunteer supporters and jurors, as the trial of Fred and Rosemary West graphically illustrated. A major recurring theme in this piece is the *lack of control* experienced by participants, in joining with a legal process which sets new and sometimes conflicting priorities over their personal desire to 'do the right thing'. Yet, the author concludes, the 'criminal justice process can … have a therapeutic value for victims of crime', if handled sensitively and effectively by the agencies and personnel involved. The pressing need here is for increasing cooperation and dialogue between therapeutic culture and the legal system, by developing existing good practice in the area of support for the immediate and indirect victims of crime.

The problematic relationship between therapy and the law is frequently noted by commentators. Judith Trowell, writing elsewhere on child protection issues, has concluded that there is 'an innate tension between a legal discourse and a clinical discourse' (2001: 90), and other writers have pointed out the gulf that exists between a legal and therapeutic worldview as applied to what constitutes evidence (Jackson, 2001). It seems fitting, therefore, to end this discussion by referring to the chapter written by a lawyer, Philip Pollecoff, who writes from a contrasting perspective. He acknowledges the real value of the therapist's contribution to the legal process. Current stereotypes of lawyers in the field of personal injury and clinical negligence may be of rapacious and unprincipled operators, the authors of the 'no win, no fee' hoardings in every hospital casualty ward, and the smooth presenters of seductive adverts on lunchtime television slots, touting for aggrieved customers. Philip offers a necessary corrective to this somewhat stereotypical vision, by arguing that 'the legal profession work long and hard in civil proceedings to *avoid* trials', perhaps contrary to the perception held by many therapists. He provides detailed and sound advice on the actual practicalities of giving evidence in court, or in presenting a report in legal proceedings, which will be welcomed by practitioners who are increasingly called upon to take on these roles. His useful advice, not the least of which is 'not speaking more quickly than the judge can write', is designed to maximise the impact of the therapist's contribution to the legal process. He notes that the boundaries are shifting between therapy and the law, notably with apparently increasing numbers of requests for therapists to act as professional and expert witnesses, providing formal recognition of the status and value of their expertise. If this activity is to be carried out effectively, then therapists need training and guidance in how to exercise these roles. What is beyond doubt, he claims, is the court's need for 'honest, impartial and learned expert opinion', which therapists, properly briefed and prepared, can play a vital role in providing. In conclusion, this book aims to contribute towards these vital steps of engagement and dialogue, by assisting in some small measure towards the empowerment of therapists and their clients within the legal process.

References

Barnett, R. (2001) 'A solicitor calls for case notes', *Counselling and Psychotherapy Journal*, 12(5) pp. 13–14.

Bollas, C. (2001) 'The misapplication of "reasonable mindedness": Is psychoanalysis possible with the present reporting laws in the USA and UK?', in Cordess, C. (ed.) *Confidentiality and Mental Health*. London: Jessica Kingsley. pp. 109–17.

Bollas, C. and Sundelson, D. (1995) *The New Informants: Betrayal of Confidentiality in Psychoanalysis and Psychotherapy*. London: Karnac.

Civil Procedure Rules (CPR) (2001) vol. 1, London: Sweet and Maxwell.

Crown Prosecution Service, Department of Health, Home Office (2001) *Provision of Therapy for Child Witnesses Prior to a Criminal Trial*. London: CPS.

Daniels, D. and Jenkins, P. (2000) *Therapy with Children: Children's Rights, Confidentiality and the Law*. London: Sage.

Foster, C., Wynn, T. and Ainley, N. (1996) *Disclosure and Confidentiality: A Practitioner's Guide*. London: Sweet and Maxwell.

Home Office (2002) *Provision of Therapy for Vulnerable and Intimidated Adult Witnesses Prior to a Criminal Trial: Practice Guidance (Consultation Document)*. London: Home Office.

Hudson Allez, G. (2001) 'Judge rules against confidentiality agreements', *Counselling in Practice*, 5(1), pp. 6–7

Jackson, J. (2001) 'A lawyer's view of evidence', in Mace, C., Moorey, S. and Roberts, B. (eds) *Evidence in the Psychological Therapies: A Critical Guide for Practice*. London: Routledge. pp. 12–26.

Jenkins, P. (1997) *Counselling, Psychotherapy and the Law*. London: Sage.

Palmer, T. (2001) 'Pre-trial therapy with children who have been sexually abused', in Richardson, S. and Bacon, H. (eds) *Creative Responses to Child Sexual Abuse: Challenges and Dilemmas*. London: Jessica Kingsley. pp. 152–66.

Sands, A. (2000) *Falling for Therapy: Psychotherapy from a Client's Point of View*. London: Macmillan.

Trowell, J. (2001) 'Confidentiality and child protection', in Cordess, C. (ed.) *Confidentiality and Mental Health*. London: Jessica Kingsley. pp. 85–94.

Legal References

Compagnie Financière du Pacifique v Peruvian Guano Co. (1882) 11 QBD 55

Gillick v West Norfolk and Wisbech Area Health Authority [1986] AC.112.

R. v Liaqat Hussain (1996) Reading Crown Court T960220

Werner v Landau (1961) TLR 8/3/1961, 23/11/1961, Sol Jo (1961) 105, 1008

Part One

THE LEGAL CONTEXT OF THERAPEUTIC PRACTICE

1

Confidentiality: A Case Study

Stephen Palmer

I'll start by setting the scene. I'm an experienced counsellor, counselling psychologist and psychotherapist. At the time of the case study, I was active in the British Association for Counselling and Psychotherapy and aware of all the codes of ethics. As I had previously edited the BACP journal, *Counselling*, and sat on the publications committee, I was up-to-date with current thinking regarding most aspects of counselling.

I practise cognitive, rational emotive behaviour, and multimodal therapy. In these forms of therapy, we usually encourage the therapist to record sessions to aid supervision. In addition, to enhance the psycho-educational nature of therapy, we would normally suggest that the clients record the sessions for their own benefit. In the comfort of their home, they often listen to the sections where they are given guidance on problems such as managing panic attacks or completing automatic thought records.

At the Centre for Stress Management where I practise, we have referrals from a number of health professionals, commercial and voluntary organisations. Clients can also contact us directly. Prior to therapy, we send the client general information about the centre, the therapy and a client checklist (see Palmer and Szymanska, 1994a; revised 1994b). As we are concerned about client exploitation, we developed this checklist to help potential clients focus on what to expect in therapy and what to ask their therapist about during the first session.

Case study

The therapy

An occupational health department of a commercial organisation referred Mary (not her real name) to us. Whenever this company had a member of staff who was stressed due to personal or work issues, they offered them about six to eight sessions of counselling financed by occupational health.

Mary's case started out no differently to the earlier clients from this organisation. She had received our details and checklist and we started the first session by her signing a simple contract clarifying fees and cancellation notice. We discussed issues relating to confidentiality. When third parties are involved such as occupational health departments it is very important to obtain explicit permission from clients as to the limits of confidentiality. We agreed that it would be helpful if we recorded the counselling sessions both to enhance my supervision and to aid her understanding of topics covered. At this time, there would have been nothing to suggest that a court case may be pending. If there were, I would not normally suggest recording the sessions.

The onset of therapy coincided with increasing relationship difficulties. Unfortunately, after a number of sessions, she had to cease counselling temporarily. As her problems with her ex-partner were escalating, and because she considered herself at some personal risk, it was agreed that it would probably be useful for me to keep both sets of the audiotapes of our sessions. I was concerned that she may need to refer to the discussions of recent life events and the audiotapes would serve as good reminders. This decision was recorded in her client notes.

Some months later she returned to counselling; at the same time, the police decided to prosecute her ex-partner. With her permission, I provided a written statement regarding the extent to which a number of incidents had affected her. This was quite straightforward as I had seen her before she had started encountering problems with her partner. I was concerned that if the Crown decided to prosecute then the defence would subpoena my client notes. My records included a range of typical personal issues that are often discussed in counselling which were not directly related to her ex-partner but could be misinterpreted by lay people or perhaps intentionally by barristers. I was also very concerned about the effect having such personal details read out in court could have upon her mental condition. She was led to believe by the investigating officer that only my statement would be referred to in court. I did not believe that this would be the case but the investigating officer assured me that this would be so. Her ex-partner was subsequently arrested for grievous bodily harm and burglary.

Prior to my appearing in court, I spoke to representatives of the British Association for Counselling and Psychotherapy (BACP), the British Psychological Society (BPS) and my insurers, Smithson Mason, regarding my legal position with special reference to the issue of confidentiality. It was suggested that I should raise this issue in court with the judge; all were unanimous in advising that an order of the court must be obeyed.

I decided to prepare for the court case by watching the training videos regarding court appearances that can be hired from the BPS (1995). These were excellent and I would recommend that other therapeutic professional bodies have a set for hire.

In court:

We did not get off to a good start. Both the defence and prosecution barristers wanted me to refer to my original clinical notes in court. As I suspected, and despite the reassurances of the investigating officer, my original statement was not going to be sufficient.

When I raised the issue of confidentiality, the prosecuting barrister representing the Crown told the judge that this was *not* an issue as far as she and Mary were concerned. After some debate between the three of us, the judge told me to continue. As far as I was concerned, this was an important part of the proceedings regarding confidentiality. The implications would be that the court could, technically speaking, photocopy my notes as evidence. At this point, I wanted to confirm that I had been formally instructed by the judge to refer to my clinical notes. I turned directly towards the judge and asked him the following question. 'Your Honour, are you instructing me to refer to my notes?' He replied, 'Yes'. I sensed that he was becoming somewhat irritated.

During the lunch break, the investigating officer photocopied all of my clinical notes. I brought to the prosecution barrister's attention the type of topics that Mary had discussed during counselling sessions which had been recorded in her notes. As far as I was concerned, these were not directly related to the court case but could be misinterpreted. The prosecution barrister then understood my resistance in referring to my notes. After lunch, in a closed session, she asked the judge if Public Interest Immunity could be applied to a number of Mary's notes; the judge adjourned the court to enable him to read the relevant notes.

It is worth noting that I was advised not to contact my client as this could prejudice the case. Over the weekend, as I was re-reading my client's notes, I became aware of the frequent reference to our audiotapes of the sessions. I would record in my notes whether Mary had listened to them or not and her general comments about the previous session. I decided to take further advice from BACP, BPS and CareAssist (the providers of my insurance scheme's legal helpline). The legal representative of CareAssist said that, even though I was only asked for my notes, my audiotapes were also relevant material especially as they were referred to in the client's notes. If I did not mention the tapes then the court might consider that I was deliberately withholding clinical evidence. They suggested that I should tell the prosecution barrister about them and also state my view that their use in court might cause my client psychological harm. It was emphasised that it was wrong to destroy records and pretend that they did not exist. This is not allowed and may lead to a charge of perverting the course of justice or to contempt of court.

In court, the judge ruled that if the client gave her permission for their use, then they would be used. The Crown implied that they would drop the case against her ex-partner if the tapes were not used. The client was left with Hobson's choice and, after a great deal of anguish, she finally gave her permission for their use. Even though we were both sitting outside the courtroom, I was not supposed to talk to her about any issue relating to the court case even though she was very distressed and I was her counsellor. Later that day I arranged via her occupational health department for a BACP Accredited Counsellor to support her through this difficult period.

The court support services had to arrange for sets of copies to be made for both the defence and prosecution barristers. I ensured that I received a receipt for the tapes from the investigating officer on behalf of the court and reminded the relevant staff of the confidential nature of the tapes.

The court was adjourned again to allow the barristers to listen to the tapes. After listening to the tapes, the Crown dropped their prosecution. However, my job regarding the materials had not quite finished. As soon as the case was discharged, I immediately followed the prosecuting and defence barristers back to their rooms and obtained their copies of both the clinical notes and the tapes. I also secured my original tapes back from the court. Again, I kept my insurance brokers informed of the outcome in case there was a claim. At no time were my client's personal details discussed with third parties, only the legal issues surrounding the case such as confidentiality, apart from explaining to the prosecuting barrister why Public Interest Immunity would be strongly preferable regarding certain client notes that she had in her possession.

The aftermath

The outcome for my client was not satisfactory as the defendant was discharged. However, she did experience fewer difficulties with her ex-partner. She was very upset about how the court had treated her and about the realisation that we had probably made an error, both when we decided to keep the audiotapes to remind ourselves of the series of incidents, and in accepting the investigating officer's word that other material would not be used. We both thought that educating therapists about some of the issues involved might be a positive step and I later put this into action.

I wrote a number of articles with Mark Scoggins, a solicitor, and Dr Roger Litton, the Smithson Mason representative who administered the BACP and BPS members' Professional Liability Insurance Scheme (e.g. Scoggins et al., 1997; 1998a; 1998b). These were republished in a number of journals and within the profession received a fair amount of publicity. I received letters and telephone calls from BACP and BPS members who explained their current difficulties regarding court cases, confidentiality and the law. I realised that many practitioners were not aware of the complex issues and in addition, had overlooked their responsibility to themselves and the profession. Some examples involved:

- Not taking legal advice on their own behalf in case they breached confidentiality;
- Not realising that they did not have to answer questions of a confidential nature unless instructed by the judge;
- Sending client notes to solicitors without obtaining a client waiver;
- Not being personally insured for professional liability and assuming their employers would protect them;
- Believing that it was acceptable to pervert the course of justice by destroying client notes or withholding relevant information;
- Keeping two sets of notes, a full set and a set for court;
- Intending to refuse to answer questions in court even if directed by the judge to answer them.

This brought to my attention the need for practitioners to receive more formal training in these issues while attending counselling and psychotherapy programmes. However, even experienced practitioners seem blissfully unaware of the many different aspects involved.

On a personal note, as we (SP and Mary) decided the case should be written about so as to inform and educate other practitioners, I have found it difficult to put the experience behind me as I am still asked to write or run workshops about confidentiality and the law. Sometimes therapists want to discuss similar issues when they meet me at conferences and often refer to the case. I know Mary would prefer to put the case behind her too.

This case study is published with the permission of the client

Acknowledgements

I would like to thank the BACP, BPS, Dr Roger Litton at Smithson Mason and CareAssist for the advice and support I received during the court case regarding confidentiality and the law. I would like to thank Mary for giving me permission to write about the case once again.

References

British Psychological Society (1995) *Expert Testimony: Developing Witness Skills*. (Training Video) Leicester: BPS.
Palmer, S. and Szymanska, K. (1994a). How to avoid being exploited in counselling and psychotherapy. *Counselling*, 5(1): 24.

Palmer, S. and Szymanska, K. (1994b). A client checklist for clients interested in receiving counselling, psychotherapy and hypnosis. *The Rational Emotive Behaviour Therapist*, 2(1): 25–7.

Scoggins, M. Litton, R. and Palmer, S. (1997). Confidentiality and the law. *Counselling*, 8 (4): 258–262.

Scoggins, M. Litton, R. and Palmer, S. (1998a). Confidentiality and the law. *The Rational Emotive Behaviour Therapist*, 6(1): 18–30.

Scoggins, M. Litton, R. and Palmer, S. (1998b). Confidentiality and the law. *Counselling Psychology Review*, 13(1): 6–12.

2

Psychoanalyst Subpoenaed

Anne Hayman

When I was subpoenaed to give evidence in the High Court about someone who was alleged to be a former patient of mine, I was placed between two conflicting moral obligations. I had to decide whether to obey the law or to abide by the rules of professional conduct. I complied with the sub-poena by attending court, but I decided I could not answer any questions about the 'patient', and I made all arrangements, including having a bar-rister to plead in mitigation of sentence, for the possibility that I should be sent to prison for contempt of court. In the event, although my silence probably did constitute a contempt, the judge declared he would not sen-tence me, saying it was obviously a matter of conscience. In this he was acting within the discretion the law allows him. Though I had no legal privilege, I was in effect given the same freedom to remain silent usually allowed to priests for the secrets of the confessional. It is possible that the judge was partly moved by the idea that any evidence I could give might only be of marginal relevance to the case.

The grounds for my decision were individual, but though some other psychoanalysts might not refuse to divulge whether they had treated a person, I think it likely that in all other respects they would feel as I did. These grounds were partly explained in the statement I made when called to the witness box. I said that it was essential to my work as a psychoanalyst and psychotherapist that people should feel free to discuss with me everything that concerns them, including matters of great inti-macy which they would not be able to reveal if there were any doubt about my trustworthiness. Indeed, one of these secrets could be the very fact that they had come to me for help. For me the need to retain secrecy was not just a moral imperative such as might exist, for example, for a general practitioner who was treating a patient for pneumonia. If such a doctor were to talk indiscreetly about his patient, he might not be behav-ing ethically, but he might still have treated the pneumonia adequately. But if I were to speak indiscreetly about a patient, I should not only be behaving unethically, but I should also be destroying the very fabric of my therapy. For people to be able to speak freely, and only then could I help them, I must supply a setting within which this could happen, and this setting was an essential part of the treatment. I had a quiet comfortable consulting-room; and when people kept their appointments I must not fail to be there; I must start and finish at the times agreed on. While they were with me there must be no interruption of the treatment; I did not talk on the phone, nor did anything besides the therapeutic task I had undertaken. I had to be completely reliable in all my dealings with my patients, and this included keeping their secrets under all circumstances. Failure to maintain any part of this essential setting would be malpractice of the same order as if the general practitioner had advised his pneumonia patient to get out of bed with a temperature of 105° and come to the surgery for treatment. My professional code applies whenever I receive anyone as a patient, whether it was someone who had attended regularly for years, or someone who had come only once, perhaps just to see what a psychoanalyst looks like.

To the judge's query whether I would still object if 'the patient' gave permission, I answered with an example: suppose a patient had been in treatment for some time and was going through a temporary phase of admiring and depending on me; he might therefore feel it necessary to sacrifice himself and give permission, but it might not be proper for me to act on this.

This example involves a vital principle. Some of the United States have a law prohibiting psychiatrists from giving evidence about a patient without the patient's written permission, but this honourable attempt to protect the patient misses the essential point that he may not be aware of unconscious motives impelling him to give permission. It may take months or years to understand things said or done during analysis, and until this is achieved it would belie all our knowledge of the workings of the unconscious mind if we treated any attitude arising in the analytic situation as if it were part of ordinary social interchange. If we allow and help people to say things with the ultimate aim of helping them to understand the real meanings underlying what may well be a temporary attitude engendered by the transference, it would be the crassest dishonour and dishonesty to permit unwarranted advantage to be taken of their willingness to avail themselves of the therapeutic situation. It would be as if a physician invited a patient to undress to be examined, and then allowed the law to see him naked and to arrest him for exhibiting himself. Where no permission has been given, the rule to maintain discretion is, of course, similarly inviolable. Patients attend us on the implicit understanding that anything they reveal is subject to a special protection. Unless we explicitly state that this is not so, we are parties to a tacit agreement, and any betrayal of it only dishonours us. That the agreement may not be explicit is no excuse. Part of our work is to put into words things that are not being said. We are the responsible parties in the relationship, so surely it is we who should pay, if there is any price to be paid, because something has not been said clearly.

But should there be any price to pay? Was I arrogating to myself an unwarrantable freedom from the ordinary responsibilities of a citizen by refusing to give evidence? Was it not rather that the attitude of responsibility towards patients was also one of responsibility towards the law? The fact that in theory people having analysis 'tell everything' should not give rise to the misleading idea that we analysts are necessarily the repositories of secrets that could help the courts if only we would divulge them. The concern of psychoanalysis is with the ever-developing unravelling of the unconscious conflicts of our patients. We know that these can affect the patient's perceptions and judgements while they are operative, hence the advice sometimes given to avoid major decisions during analysis. We are not seeking the 'objective reality' the courts want, and generally we are not in a position to give it to them. Over the years we may hear a number of different versions of the same event, each completely sincere, but varying with the changing emotional focus of the analysand, each version being a clue to another level of unconscious conflict. To report on whichever is momentarily in the ascendant could mislead a court as, for example, a report on an applicant's blood-pressure after a night of vomiting could mislead an insurance company. I would suggest that in principle there may be less conflict between our moral obligations to the law and to the rules of professional conduct than would appear at first sight. If a psychoanalyst or psychotherapist wished to offer a patient's description of an event as objective evidence, it would be necessary to produce every version of the event, explaining the differences by detailing all the known underlying meanings; with the misleading probable result of the court's either accepting one version unequivocally, or discrediting therapist or patient as unreliable. Justice, as well as our ethic, is likely to be served best by silence. X.

Hayman, A. (1965) "Psychoanalyst subpoenaed" *The Lancet*, 321, 16th October, pp.785–6 © The Lancet

Anne Hayman has recently added the following postscript to her original anonymous article.

This principled stand against saying anything at all apart from my name etc (including not saying whether or not the person concerned had ever been a patient of mine, so there was no question whatsoever of my giving any evidence) aroused no obvious outside interest; and there was no response when *The Lancet* referred to the article twice within the following year.

   It has been available as potentially advisory within the British Psycho-Analytical Society but there has been little resort to it, and perhaps rather little need. However, within the last year it has been used as a reference point in ongoing discussions on ethics within the International Psychoanalytical Association.

3

Legal Pitfalls in Counselling and Psychotherapy Practice, and How to Avoid Them

Gideon Cristofoli

As a solicitor I tend to see clients once they have made errors that have got them into disputes with their own clients. In this chapter I aim to provide the legal background to the psychotherapist/client relationship and point out some of the pitfalls.

At the root of the relationship between a therapist i.e., a counsellor or psychotherapist, and their client is a contract. Simply, a contract is where one party agrees to provide something in consideration for something else from another party. In everyday life there are numerous contracts being formed and completed. Every time a person goes into a shop, he or she is offered an object for sale at a certain price, agrees that price, pays the money and receives the object. In the case of a therapist or psychotherapist, they provide a service and receive in consideration for that service a payment of money. In legal terms it is the same whether it is the provision of legal services, therapy or gardening.

Terms of the contract

The details of the particular contract can however be broken down into a number of terms. If these terms are clear and obvious and can be simply identified they can be viewed as express terms of the contract. Most professionals giving a service should at least have a written agreement whereby they will provide a service for a certain time at an hourly rate. If this hourly rate is agreed before the psychotherapy session is begun, then the client is under an obligation to pay the appropriate sum for the time the session took. If there is no agreement before the service is provided how does the client know what to expect and how does the therapist think that the charges can be justified? It is therefore very good practice to have a set of standard terms and conditions which can be handed or posted to every client at the beginning of the client/psychotherapist relationship.

Therapist

Standard Terms and Conditions

1 Definitions

    1.1 'The Client' means the person who agrees to buy the service from the Therapist.

    1.2 'The Therapist' means Therapist of [address].

    1.3 'The Service' means the provision by the Therapist to the Client of the services as agreed between the Therapist and the Client.

    1.4 'The Therapy session' means the period during which the Client employs the Therapist to prescribe the services.

2 Price

    2.1 The price shall be the Therapist's quoted price which is exclusive of VAT. It shall be calculated at the rate of £xxx per hour ('the hourly rate').

    2.2 The price shall be quoted for the agreed Therapy session. If any further period of therapy is required then a further sum will be payable.

3 Payment

    3.1 Payment shall be due immediately after the Therapy session and if payment is not received the Therapist may terminate this agreement.

4 Appointments

    4.1 Appointments may be rescheduled entirely at the discretion of the Therapist.

    4.2 In the event that the Client wishes to reschedule an appointment, the Client must give at least 48 hours notice to the Therapist and will be liable for payment of a cancellation fee for the missed appointment calculated at the hourly rate for the length of the session missed.

5 Limitations of Liability

    5.1 The Therapist shall not be liable for any consequential or indirect loss or loss of profit suffered by the Client in relation to the services supplied.

    5.2 The Therapist's total liability to the Client for any default act or omission in connection with this agreement and the provision of the services shall be limited to the price paid for the Therapist Period.

    5.3 The Therapist gives no guarantee that the therapy and the provision of the services will result in an improvement to the Client's mental or physical condition or general well being, as each individual client reacts in a different manner to therapy and it may be necessary for a client to undergo an extended period of therapy before any improvement may be apparent, if at all.

6 Warranties

The Therapist warrants to keep all information provided by the Client confidential save for clinical supervision and where the Therapist is required by law {or a strong moral obligation} to disclose some material facts and information to a third party.

7 Complaints Procedure

7.1 The Therapist is governed by the ethical and professional guidelines of the Therapist's professional body, The xxxxxxxxx Institute.

7.2 At the first instance, if the Client has any wish to complain they are asked to address their complaint to the Therapist who will endeavour to satisfy the client.

7.3 If the Client is then not satisfied they are invited to contact the Therapist's professional body The xxxxxxxxx Institute at [address].

8 Termination

8.1 The Therapist may terminate this agreement at any time by giving written notice to the Client. The Therapist need give no reason for the termination.

8.2 The Client may terminate this agreement at any time by giving written notice to the Therapist.

8.3 Upon termination all outstanding fees shall become immediately due and payable.

Figure 3.1   *Standard Terms and Conditions Document*

This is a standard terms and conditions document which could be easily tailored to the individual needs of any therapist. It sets out the basic essential details that any client may wish to know and can protect the therapist from unnecessary disputes and complaints from a difficult client.

The standard terms first identify the parties involved. They then establish a basis for charging and give an hourly rate, and then detail when payment must be made. It provides the opportunity for the therapist to reschedule appointments and makes the client liable for failing to attend appointments.

The terms then seek to limit in some way legal liability. It is not legally possible to exclude liability for a personal injury or the death of a client, but it is often wise to try to restrict financial loss. Unfortunately, it is in the field of personal injury that counsellors and psychotherapists are most greatly at risk because they are dealing with an individual's health. Under the warranties section, the therapist can provide some agreement to the client to protect confidential information, and could also give promises about the quality of service.

Having a complaints procedure is useful to allow the therapist to resolve problems at an early stage. It needs to be provided carefully so as to avoid the impression that the therapist often receives complaints or is encouraging them. It is sensible for the therapist to check the existence and nature of their professional body's complaints procedure and how its powers are wielded. There is a necessity for professional bodies to treat all complaints against their members with the utmost seriousness in order to protect the standing of their members, the body and the profession. However, this can lead to individuals becoming involved in a long and painful process of defending a complaint against them, which has no reasonable grounding whatsoever. It is useful to check that the professional body has a procedure for determining if there is a *prima facie* case before the full complaints procedure is set under way. With the termination clause, the therapist has reserved the right to end the relationship with the client at any point. For instance, if the client were to become very difficult or fail to pay the therapist, it will be useful to have this clause. These terms and conditions can be contained in a letter or brochure to make them more customer friendly. It is also good practice to talk the matter through informally with the client before presenting them with the document.

In addition to these express terms, it is normal for the law to imply certain terms into the client/therapist relationship. The Supply of Goods & Services Act 1982 implies into any contract for the provision of services a number of basic terms. The term that is relevant to the client/psychotherapist relationship is the implied term that the latter will carry out their work with reasonable care and skill. It is upon this implied term that most court actions are founded against professionals.

If a psychotherapist can be found to be in breach of this implied term, then the client can claim damages arising naturally from the breach. These damages can fall into two categories:

- *the financial loss*, being the cost of the treatment and any consequential financial loss that can be justified
- *damages for any personal injury* the client has suffered as a result of the treatment which was not carried out with reasonable care and skill

Negligence

Parallel to this claim for breach of contract a client can claim against a therapist for negligence. When discussing professional services, words such as 'incompetence', 'mistake' and 'misconduct' are often used. In legal terms, the only concept that really is of importance is negligence. Like many terms in the law, it is defined by other terms.

First, a *duty of care* between the therapist and the client must be established. It is generally accepted and has been found in case law that this duty of care exists, whether the client is in the public or private sector. It is then necessary for it to be established that there was a breach of that duty of care, similar to the claim for breach of contract.

It is necessary in negligence to demonstrate that the treatment fell *below the standard of a reasonably competent therapist* occupying that particular post. This test is called the '*Bolam test*' and was established in a case in 1957 called '*Bolam v Friern Hospital*'. I quote from the case as follows:

> but where you get a situation which involved the use of some special skill or competence then the test as to whether there has been negligence or not is not the test of the man on the top of the Clapham omnibus because he has not got this special skill. The test is the standard of the ordinary skilled man exercising and professing to have that special skill. A man need not posses the highest expert skill. It is well established law that it is sufficient if he exercises the ordinary skill of an ordinary competent man exercising that particular art. (Mc Nair, J. at 121).

It has been found that there is a good defence to a claim for negligence if the defendant can demonstrate that a substantial body of reputable practitioners would have acted in the same way as the defendant in those circumstances.

The third element that must be demonstrated for a claimant to succeed in a claim for negligence is that of *consequential loss*. This is the demonstration that some injury has resulted directly because of the breach of duty. In counselling and psychotherapy this injury will undoubtedly be a psychiatric injury or originate as a psychiatric injury. The law is rather strict on the proof of an injury of this nature and it has been shown that it is only possible for a claimant to recover damages if the claimant can bring himself within one of the closely defined categories of recognisable psychiatric conditions. At this point, I would like to raise a problem. The obvious question is, if a client comes to you with a recognisable psychiatric condition, then does he fulfil this requirement if the client gets worse and he wishes to blame you?

This issue can be largely answered by viewing the *defence of causation*. It is necessary for a link to be established by a claimant between the breach of the duty and the consequential loss. The claimant must demonstrate that the action of the psychotherapist in fact made the condition worse. This is a very difficult thing to do. Where medical or scientific evidence is ambivalent or suggests that there could be a number of causes of the claimant's deterioration in a psychiatric condition, then the claim will fail.

If a claim is successful then there must be an assessment of what the claimant can receive as *compensation*. Damages are assessed taking account of a number of factors including the ability of the claimant to cope with life, the effect on the relationship with the claimant's family, the claimant's future vulnerability and prognosis. If the claimant succeeds with the claim of a psychotherapist making an individual's condition deteriorate, the court will try to measure the degree to which these factors have changed.

Damages are awarded for the pain and suffering that results from the act of negligence. If an individual were to develop a recognisable psychiatric condition from a normal state they could easily receive basic damages of between £25,000 and £50,000. Added to this can be damages for future loss of earnings and also a claim for the cost of caring for the individual. These can reach hundreds of thousands of pounds.

With this exposure in mind it is advisable for a therapist in private practice to have some form of indemnity insurance to protect against claims for damages. A solicitor is not allowed to practice without this insurance, lest the advice he gives is negligent and results in someone having a loss and wishing to sue him. It would be sensible for all professionals providing a service to follow this example.

Private practice

There are a number of specific pitfalls which could expose a psychotherapist to difficulties or actions in private practice. The first and most obvious one is that of actually receiving payment. If the therapist does not have a written express agreement with the client then there is always scope for the latter to argue about how much has actually been agreed to be paid or stating that the service has been provided as a favour. The simplest way of keeping track of costs is to ensure that each individual consultation is paid for immediately after the consultation. If someone's cheque bounces or they do not pay, then they do not have another consultation and the therapist writes off the cost of one session.

If, however, a therapist allows someone to have three or four months worth of consultations before rendering an invoice they might be surprised to find that the client doesn't pay up. The difficulty is then to try to recover an amount of money that a therapist may be loathe to write off. It may be necessary to try to recover the money through taking action in the Small Claims Court. This can be a stressful and frustrating experience, as the client will undoubtedly now raise the concept that the therapy was unsatisfactory, and in fact had made his or her condition worse.

Dependency, touch and consent

These three issues, of getting too close to a client, having physical contact with a client and actually getting consent from a client before moving on to the next stage of psychotherapy are interrelated. It is

widely understood that some therapists use touch as part of the therapy
and so it is important that the client understands how touch is being used
and gives consent to such treatment before it is undertaken. It can be
very easy for a client to misunderstand touch, interpreting it in a sexual
context and, before the psychotherapist knows it, they have allegations
of serious malpractice filed against them. The therapist might cease treating a client who has misunderstood the treatment and romanticised the
relationship but the problems may not end there. A 'scorned' client is
likely to turn bitter and may complain to the professional body, sue or
harass the therapist. Harassment can be very unpleasant, if clients, seeking to become involved in a counsellor's life, make numerous phone calls
or begin stalking. If a therapist receives such harassment, there are a
number of remedies available, both criminal and civil. One can apply for
an injunction or use the Protection from Harassment Act 1997. However,
if matters have got that desperate, the therapist's first step should be to
seek the help of a solicitor.

If proceedings for personal injury are pending, a civil court is likely to be
considerably less sympathetic to a therapist who has such allegations made
against them. It may be difficult to find a body of reputable practitioners
who would support such treatment in a claim for negligence. There is also
the greater risk that a client may allege assault and battery against a therapist resulting in a criminal investigation. To avoid such problems it is sensible to obtain a letter of consent to the treatment signed by the client.
This letter should establish that the client is aware of the intended treatment and understands its context and agrees to it proceeding.
A simple letter of consent could take this form:

> I xxxxxxx of [address] consent to undergoing therapy from yyyyyyyy that
> involves physical contact and I understand and confirm as a client of
> yyyyyyyy that I do not consider this physical contact to be intrusive and I
> agree to its use as part of the therapy.

It is useful to try to identify early on in a client/therapist relationship
if a client is going to be difficult or even dangerous to work with. If a
client has been to numerous therapists beforehand, has only negative
things to say about them and has filed complaints, it is fairly easy to see
that the current therapist may be next in line. The therapist should consider whether he or she really wants to take them on and be exposed to
the inevitable complaints and criticism to come.

Contracts and supervision

A number of difficult issues can arise when applying legal concepts to
the therapist's professional practice. The classic situation of a therapist

drawing up and working to a contract containing both therapeutic and legally binding features may be the norm in private practice, but may be less easily applicable elsewhere. Some therapists work as paid employees of organisations such as an NHS Trust, or of an agency providing a counselling service. In the latter situations, the therapist's legal liability is held by the employer, based on the concept of vicarious liability, whereby an employer carries legal responsibility for the actions and mistakes of staff performed as part of their work activity. Some therapists are very familiar with this concept, and find it reassuring that their employer can bring the resources of their legal department to bear, in the case of threatened litigation. Other therapists may feel that the concept of vicarious liability is somehow at odds with their own wish to take full clinical responsibility for their own professional work with clients. In fact, vicarious liability is simply the legal form taken here by professional liability, which is defined in this context by *employment factors*, rather than by the level of professional expertise displayed by the therapist as a practitioner. There is, furthermore, a legal argument that vicarious liability will also apply to therapists working in an unpaid, voluntary capacity, where the volunteer is essentially working 'as if employed', in terms of their level of responsibility for client work.

Supervisors also represent something of a special case in terms of legal liability. Supervisors carry legal liability for their work in supervising the therapist, but do not appear to owe a direct duty of care to the client as such. This is apart from the normal duty of confidence, which is owed to both supervisee and client. The main line of legal liability will be to the supervised therapist, primarily via the terms and conditions of the contract, which was presumably established at the outset of the supervisory relationship. This could, in fact, take the form of a suitably adapted version of the contract outlined earlier. One word of warning – both therapists and supervisors are often guilty of using the term 'contract' rather freely, in a way that might suggest it carries legal weight, as well as fulfilling a therapeutic purpose. Agreements, either between the therapist and client, or between therapist and supervisor, which do not contain an element of 'consideration', i.e. an exchange of goods or money for services rendered, will not qualify as a contractual arrangement in legal terms. Many therapeutic agreements will not necessarily qualify, therefore, as legally binding documents.

Records of therapy

Another problematic aspect of psychotherapy practice concerns the value and status of notes taken of therapy sessions by the therapist. While these can prove useful as an *aide-mémoire* for the therapist, enabling him or her to provide a high level of professional service, the notes may also come to fulfil other, unintended purposes in the context of legal proceedings. Clients have wider rights of access to therapists' notes under recent data protection legislation (see Chapter 6), and the therapist is unable to prevent these notes being accessed via the legal process of discovery in the case of court action (see Chapter 3). Given that the therapist has no access to claiming privileged status for these recordings, some therapists may conclude that note taking may contribute to a potentially damaging degree of personal and professional disclosure in the public arena of a courtroom, for which these notes were never intended. The therapist may therefore conclude that a minimalist approach to note taking would serve both as an efficient record of the therapy provided to the client, and would also reduce the risk of detailed notes being used in later court proceedings.

However, an alternative view is that detailed note-keeping could provide the means for an effective defence in the event of being sued or made the subject of complaint by an aggrieved client. Detailed record keeping, particularly where the contractual and therapeutic relationships with the client become problematic and conflicted, may well be a necessary safeguard to provide evidence of the therapist's level of professional service, and of attempts to resolve points of contention which may have arisen. Given that many therapist-client problems appear to be relationship-based in origin, rather than contractual in a strict sense, it may also be wise to consider the value of making an apology to an aggrieved client at an appropriate stage. However, this needs to be expressed prudently, with the necessary proviso that this is not equivalent to an admission of responsibility for any damage claimed by the client arising from the therapy itself. Therapists facing this difficult situation are strongly advised to liaise closely with their professional indemnity insurance company, and to comply strictly with the terms of their insurance policy, in addition to obtaining appropriate legal advice. Where the therapist becomes involved in litigation with the client, or in complaints procedures, which are increasingly quasi-legal in form, then the nature of supporting documentation, such as leaflets outlining the nature of the service, and brochures indicating potential limits to confidentiality, may well prove to be strongly supportive material in providing an effective defence against a client's unfounded legal case or complaint. Clearly, the need for such a defence will prove to be exceptional, but the increasing trend towards legal resolution of disputes suggests that the therapist should take necessary steps to protect their professional reputation and livelihood.

Conclusion

The therapist should be aware of the structure placed upon the psychotherapist/client relationship by the law. It is important to establish the terms of contract to avoid misunderstanding. There is a basis for an individual who has a recognisable psychiatric condition to bring a claim for personal injury. It is not easily proven, but with care can be easily avoided. The therapist also needs to consider carefully the stance to be adopted towards record keeping, in the light of its potential role in litigation. Accurate contextual documentation about the nature of the service provided will enable clients to be better informed prior to engaging in the contract of service, and will prove to be valuable defence material, should legal action arise.

Legal references

Bolam v Friern HMC [1957] 2 All ER 118.

4

Taking Legal Action Against a Therapist for Professional Negligence

Inge Power

In 1990 I would have described myself as a reasonably competent businesswoman with a stable marriage and a thriving family. I'd say I was pretty down-to-earth and level-headed – not at all the type of person to let myself be swept off my feet by a new-age pseudo-psychiatrist. My husband and I had spent all our married lives working together raising our three children, building up our business, and supplementing our income by alternative ventures wherever possible.

I first met Dr X at an alternative therapy weekend workshop, where he had been invited to do a two hour guided meditation. He introduced himself as a former NHS doctor with a specialist interest in a holistic approach to medicine. I was intrigued by him. He told us a little about his own brand of alternative therapy, which he described as the most powerful form of psychotherapy known. I found the guided meditation session very moving; in fact I became a little tearful, and after the session he spoke privately to me – he took both my hands in his, looked into my eyes and told me he believed I needed his help. His offer seemed warm and sincere, but I hesitated. As I understood him, he was offering me therapy. At that moment I really wasn't sure I either wanted or needed any form of therapy.

A few days later, Dr X telephoned me. He wanted to persuade me to attend his own alternative therapy weekend workshop. He sounded so enthusiastic and inviting that I let my curiosity get the better of me, and I agreed to attend. He asked a string of medical questions because, he explained, the therapy was very intense.

There were about 18 people at the workshop. A number of the participants knew each other and it appeared that Dr X had met each of us previously. I gathered some of them were his private patients. Dr X introduced himself again as a medical doctor and a psychiatrist with a special interest in alternative therapy. He went on to tell us that his own branch of alternative therapy was probably the most intensive form of psychotherapy known and that he was currently the only qualified practitioner of this method in the UK. He really gave a very powerful impression that he was an expert in this field. He described the process of therapy in terms which sounded quite alarming, mentioning, for example, past lives and out-of-body experiences. I should have left at that point. I wish I had. But after expressing some misgivings, I agreed to stay, because I honestly believed I was in the care of a highly trained practitioner, a medical doctor and a psychiatrist, who was fully qualified to practise this particular form of therapy.

The weekend was very intensive, based on group sessions throughout the day and evening. Dr X led each session. The therapy itself was a powerful emotional experience for me. As participants, lying on the floor, we were put into a state of relaxation, attaining an altered state of consciousness by a combination of deep breathing and evocative music. In this altered state, events and emotions emerged from the sub-conscious, over a period of 2 to 3 hours, and afterwards, we processed those experiences by talking them through as a group. During my first session I was in a trance for about 3 hours, reliving some painful childhood memories. I came round in floods of tears, to find Dr X lying beside me, under the blanket, with his arms around me. He held me in his arms, comforting me for several minutes. Oddly, I recall that he made an incongruous comment just before we both got up. He said 'Oh, by the way, in case you're wondering, I'm not gay.' His remark seemed odd and out of context. Looking back on this, I now wonder if he was trying to sow the seeds of closer personal connection with me. I certainly found him attractive, almost charismatic, with tremendous physical charm and presence. It seemed almost that he could offer me the key to transforming my whole life at that stage, if I could only summon up the confidence to place my trust in him.

During the weekend, I felt emotionally as if I had been 'hit by a sledgehammer' and as if something hugely significant had shifted within me. I had a number of very strong experiences. For example, I was in a 'trance' reliving my mother's suicide years earlier, begging her not to take the tablets – something I dearly wish I had been able to do at the time. Later the same weekend Dr X invited me to participate in a healing ceremony. He laid me down, with my eyes shut, and told everyone in the group to massage and fondle me and to project love towards me. He had emphasised to us that all illness is psychosomatic, that tumours are caused by negativity, and that his own form of therapy had released me from that negativity. He told everyone else to go for a cup of tea, and he stayed and hugged me quietly for a while. When they returned, I believed I was 'healed'. In fact, at that time I was awaiting treatment for a troublesome polyp, and from that day I ignored the symptoms. I cancelled the investigative operation which had been booked and imagined I no longer had a problem. I had already fallen so far under Dr X's spell, it never entered my head that I was making a big mistake which would subsequently result in a life-threatening tumour needing major surgery.

From our first meeting, and throughout most of our association, Dr X showed me a great deal of personal attention. He frequently gazed into my eyes, hugged me, massaged my neck and shoulders, and kissed me. I confess, I revelled in this display of warmth and affection, and I was amused by his rather audacious sexual innuendo. Not at all the way a therapist should behave towards his client – but how was I to know – I'd never been in therapy before. Towards the end of the weekend, close to the time for going home, Dr X came and sat with me. He pointed out two women he'd been talking to who were not part of our group. He said they were psychic. They had apparently told him that his own partner, Y, was not coming back to him, and that he had met someone special who was going to take her place. I was bowled over at the way he confided this to me. I recall asking myself whether he was trying to tell me that he looked on me as that 'someone special'.

It was common for participants in Dr X's group therapy sessions to continue to be immersed in emotion for some days afterwards – that was certainly my own experience. Hand in hand with the emotions attached to the particular session, I experienced an amazing feeling of euphoria. It took me years to appreciate that this was not, as I had naively believed, a state of bliss – it was simply a symptom of oxygen deprivation during the therapy.

I attended a group follow-up meeting a few days later, at Dr X's house. I was the last to leave that meeting and Dr X made me coffee before my drive home. He mentioned that he was looking for an alternative Centre for his workshops, so I told him about my Guest House. We agreed to give some thought to the possibility of running his courses there. It seemed a good idea to look at the potential of a joint venture, which had the makings of a promising and exciting new departure.

Dr X encouraged us all to keep in touch with him, particularly if we had emotional issues we wanted to talk through. A few days after the follow-up meeting I was talking to him on the phone, when he suddenly interrupted me. He suggested I should see him privately, on a one to one basis, saying his fee was about £85 per hour. I expressed some concern at the fee. Dr X asked me how much I'd earned from my business in the last three years, and what I'd spent it on. When I explained that my income went to my home and my family, he asked me straight out 'Isn't it time you spent some of it on yourself?' Goodness knows why I fell for that argument, but I agreed there and then to start having private therapy sessions with him.

My first private session was at Dr X's home. It was a warm sunny day and we had the session outside in the walled garden. He told me straightaway that he would only work with people he liked, and that he liked me and therefore he would work with me. Even then, I remember feeling a veiled threat in this remark, thinking 'I mustn't say anything this man doesn't like, or he'll refuse to see me'. He took a brief history and discussed my background. He seemed to talk about himself rather a lot and there was plenty of sexual innuendo, which embarrassed me, although I didn't say so at the time. He told me I was actually very repressed, and that he intended to do something about that. Dr X asked me what goals I would like to set myself for my treatment plan over the course of the next 12 months. I remember saying that I had a problem at the time with my low self esteem. Also, I was always worrying about money. Dr X said that we could think of more matters to work on as we went along. He suggested a treatment programme for 12 months consisting of monthly one-to-one sessions, small group sessions, and residential weekends. These would be psychotherapy sessions, including guided imagery, meditation and counselling. Before I left, he phoned a former colleague of his, Mrs Z, and he told me they would come to my house the next morning to discuss the possibility of the joint venture we had been discussing. He walked back to my car with me, with his arm around me, and kissed me before I got in the car. He continued to behave towards me in this rather intimate way at most of our meetings and I gradually came to accept this as a normal part of our relationship.

The following day, Dr X came to my home with Mrs Z, a professional colleague. He again greeted me with a hug and a kiss, and then he met my husband. Dr X and Mrs Z both talked very enthusiastically about his work in alternative therapy and the sort of courses they ran. They said they loved the place and we all discussed the possibility of extending the buildings for his purposes. I was totally sold on the man, and I had no problem silencing my husband's misgivings. From that day on, Dr X and I were in almost daily contact, eagerly planning the development of our new therapy centre. I had no appreciation whatever of the way Dr X was exploiting and manipulating our relationship. I felt honoured that he had chosen to work with me, and innocently oblivious to the fact that he was using our premises, our money and our hard work to promote his own career.

Dr X taught me to meditate and told me that meditation produced the most intimate communication it was possible to have between people. He said he wanted me to meditate twice a day for 20 minutes at the same time as him each day. My experience when I meditated was a feeling of being lifted out of my body and I felt a loss of boundaries, in that I seemed to be able to feel other people's emotions. My mind would sometimes become crowded with fear and anger which did not seem to relate to my own life. It also seemed to increase my sense of trust in Dr X. I continued regular meditation for about a year, with Dr X frequently reminding me that I must keep it up.

In fact, I did eventually stop meditating, because I began to have what I would now see as paranormal experiences. In addition, some of the feelings and events I encountered during my therapy were extremely powerful, and could best be described as 'transpersonal experiences'. Some of my experiences were pretty bizarre, and it was during this time I began to believe that I had strong psychic powers. Several times during therapy, I relived long-forgotten traumatic experiences from my past. These included my mother's suicide, a distressing incident in childbirth and a frightening wartime memory. I had some very disturbing 'dreams' in which I was a little Polish girl, being rounded up from the Ghetto and taken to the gas chamber. The 'memory' of this was very vivid and detailed, right up to and even beyond the moment of my death. These profoundly disturbing events were experienced in minute detail. For a while I was absolutely convinced I had been this little girl in a past life.

I now understand that I was starting to lose touch with reality and on the verge of a degree of personality disintegration, as a result of exposure to too many unresolved issues from my sub-conscious. But at the time I was completely immersed in those experiences, with absolute confidence in my therapist.

At one of the group therapy sessions, I relived my own birth, and because I found this 'memory' very distressing I sat up and told Dr X I didn't want to continue with the session. I told him I felt desperately lonely at that moment. I was re-experiencing the feeling of separation from my mother after my birth. He sat by me, cradling me in his arms, rocking me gently and maintaining eye contact with me. I felt completely transfixed. In those moments, as I can now understand it, my feelings for him replicated those I would have had towards my own mother. In my trance-like state, he had managed to become a part of my subconscious experience. From that day on, I felt totally dependent upon him, but at that time I had no idea why. As before, he behaved very warmly towards me all weekend, and we spoke more about our plans for the Centre. He encouraged me to announce our plans to the whole group.

Soon after this, I began to feel uncomfortable about my emotional dependency on Dr X. I became very distressed, not least, I think, because my feelings towards him seemed to be at odds with my commitment to my marriage. My next therapy session only served to heighten my feelings, and I was unable to talk this through with Dr X after the session. I saw this as an emotional problem which I needed to resolve with him as soon as possible. Falling in love again was the last thing in the world I wanted. I loved my husband and my family, so why on earth did I feel this way about Dr X? It certainly wasn't making me happy. I cried all night and rang him in the morning. I was still very upset and confused and I asked him 'How do you cope with a patient who falls in love with you? Does this mean we will have to stop working together?' Dr X reacted by saying 'How could you, of all people, say that? Of course we can'. Then he said he felt flattered but that my feelings had nothing to do with reality and would soon pass. I made up my mind I would never mention it again, whatever my real feelings. This was my own problem, and somehow I would have to find a way to get over it.

In fact, by that time, my dependency had reached the stage where I was totally mesmerised by Dr X, who could do absolutely no wrong in my eyes. He continued to see me as a patient, subjecting me to more intense emotional experiences. During the months that followed I worked feverishly to promote his courses and to build and set up the Centre we were planning to run together. It was an incredibly confusing period for me. At times he would show me great affection, telling me that I was a very special person, holding me in his arms. Then, at other times, he would become aggressive and dictatorial for no obvious reason. Every time he contacted me, whether for business or for any other purpose, he treated it like a therapy session, always probing. There seemed to be no respite from the soul searching he required of me. He kept insisting on prolonged eye contact with me and I felt totally dis-empowered by this. Dr X had achieved complete control over me, and I felt totally dependent on him.

I now understand that I was actually experiencing 'transference' – a valuable tool for change in the hands of a competent therapist. Sadly, in my case, I was not in the hands of a competent therapist. To all intents and purposes, I now perceived Dr X as a loving but all-powerful parent. My psychological state at that time was rather like that of a helpless young child, even though I had no insight or understanding of this at the time. I felt an impelling need to be near him and at the same time I felt afraid of him. My overwhelming feeling was a loss of separateness – as if he and I were inextricably enmeshed so that I could no longer function unless he pulled the strings.

Over several months, our plans and efforts for the Centre gathered momentum. Then Dr X and I had a major row. His professional colleague, Mrs Z, stayed at my house for the weekend, and told me out of the blue that Dr X had arranged to run a series of courses, not at our planned joint centre, but at a completely different venue – in fact, at what was, at least in purely commercial terms, a rival establishment. I was absolutely horrified, because we were by this time financially committed to the Centre, and the building work was now at an advanced stage. Dr X had led me to believe that he was totally committed to the Centre we were planning, so I drove to his house there and then. I was puzzled and annoyed so I asked him straight out for an explanation. Dr X's response completely took the wind out of my sails. He simply asked in a very cool way 'What has this got to do with you?' I was staggered by this reaction, which felt like a denial of all our plans. Then he told me something else which sent me reeling. He had been discussing me with my closest friends and they had, he said, warned him about my motives for wanting to work with him. I felt totally humiliated. I was so hurt that my friends – people I had trusted – could have been so spiteful. It hadn't occurred to me that this man, with his magnetic powers of attraction, had delighted in cultivating a growing entourage of sychophants, all vying for his affection and scheming against anyone they thought might be a rival.

Dr X had been planning to come to see me to discuss dates of courses. However, after this bitter argument, he telephoned me and, after another heated exchange, said that he had finished with me and with the Centre. There was no mention at all of my therapy. A few days later, Dr X seemed to back-track in a dramatic and unexpected fashion. He wrote and said, among other things, that he had decided to open our joint Centre exactly as planned. He said that, for the time being, all communication between us should be through his colleague, Mrs Z, and that we would need to meet before the next group therapy meeting, and that his partner, Y, would be there to 'supervise' the meeting between us. Again there was no mention about what was to happen to my personal therapy with him. I thought I had been left in a state of emotional dependence, with my business plans hanging by a thread.

The whole family had worked very hard to complete the Centre in time for the agreed opening date. By this stage, our plans had passed the point of no return. Three weeks later, I had a telephone call out of the blue from Y, basically ordering me to meet with Dr X in his house the following day. I had pretty well given up hope of a reconciliation by this stage, and I expected that we would just shake hands and part amicably. However, when I arrived for the meeting, Dr X tried to hug me, and then conducted a meditation session with Y and I. In retrospect, I now wonder if this may have been set up to try to get some degree of control over my mind before the meeting itself. All he would say at the time was that we should meditate 'in order to keep our discussions focused'.

After the meditation session, the three of us went out and sat in the garden. I felt very uncomfortable so I decided that I must apologise for the row and then simply leave. However, Dr X again nonplussed me by saying 'Right, you are now going to appoint me Medical Director of the Centre and I am going to accept.' He then went on to set out all the courses he was going to run, while Y sat taking notes. I thought I was dreaming! I told him how wonderful that sounded, feeling enormously relieved. Dr X hugged me warmly and said that we had years of work ahead of us. Dr X said that, because of our continuing business plans, he did not think we should continue with one-to-one therapy sessions. However, he insisted I should attend the next group session. I was still left feeling uncertain and confused by the abrupt end to my therapy, but he told me it was up to me to find another counsellor to continue the work started with him.

Next day Dr X wrote me a formal letter confirming our discussions and our joint plans for the Centre. This letter referred to my role being put on a 'formal professional basis' and, in particular, my need to 'respect those boundaries'. His letter was generally a great relief to me, as it appeared to formalise our plans and our business relationship and outlined the range of courses we would run, 'on terms to be agreed'. He phoned me while I was reading the letter and asked if I was happy with it. He seemed to be every bit as pleased as I was and we agreed that I would send him a formal response accepting his proposals and appointing him as Medical Director. He rang me back the next day to thank me, and to discuss progress with the building and promotional work we needed to do together. Suddenly my future looked pretty good again.

Within weeks we opened our Centre with a grand launch attended by over forty doctors and therapists. It was a very exciting occasion for me. Dr X told me he was delighted with the work we'd done – far better than he'd expected – and he presented me with a beautiful bouquet, including a dozen red roses. That night I revelled in their perfume, but within a week I had to face up to the thorns that were part and parcel of my relationship with my new business partner.

We arranged a business meeting at the Centre a few days after the opening night. Dr X arrived with his partner Y, over an hour late, and we sat round the table and began to look at the Centre's financial arrangements. When we started to discuss the programme of courses, Y asked Dr X if he really wanted to be committed to all this, bearing in mind all the other interesting projects he might be doing. When he started talking in the same vein, I was totally dumbfounded. We had completed a major building and refurbishment programme for him in only 16 weeks. In addition, we had successfully promoted the Centre's work, resulting in considerable interest at the launch only 3 days earlier. I simply couldn't find words to express my shock. I pulled his letter of agreement out and asked him why on earth he had written it. He said I really didn't realise what an important doctor he was. I tried to say that of course I did but he became angry, hammering on my table, shouting 'Oh no you don't!'. Then he said 'You see, it's all a matter of boundaries.' I could no longer hold back my tears of frustration and confusion and rage. Dr X used the expression 'boundaries' only when it suited his purposes. It always upset and confused me. I had in the back of my mind that he was using it as an ongoing provocative taunt, referring back to my rather clumsy attempt to try to sort out my feelings for him earlier in the year. He knew exactly how to hurt me. Y announced that they were leaving. While she was out of the room, Dr X took me in his arms and once again told me I was a very special person. Then he promised me 'Whatever else happens, I will always be your friend'. Then they left. Once again the bottom had dropped out of my world.

The next day, Y rang me to say that she thought I'd misinterpreted Dr X's intentions. She started to lecture me at length about expecting too much of him, and she told me he had never planned to run courses at the Centre. A few minutes after her call Dr X rang me back and apologised to me, saying that nothing had changed and that our plans could still go ahead. This was so utterly confusing for me. From then on Dr X was completely unpredictable, one day warm and enthusiastic, the next day highly critical and aggressive. At those times he would often warn me that unless I complied with whatever he happened to want on that day, he would pull out of the Centre. I started to become very depressed and anxious. Whenever I was with him or talking to him, I became nervous and inhibited.

The final blow came when Dr X rang me unexpectedly, before he had run any courses at our Centre, and told me that he had secured a job with a prestigious alternative therapy provider over a hundred miles away. I was completely devastated by this news. I had lost my therapist, my business partner, and the person I had come to regard as the source of my strength and inspiration. He absolutely refused to meet me or to discuss the mess he'd left me in. During this period I was very confused and my mental state steadily deteriorated. I had been suffering from bouts of quite severe depression, which I related to my fear of Dr X letting me down. I now felt totally abandoned, and in the months that followed I twice came close to suicide. I could not sleep at night and paced the house. During the day, I couldn't keep awake. At times I couldn't eat but at other times I ate compulsively. Sometimes my arms shook uncontrollably. I avoided all my friends, and left the room whenever we had visitors. I rarely went shopping and when I did I usually came home in tears.

Altogether, I was in a very bad emotional state by now, even though I still believed that there must be some way that Dr X and I could discuss the situation and reach an understanding with one another. Because I still held him in such high esteem, I could only view what had gone on as being my fault, but I still could not understand what I'd done wrong. I felt isolated and helpless. Around this time, I was under the care of the Community Mental Health Team for about eight months.

Support and understanding from my husband, family and friends was my lifeline at this difficult time. I had also made contact with a member of POPAN (Prevention Of Professional Abuse Network) because I believed she might be able to mediate between Dr X and myself. It was with her help that I gradually began to realise that Dr X's dual relationships with me had been absolutely unethical and very damaging. I received regular telephone counselling from POPAN, and my counsellor gradually helped me to understand what had happened to me during the course of my relationship with Dr X. I learned about transference and realised for the first time that my dependence on Dr X must have stemmed from the session when I had relived my birth. I had other valuable

insights which were a big help to me in making sense of my fragile
emotional state. One article I read about an abusive relationship within
counselling training in the USA was particularly valuable in helping me
to make sense of my own experience (Anonymous, 1991).

One further development was particularly significant in changing my
attitude towards Dr X. I was advised by a friend to check up on Dr X's
professional qualifications. Up to that point it had never once occurred
to me to doubt that he was a psychiatrist – a claim he had often made to
me and to others. However, in response to my enquiry, I learned from the
Royal College of Psychiatrists that Dr X had never been registered as a
psychiatrist. Intellectually, I could now accept that this man had misrepresented his qualifications and had been out of his depth in his so-called
therapeutic work, and that he had been exploiting the transference
between us for his own ends. Complete emotional acceptance, however,
was to take very much longer than intellectual acceptance.

Gradually, my anger at Dr X grew to the point where I began to consider taking some kind of legal action against him, although the grounds
for action were not initially clear. Apart from the hurt and psychological
pain he had put me through, I had also incurred substantial financial
losses through his withdrawal of support for the Centre at a critical stage
of its development. Without his enthusiastic encouragement, we would
never have invested our time and money so heavily into a somewhat
risky business venture, completely outside my own area of expertise. At
every stage, my usually clear-headed business sense had been fatally
undermined by my desire to please and gain the full approval of Dr X. In
considering legal action, however, one of the initial problems lay in finding a solicitor with sufficient understanding of the issues involved in
inappropriate exploitation of the therapeutic relationship, transference
and dual business-therapy relationships. After three false starts I was
introduced to one of the very few solicitors, at the law firm Frank Allen
Pennington, who specialise in claims involving psychological issues. This
solicitor managed to track down the key legal case of *Werner v Landau*,
and then things started to move. In *Werner v Landau* the judges had
taken the trouble to get to grips with the difficult issue of inappropriate
exploitation of transference in therapy, had recognised the serious damage
caused, and had ruled against the psychiatrist. Winning a case against a
former therapist is by no means easy, and ultimately, after seven gruelling
years I had to be content with receiving a notional sum of £15,000 as an
out-of-court settlement, rather than having the satisfaction of winning
my case in court.

While this sum can never compensate for the damage I had been
caused by Dr X, it was far more than recognition that I had been wronged
by his arrogant and callous behaviour. Dr X had refused to have anything
to do with me since he had abandoned our Centre. I had never been

given the opportunity to resolve all the unfinished business between us. For me, it was absolutely essential to be able to confront him with the enormity of the damage he had done to me. Once we had reached the stage of exchanging evidence, he capitulated and made an offer into Court straight away. At that stage I knew, with a sense of triumph, that I had broken the hold he had over my life.

Dr X had drawn me by degrees into a powerful psychotherapeutic relationship, to which I would never have consented had he not misrepresented his qualifications to me. He had exploited that relationship for his own purposes by inducing in me a state of unquestioning trust and dependency in him, which damaged my physical and mental health, and undermined my family life. He had caused a major ongoing interruption in my career and business activities, severely limiting my earning ability. It took seven years of intermittent therapy and medication to neutralise the compulsion I felt to convert Dr X's initial vision of our Centre into reality, and to reach my current state of equilibrium.

My purpose in writing this account, painful though it has been, is to alert others to the potential dangers lurking in the therapeutic relationship, when the powerful feelings unleashed in the vulnerable client can be manipulated and exploited for gain by an unscrupulous charlatan.

References

Anonymous (1991) 'Sexual harassment: A female counseling student's experience', *Journal of Counseling and Development*, 69: 502–6.

Legal references

Werner v Landau (1961) TLR 8/3/1961, 23/11/1961

5

Transparent Recording: Therapists and the Data Protection Act 1998

Peter Jenkins

Most counsellors and psychotherapists will be familiar with the fact that their clients enjoy a legal right of access to records kept on computer. This right applied under the former Data Protection Act 1984 (DPA 1984). They will also know that clients possess similar rights of access to personal records in the areas of health, education, and social work, under similar legislation. The principle of greater access of citizens as 'data subjects' to information kept on file was established after Graham Gaskin, a young man formerly in residential care, won his case for access to his social work file at the European Court. Access is, however, *qualified*, rather than total. Restrictions limiting access to information have taken various forms in the past, including a requirement for counselling prior to obtaining access to adoption information, under the Adoption Act 1976, or the operation of time limits protecting information recorded prior to the legislation taking effect, and above all, provision for access to be denied where it may cause the applicant or others 'serious harm'.

Clients' rights of access to personal files have taken a further step forward under the Data Protection Act 1998 (DPA 1998), introduced to comply with European Directive 95/46/EC. This radical piece of legislation substantially widens the rights of clients to information kept on file, including information kept in handwritten records, rather than simply on computer (Carey, 1998).

There has been some uncertainty about precisely how the new legislation will affect therapists (BACP, 1998). (The term therapist will be used here as a generic term to apply to both counsellors and psychotherapists.) The use of computerised therapeutic records may be increasing (Ross, 1996), but many practitioners may well still keep much client material in

(The following extract from *Counselling*, 10(5), pp. 387–91 is reproduced with kind permission of the British Association for Counselling and Psychotherapy – holder of the copyright.)

manual form, rather than on computer. The situation is further complicated by the fact that, for many counsellors and psychotherapists, there is an absence of any specific legal requirements to keep records as a profession, unlike that applying to nurses, for example. The broad range of organisational contexts in which therapists work can also impose a wide variety of styles and requirements for record keeping (Easton and Plant, 1998). Despite this, however, therapists belong to a professional culture where record keeping is seen to be important for a complex set of purposes, ranging from personal reflection to professional development. The extension of clients' rights of access to manual records (probably the most favoured form of record keeping for many therapists) thus poses a number of important issues to be resolved, beyond that of simple knowledge of, and compliance with, the law.

Purposes of record keeping

The changes in the law need, first, to be placed in the context of the professional culture of counselling and psychotherapy, and of the rationale for the emphasis placed on recording within professional training and practice. McMahon (1994) suggests that there are a number of specific purposes for keeping records, including the following:

- as memory aid
- to monitor client progress
- for administrative reasons
- to aid process of referral
- for training/accreditation purposes
- to assist therapeutic audit
- for legal reasons
- for internal complaints procedures
- as a tool for reflection

McMahon suggests a wide range of justifications for recording, from keeping brief notes as an *aide-mémoire*, to writing detailed case studies, which may be required for the purposes of further training or for professional accreditation (Parker, 1995). Case studies as a specialised form of recording, in turn, may pose particular problems regarding client confidentiality, given the appreciable danger of client self-recognition in the event of wider publication (Bond, 2000: 12–13).

   Keeping therapeutic records on clients may be a clear agency requirement, and one that is increasingly emphasised with the need to demonstrate cost-effectiveness to management bodies, or to external funding organisations. It was previously an ethical requirement by BACP that practitioners inform clients of any records that were kept, under section B.4.3.4 of the former Code of Ethics (BACP, 1998). Under the current BACP *Ethical Framework*, counsellors are encouraged, but not required, to keep records of client work. In addition, the *Framework* states that 'Practitioners should take into account their responsibilities and their clients' rights under data protection legislation and any other legal requirements' (BACP, 2002a: 6). It is probably the area of records kept for personal reflection which may prove to be most problematic for counsellors and psychotherapists, given that these recordings may well be highly personal and speculative by their very nature. Despite the importance accorded to recording within the professional culture, McMahon (1994) also notes that it is rarely taught in a systematic way on training courses, although useful guidelines are available (Bond, 2000; Davy, 1999; du Plessis and Hirst, 1999). In addition, there seems to be a pervasive uncertainty among counsellors and psychotherapists about the length of time that records should be kept (Easton and Plant, 1998). From a narrowly legal perspective, it has been suggested that the relevant time limit of 6 years should apply (Cristofoli, 1999; Jenkins, 1997). This period (plus a year as a safety margin) corresponds to the time limits for bringing certain types of legal case against the counsellor or psychotherapist, and is used by lawyers as a basic principle applying to their own record keeping practice.

Requirements for data protection

The Data Protection Act (DPA) 1998 came into effect in March 2000. It is a complex, detailed piece of legislation, which requires careful interpretation and guidance. It starts with a wide, all-inclusive definition of data processing, and replaces the earlier concept of 'data user' with the more specific terms of 'data controller' and 'data processor'. Counsellors and psychotherapists who themselves hold personal data on their clients are thus 'data controllers'. The term 'data processors' refers, broadly, to computer bureaux. Where therapists keep records which are further processed by their agency, such as a voluntary organisation, then the organisation will indicate the named person to act as the data controller.

The change in focus within the Act is significant, in that it signals a clear political purpose behind the law. The extension of citizens' rights as 'data subjects' is part of a wider cultural change within society, according to the officers of the former Data Protection Commissioner, now Information Commissioner (Interview with DPR, 1999). Together with the Freedom of Information Act 2000 and Human Rights Act 1998, the Data Protection Act 1998 represents a profound opening up of the structures of civil society to wider scrutiny and transparency. It is taken as a fundamental right of citizens to know what records are being kept about them, subject to necessary restrictions needed for the operation of taxation, national security, and the justice system. Given the widest possible commitment to this new spirit of openness, the full extent and implications of the Act cannot be captured in brief official guidelines, but will await the future decisions of the courts, in resolving key test cases concerning rights of access. The Act is therefore far wider in its potential scope than simply posing a new set of regulations concerning the keeping of records. It marks the start of a major cultural change, with a particular challenge to counsellors and psychotherapists as a professional group, because of the very centrality of recording within their established practice (cf Jenkins, 2001; Jenkins and Palmer, 2000).

One possible response might be for counsellors and psychotherapists to adjust to what is now required by the letter of the new law, in other words, to adopt what the officers of the Information Commissioner term a 'minimal compliance' approach. It is interesting from this point of view that the number of prosecutions of counsellors and psychotherapists under the former DPA 1984 has been almost non-existent in the past, with probably only one case linked to an agency providing counselling-type services. In terms of monitoring compliance in the related area of health services, an estimated 2,500 General Practitioners were thought, at one stage, to be risking fines by failing to register under the DPA 1984 as required. In 1997, a GP was, in fact, the subject of a prosecution for failure to register correctly (Smith, 1998).

There is a danger, however, of seeing the law in terms of simple compliance, rather than in coming to terms with what it represents as a sea-change in public attitudes towards the limits of professional accountability and confidentiality. Counsellors and psychotherapists need to go beyond simple *compliance* to grasp the real purpose of the Act, and to consider the serious implications for their own practice.

The Data Protection Act 1998 covers a number of key aspects, about which counsellors and psychotherapists need to be well informed. These include the revised principles for data protection, issues concerning client access to manual records, new categories of data requiring safe handling, and the time scales for implementation. Under the Act, personal data means information relating to an identifiable living person. As said, the revised definition of data processing covers almost any conceivable use or handling of such information. As the Introduction to the Act states, this 'is a compendious definition and it is difficult to envisage any action involving data which does not amount to processing within this definition' (DPR, 1998: 6). The intention to capture and regulate the widest possible access to such data is made very clear, given the Act's breadth of remit. The principles of the Act are slightly revised and amended from the 1984 version. Personal data is to be:

1   Processed fairly and lawfully
2   Obtained only for one or more specified lawful purposes
3   Adequate, relevant and not excessive for their purpose
4   Accurate and kept up to date
5   Not kept longer than is necessary
6   Processed in accordance with the rights of data subjects
7   Protected against unauthorised use or loss
8   Not transferred outside the European Economic Area (i.e. the 15 EU members states, plus Iceland, Liechtenstein and Norway) unless subject to similar levels of data protection

These principles are broadly similar to those of the DPA 1984. The crucial change lies in the extension of the rights of clients, or data subjects, to information kept in the form of *manual records* – information previously unavailable under the 1984 Act. However, the situation is made more complex by the fact that clients already enjoy substantial rights of access to their own education, health and social work files, i.e. 'accessible records', under a range of similar legislation and regulations. The DPA 1998 specifies that where such information is part of a health record kept by a health professional, then the client will already possess a qualified right of access, for example, under the provisions of the former Access to Health Records Act 1990. Section 69 of the DPA 1998 refers to those who are identified as 'health professionals' for the purposes of the Act, under yet another piece of legislation, the Professions Supplementary to Medicine Act 1960. This is a rather fragmented and incomplete list, referring, for example, to clinical psychologists and child psychotherapists, but not to counsellors and adult psychotherapists as such. Client access to handwritten therapeutic notes would depend here on whether the notes were kept as part of a specific 'health record'. If they were not defined as part of such a record, then access would still be possible, if the type of manual recording system being used met key criteria. The Introduction refers to a 'relevant filing system', meaning 'any set of information relating to individuals … [where] the set is structured, either by reference to individuals or by criteria relating to individuals, in such a way that specific information relating to a particular individual is readily accessible' (DPR, 1998: 3).

According to Iain Bourne, Data Compliance Manager at the Office of the Data Protection Registrar, purely manual counselling records will not require to be registered or 'notified' under the terms of the Act:

> If you've only got information which falls within a 'relevant filing system', ie non-automated files, or you've only got a relevant filing system and non-automated accessible records, i.e. paper-held records, you do not need to register, where that is the only data you have. If you also have automated records, you do have to register under the Act. (Interview with DPR, 1999)

The purpose of the Act in adopting a catch-all definition of data processing is to widen the rights of citizens to information being kept on them, with certain narrowly defined exemptions. Although the previous legislation is to be repealed, clients' rights of access to health, education and social work records will remain as established rights in law, covered by specific Statutory Instruments. The actual effect of the Act is to target manual files of a highly specific kind, or those held in combination with a computerised system, on a PC for example. Counselling and psychotherapy client files held solely in the form of a card index, not linked to a computer database, do not therefore require notification, according to the above authority.

However, even if a therapist was not required to notify the Information Commissioner, on the basis of solely holding purely *manual* files, he or she would still be required to work to the principles of the legislation concerning the transparency of their systems for holding information. If a client requested access, then the counsellor would have to disclose to them their 'registerable particulars', outlining the general nature of the records kept within 21 days. This would be the case even if the therapist concerned was not formally registered (or 'notified' in the new terminology) under the DPA 1998. According to Ian Miller, Data Compliance Officer with the DPR, 'somebody holding purely manual records in counselling, even though they wouldn't have to notify or register with us, they would still have to have an understanding of the principles that they are required to abide by' (Interview with DPR, 1999). This would apply, for example, to the proposed transfer of client data outside the European Economic Area. Similarly, a counsellor or psychotherapist planning to take client records to the United States, would need to be aware that data protection standards there are not set at a federal level, but vary significantly from state to state.

The question remains as to *why* the therapist might not want to offer open access to their manual records, even though some manual records fall outside the requirement for notification. As outlined above, much counselling and psychotherapy recording would be in an 'objective' format for evaluation and/or agency purposes. However, some records might contain more personal, reflective material which, if disclosed, could be thought damaging to the therapeutic alliance. McMahon gives hypothetical examples that may well be representative of much therapeutic recording, in terms of the practitioner's subjective and personal responses to the client and to the process of therapy, such as:

'I suspect that E hooks into my not o.k. child.'
'I find E particularly draining to work with.'
'I really dislike K and do not know why – take to supervision.'
'I find myself wanting to "mother" J and I shall take this to my next supervision session' (1994: 264).

The tradition, indeed the *necessity*, of recording such highly personal and subjective responses is well established in counselling and psychotherapy training and practice. Therapists may need to rethink this approach if they are reluctant to share these personal reflections with their clients. Where the client material is very sensitive in nature, for example, concerning erotic or counter-transference material, then its disclosure outside the therapeutic context can have serious repercussions for the perceived professionalism and competence of the practitioner. This happened in the case of Dr Margaret Bean-Bayog, a psychiatrist in the United States. Her detailed and sexually explicit personal therapeutic records became evidence in a malpractice case, following her client's suicide. Although the case was settled out of court, without an admission of liability, her license to practise was subsequently withdrawn by the state of Massachusetts (McNamara, 1995). It needs to be remembered that, outside of data protection law, clients can, in any case, gain access to their own records through the legal process of 'discovery', given that counsellors and psychotherapists do not possess anything approaching the degree of professional privilege enjoyed by solicitors regarding confidential protection for client files (Bond, 1998).

Sensitive personal data

The Data Protection Act 1998 introduced a category of information requiring special consideration, which has a particular relevance to counsellors and psychotherapists. The broad category of 'sensitive personal data' consists of information recording the data subject's racial or ethnic origin, political or religious beliefs, trade union membership, history of offending or court sentences. More relevant to counsellors and psychotherapists is the fact that sensitive personal data also includes information about a person's mental or physical health and sexual life. Handling such information now requires the *explicit* consent of the client, unless the processing is carried out for medical purposes, by a 'health professional', or by a person owing a duty of confidentiality equivalent to that of a health professional. Whether counsellors and psychotherapists would qualify under the latter grounds has yet to be definitively established by a court of law, and is still subject to ongoing debate (Bond, 1998). Recording this category of sensitive personal information now places a requirement on the therapist to obtain the client's explicit consent. This is defined in the original Directive as 'any freely given specific and informed indication of his wishes by which the data subject signifies his agreement to personal data relating to him being processed' (Article 2 (h), Directive 95/46/EC). This implies an *active* process of giving consent, rather than one where the client is assumed to have given it, for example, by the client having failed to return an opting-out card or leaflet.

Counsellors and psychotherapists need to be scrupulous in working to the principles and requirements of the Act, by clearly obtaining client agreement for recording sensitive personal data. Further, it should become the case that therapists strive to develop 'best practice' in promoting client rights as citizens concerning the use of personal information. Gaining explicit client consent has become more widespread as established practice in other professional activities. The General Medical Council, for example, now requires written patient consent for inclusion in research and publication (GMC, 1998). It needs to become established 'best practice' for clients' explicit consent to be obtained for therapeutic records as a matter of routine.

Time scales for implementation

The complexity of the law means that it will be phased in over a period of time, to enable individuals and organisations to comply with its requirements. The provision for client access to manual records is thought to pose major problems in certain areas, such as personnel departments in large companies, which need addressing carefully. Personal data which was being processed prior to 24 October 1998 had until 2001 to comply with the new law. Data recorded manually and processed before the starting date of October 1998 has a further transitional period, up to 2007, to comply with the Act. The transitional periods refer to complex combinations of data kept on computer and in manual systems. The regulations are complex, and as the Introduction admits, not entirely clear, requiring further guidance and regulations to be issued by the Home Secretary at a future date.

The Act presents a major challenge to established practice within the counselling and psychotherapy profession, particularly in terms of recording the therapist's subjective evaluation of their own process, and of the developing therapeutic relationship with the client. This kind of challenge has, however, been experienced and met by other professional groups in the past. Social work recording used to contain a mix of 'task' and 'process' elements prior to the regulations opening up case files to client scrutiny. This shift required the conscious adoption of a more focussed and accountable style of record keeping, often negotiated and shared with the client (Gelman, 1990; Payne, 1989). In the field of psychiatry, one small scale research project suggests that even extremely sensitive information about a client's diagnosis can be shared with them, with usually positive outcomes for the working relationship (Kosky and Burns, 1995; Laugharne and Stafford, 1996). Counsellors and psychotherapists need to adapt to the revised legal requirements by reconsidering the type of data that is recorded, and the ways in which this can be shared, if necessary, with clients. It may be the case that personal reflections will no longer be recorded, even manually, to avoid the likelihood of clients' gaining access to material which may be misconstrued. There does seem to be a small but discernible trend for some therapists and their employing agencies no longer to keep any records. This is intended precisely to *prevent* their subsequent disclosure, although this is more with reference to discovery by the courts, rather than to access by clients under data protection law.

Implications of data protection law

There are a number of key implications arising from the Act, both for organisations providing counselling, and for individual therapists. Agencies clearly need to notify the Information Commissioner if involved in processing personal data. Futhermore, a full audit of all forms of recording undertaken by the staff of the agency should be carried out. In counselling organisations, this will often comprise a wide range of activities, not all of which may be known to or fully appreciated by management. Recording may include audio- and video-taping of work with clients, production of formal agency records of client contact, and also of more informal 'process' notes or *aide-mémoires* for use in supervision. Implementing a clear policy on data protection requires that the organisation has a firm grasp of the many ways in which data is actually being recorded and processed in its name. Organisations need to undertake a risk assessment, in order to identify forms of recording which may be incompatible with data protection law. For example, counsellor process notes kept may be kept 'off-site' in insecure and unaccountable formats, thus restricting client entitlement to gain access to notes as a data subject. Agencies may also compile 'risk registers' of clients posing a risk of violence or aggression towards staff, to which client access may be denied. Information on data protection practice needs to be conveyed clearly to clients, concerning their rights to access notes. Overall, organisations may wish to review their policy on record keeping, and consider opting for a proactive rather than reactive stance towards client access. This may be considered as an entitlement and as a norm of good practice, rather than as an event signalling client distrust and as a feared precursor of a formal complaint about the quality of the service.

Similarly, therapists may take the challenge of the law as an opportunity to review their own values and practice with regard to recording. Of necessity, this must entail a reconsideration of the status and worth of process notes, as a form of covert professional recording which is increasingly at odds with a developing culture of openness and transparency. All forms of recording need to be put under careful scrutiny. Supervision notes, for example, may be exempt from the client's right of access, where the client is not identifiable. Other forms of recording, for example, such as case studies, are problematic, obviously requiring client consent and anonymisation, but which do not hold a clear status as an integral part of a client's overall record. Process notes might be kept simply as short-life notes which are routinely destroyed immediately after use as prompts in supervision.

Therapists need to think carefully about the content of recording, in the light of data protection principles. The Act extends client access from records of *fact* to those containing *opinions about and intentions towards* the client. Anecdotally, much therapist recording appears to contain much subjective material about the counsellor's personal responses to the client. For example, Mearns suggests up to 20 possible topics for supervision, only one of which actually relates to what can be described as direct observations on the client (Mearns, 1997: pp. 82–3). Structuring therapy notes in terms of three separate headings such as Facts; Opinions; and Intentions, might bring this point home in a salutary and instructive way to therapists trying to calibrate recording with the spirit and letter of the law. Elsewhere, a format for distinguishing recording in terms of material which is core, critical, simply circumstantial or even questionable is suggested as a guide (Jenkins, 2001: 4).

The complexity of data protection law arises from the fact that therapists do not sit neatly in boxes, but practice across a wide and growing diversity of settings. In specific settings, such as health, education and social work, records are covered by pre-existing regulations, and are thus termed 'accessible' records. There are governed by specific regulations in the form of Statutory Instruments, with distinct provision for limiting client access in the case of 'serious harm', either physical or psychological, arising to the client or to a third party. There are key issues relating to these more specialised forms of record, of which therapists need to be well informed. For example, there is an apparent conflict of parental and child rights concerning access to counselling notes comprising part of a child's educational record, which remains to be clarified via regulations or case law (BACP, 2002b: 19). In the medical field, where therapists are increasingly working in primary and secondary care settings, therapy records comprise part of the patient or client's health record. This may present problems in a multi-disciplinary team setting, where sensitive client material disclosed in a therapeutic context is potentially accessible by other team members without a demonstrable 'need to know'. This issue is likely to gain added significance in the light of accelerating moves towards the adoption of Electronic Patient Records in the NHS in the coming period.

Conclusion

The Data Protection Act 1998 extended established rights of client access from computer records to both computer and manual files. This presents a problem of adaptation by the counselling and psychotherapy profession, in that its recording has often contained highly subjective personal reflections in the past, which were not originally intended for sharing with the client. The experience of other professional groups, such as social work and medicine, may be a useful guide in some respects here. The regulations concerning the Act are complex, but contain exemption from the notification requirement for certain records solely kept in manual form. Despite this, the wider purpose of the Act is clearly to extend the rights of clients as citizens, and to increase the extent of professional accountability for handling personal data. The adoption of best practice will require counsellors and psychotherapists to work within the *spirit* of the Act, rather than to work simply on the basis of minimal compliance. Such best practice requires obtaining the explicit consent of clients for the recording and handling of new categories of sensitive personal information, itself the lifeblood of the therapeutic process. Ultimately, the central concept of therapeutic recording will be tested, and will perhaps even be radically reshaped, by the extension of clients' rights in the field of data protection and access to records.

References

Bond, T. (2000) *Standards and Ethics for Counselling in Action*. (2nd edition) London: Sage.

Bond, T. (1998) *Confidentiality: Counselling and the Law*. Rugby: BACP.

British Association for Counselling and Psychotherapy (1998) *Code of Ethics and Practice for Counsellors*. Rugby: BACP.

British Association for Counselling and Psychotherapy (1999) 'Getting in on the Act', *Counselling Matters*. No. 1: 12.

British Association for Counselling and Psychotherapy (2002a) *Ethical Framework for Good Practice in Counselling and Psychotherapy*. Rugby: BACP.

British Association for Counselling and Psychotherapy (2002b) *Good Practice Guidance for Counselling in Schools*. Rugby: BACP.

Carey, P. (1998) *Blackstone's Guide to the Data Protection Act 1998*. London: Blackstone.

Cristofoli, G. (1999) *Personal communication*. Bookers and Bolton, Solicitors to UKCP.

Data Protection Registrar (1998) *The Data Protection Act 1998: An Introduction*. Wilmslow: DPR.

Davy, J. (1999) 'How to write a client case study', in Bor, R. and Watt, M. (eds) *The Trainee Handbook*. London: Sage. pp. 35–60.

Directive 95/46/EC, *Official Journal of the European Communities*, L281, Vol. 38, 23/11/1995.

du Plessis, P. and Hirst, F. (1999) 'Written communication about clients', in Bor, R. and Watt, M. (eds) *The Trainee Handbook*. London: Sage. pp. 87–106.

Easton, S. and Plant, B. (1998) 'Practical approaches: Clients' notes – how long should we keep them?', *Counselling*, 9(3): 188–90.

Gelman, S. (1990) 'The practicalities of open access record systems', *Journal of Social Welfare Law*, 4: 256–69.

General Medical Council (1998) *Seeking Patients' Consent: The Ethical Considerations*. London: GMC.

Interview with officers of Data Protection Registrar (1999) 31 March.

Jenkins, P. (1997) *Counselling, Psychotherapy and the Law*. London: Sage.

Jenkins, P. (2001) *Access to Records of Counselling and Psychotherapy* (BACP Information Sheet). Rugby: BACP.

Jenkins, P. and Palmer, I. (2000) *Record Keeping and the Data Protection Act 1998* (BACP Information Sheet). Rugby: BACP.

Kosky, N. and Burns, T. (1995) 'Patient access to psychiatric records: Experience in an in-patient unit', *Psychiatric Bulletin*, 19: 87–90.

Laugharne, R. and Stafford, A. (1996) 'Access to records and client held records for people with mental illness: A literature review', *Psychiatric Bulletin*, 20: 338–41.

McMahon, G. (1994) 'Practical approaches: Note taking', *Counselling*, 5(3), pp. 183–4; 5(4), pp. 264–5.

McNamara, E. (1995) *Breakdown: Sex, Suicide and the Harvard Psychiatrist*. New York: Pocket Books.

Mearns, D. (1997) *Person-Centred Counselling Training*. London: Sage.

Parker, M. (1995) 'Practical approaches: Case study writing', *Counselling*, 6(1): 19–21.

Payne, M. (1989) 'Open records and shared decisions with clients', in Shardlow, S. (ed.) *The Values of Change in Social Work*. London: Tavistock/Routledge. pp. 114–34.

Ross, P. (1996) 'Paperless client records', in Palmer, S., Dainow, S. and Milner, P. (eds) *Counselling: The BAC Counselling Reader*. London: Sage/BAC. pp. 474–84.

Smith, N. (1998) 'GPs face data protection fines', *General Practitioner*, 10 April, p. 10.

Legal references

Statute:

Adoption Act 1976
Access to Health Records Act 1990
Data Protection Act 1984
Data Protection Act 1998
Freedom of Information Act 2000
Human Rights Act 1998
Professions Supplementary to Medicine Act 1960

Acknowledgement

The assistance of Iain Bourne, Data Compliance Manager, and Ian Miller, Data Compliance Officer, of the Office of the Information Commissioner, in researching this article, is gratefully acknowledged.

6

Preparing Reports and Presenting Evidence in Court: A Guide for Counsellors and Psychotherapists

Philip Pollecoff

It comes as a surprise to most non-lawyers that the legal profession works long and hard in civil proceedings to *avoid* trials. This is because trials are risky, expensive and nerve racking for the participants. It is better that lawyers resolve disputes wherever possible by settlement. Accordingly, most cases never reach a trial. The Legal Services Commission, which funds public law cases such as care cases and assists litigants on low incomes in civil and family disputes, is also prudent regarding funding a case to trial.

Purpose of appearing in court

The main objective of any preparation for the court is to assist it in its task of justly resolving a dispute or examining a situation. A witness statement or a report forms part of the evidence placed before the court and the parties concerned to be weighed at a trial. Therefore, when a therapist (i.e. counsellor or psychotherapist) is asked to give evidence, or is initially approached to write a report, it is important that he or she bears in mind the requirements of:

- writing a report of sufficient clarity that does not raise more questions than it answers
- helping the parties reach a truer understanding with a view to resolving the dispute

When initially approached, and before actually tackling the report, it is crucial for the therapist to recognise in what areas the answers or information is lacking. Sometimes, the true position is that there may be no easy answers to a given scenario and degrees of risk, whatever course of action is adopted. It may be that the therapist's expertise is insufficient and so another expert is more apposite.

There could be a conflict of interest, or the therapist could have developed a relationship with the subject of the report, which would cloud objectivity. Competing needs should be considered with clarity. When approached to give evidence, it is easy to become flustered if the situation is messy. However, a therapist should pick apart those aspects which are confusing and should not panic at the thought of giving evidence in court. Instructions should be clarified and the rules of the particular tribunal for whom the report is requested must be investigated. If the therapist is instructed by solicitors, the latter can assist in this task.

One of the best ways of becoming clear as to the purpose of the report is to discuss with those requiring it:

- the limitations of any knowledge or expertise
- the amount of time needed to prepare the report
- the number of additional interviews with the parties, where relevant
- the issues that the counsellor is prepared to address

It is perfectly proper to state at the outset that the therapist is qualified to give an opinion on issues x and y, but not on z. When requested to write a report, the therapist should prepare a report on the agreement that it will form not only the basis of any oral evidence, but will be the *sum total* of the oral evidence. In other words the report needs to answer all the questions that are likely to be raised. The most difficult report can be written without too much hardship, if a cool methodical approach is taken.

Counsellors and psychotherapists are in a unique position when asked to give evidence, for the following reasons:

- Unlike other professionals, they do not necessarily keep detailed notes of each session held with a client.
- Their qualifications as quasi-psychologists may be thrown into doubt, or at least examined against their opinion, as to the degree of expertise they can claim in making a particular judgement.
- Therapists perceive the adversarial legal approach as being contrary to the culture of therapy, in that lawyers wish to analyse *facts* and therapists are more concerned with *motivation*. This perception is somewhat misconceived. However, while the court room and the law are considered an alien environment for therapists, these concerns must be addressed.
- Problems can arise regarding client confidentiality in the context of presenting reports or giving evidence.

Wherever possible these problems should be addressed before any commitment is made to acting as a witness. The courts rely on the evidence presented at the trial to such a degree that in 1961 Lord Justice Parker commented that: 'A Judge is not supposed to know anything about the facts of life until they have been presented in evidence and explained to him three times'. This is a slight exaggeration. However, the facts must be presented before the court, with supposition and assumption being distinguished from factual information. The expert advises and the Judge decides on the basis of all the evidence. The court can come to a conclusion that is contrary to expert opinion in certain circumstances.

However, expert evidence is relied on by the courts on a daily basis. For example, in clinical negligence claims, the claimant must prove the vital element of a breach of duty of care. The Judge will rarely be in a position to make any decision in this regard without some medical evidence, and a medical report is now an essential element of the pleadings in a personal injury claim.

If a therapist is requested to make a statement or write a report, the very first step before agreeing to participate is to find out on what basis the evidence is being requested. For instance:

An expert witness   An expert witness gives evidence *both* of fact and opinion. A distinction can be drawn between the *opinion* of the expert and the *facts* of the case: '... those who call psychiatrists as witnesses should remember that the facts upon which they base their opinions must be proved by admissible evidence. This elementary principle is often overlooked' (*R v Turner* [1975] Lawton LJ at 840). Experts are entitled to give such opinion as evidence because of their qualifications and experience in their field of expertise. Evidence is given in the form of a report.

A professional witness   A professional witness gives mainly factual evidence, but can give opinion based on their professional qualifications and experience. Evidence is given in the form of a statement. This statement may be read out in open court without the need for them to give evidence, unless it is disputed by the other party.

A professional witness statement may, for example, be a statement by a surgeon verifying the time and cause of death in a road accident case. The element of opinion may be regarding cause of death and may not be disputed. Or it may take the form of a statement from a counsellor describing a course of attendance and the nature of any intervention made. The nature of the intervention may have an element of opinion and again may not be disputed.

A witness of fact   A witness of fact merely gives evidence as to what happened in a case e.g. a therapist recalls that a client attended on a series of given dates and times. The primacy of factual evidence depends on the nature of the case. The parties may need to know that X undertook a course of counselling on given dates and is willing to undertake further counselling for, say, anger management. The success or failure of the previous therapy is not at issue. The issue is that X is willing to tackle the problem. A brief note from the therapist is all that is required. It is unlikely that a Family Court will insist on a formal witness statement. On the other hand, the same evidence may provide an alibi to a murder case. In such circumstances, the therapist will be asked to show his or her diary and other material evidence, to corroborate the facts.

It is important at every instance to grasp the *purpose* for which the evidence is being required and to appreciate the *proportionality* or *seriousness* of the evidence. Furthermore, different rules govern the criminal and civil courts. The Family Court has its own guidelines regarding the presentation of expert evidence where children are concerned, primarily in abuse cases. So, before accepting instructions, a therapist should request in some detail the *nature* of the evidence required. Also, it is important not to take the response at face value, because there is often a significant degree of 'creep' regarding evidence. This is illustrated by the following example. Counsellor X is asked to give a short statement to the solicitors for her client, Mrs Y. This confirms the fact that Mrs Y is receiving counselling for emotional trauma experienced during her marriage. Counsellor X writes a four-line note, which Mrs Y exhibits in her witness statement as corroborative evidence regarding contact proceedings concerning her children. If this evidence is not accepted, the court may request a more detailed report from counsellor X, or the court may request an independent counsellor to write a report on Mrs Y. The latter, in turn, will contact counsellor X for more information, or counsellor X may be called to give evidence at the hearing of the contact issues.

To summarise, whenever a report is being requested, before accepting the instructions, a therapist should:

- ascertain the purpose for which the evidence is being required
- discover whether it is a report requested by the court, or a joint report, i.e. for both parties to the proceedings
- clarify whether the request is to be a witness of fact *or* an expert witness
- request sufficient background information as necessary
- ensure familiarity with all significant developments in the case, requesting updates from those instructing as necessary
- adhere to any time limits, as most reports are timetabled by the court

Reports in civil proceedings

It has long been recognised by the judiciary that expert evidence has often been abused in its use in the civil justice system. As part of the general reforms known as the Woolf Reforms presented in *Access to Justice* (1996), the system of civil justice was overhauled and a new policy implemented regarding expert witnesses. Under the *Civil Procedure Rules (The White Book)*, part 35 of which governs expert witnesses, an expert is defined as 'an expert who has been instructed to give or prepare evidence for court proceeding' (Civil Procedure Rules, part 35 r 2). Under CPR Prt 35 r. 3:

(1) It is the duty of an expert to help the court on the matters within his expertise.
(2) This duty overrides any obligation to the person from who he has received instructions or by whom he is paid.

Expert reports are addressed *to the court* and not to one particular party to any proceedings. Such reports are commonly either ordered by the court, or by a joint letter of instruction from the parties concerned. Experts' reports are therefore no longer partisan. The court insists that the expert acts on behalf of the court rather than of a party to the proceedings. However, under CPR part 35 r 14, the expert can apply to the court for directions to assist him in carrying out his function as an expert witness and he may do so without giving notice to either party. Accordingly, if for any of the reasons outlined at the beginning, a therapist is in a dilemma regarding giving expert evidence in a civil case, he or she can apply to the court for directions.

Occasions may still arise when a therapist is asked to undertake a report on behalf of one party, or indeed such a report has arisen before proceedings and the therapist is then called to give evidence. This is likely to arise in Employment Tribunals and employment law cases, as when counselling has been provided for a worker who has complained of harassment. The therapist's report may be supplemented by that of the clinical psychologist initiating the referral. When writing the report, it should be borne in mind that it could be used in evidence. Extra care should be taken to make the report inclusive of all relevant facts.

In medical negligence cases, the expert is required to advise on the doctor's medical practice in relation to the damage allegedly suffered by the patient. The standard applied to the defendant in medical negligence cases is the well-known *Bolam* test, which is essentially a form of professional peer defence. This defines negligence in terms of failure to act 'in accordance with a practice accepted as proper by a responsible body of medical men skilled in that particular art' (*Bolam v Friern HMC* [1957] at 121). This test would also be applied to allegedly negligent cases of counselling, psychotherapy and psychological testing or treatment (*Werner v Landau* (1961); *Phelps v Hillingdon LBC* [1997]). Negligence would be established on the basis of expert evidence on whether the therapy in question was consistent with that of 'a body of competent respected professional opinion' (*Bolam* [1957] at 121).

Following the *Bolitho* case [1997], it has been held that expert opinion has to demonstrate that the course of action taken by the practitioner was *logically defensible*, as well as being consistent with standard practice according to the *Bolam* test. It is thought that this additional requirement for the expert's report will actually apply only in rare cases of medical negligence, and will probably be even rarer still in cases of negligent psychotherapy.

Sometimes, in a personal injury claim, a therapist's report may be required as well as a medical report, to be annexed to the claim at the start of the proceedings. This is written on behalf of the claimant to support the claim, although the same expectation of impartiality is implicit in the objective standing of the report. The report will be addressed to the court and not to instructing solicitors. The instructing solicitor will require the addition of a statement of truth in accordance with the *Civil Procedure Rules*. This is a statement on the bottom of the report that states: 'I believe that the facts I have stated in this report are true and that the opinions that I have expressed are correct.'

In the report, the expert must confirm that they understand their duty to the court and have complied with that duty. The report will contain the expert's qualifications, any literature relied upon in preparation of the report and the substance of the solicitor's instructions to the expert. It should be noted that, once the report has been filed with the court and disclosed, any party may use the report at the trial. Accordingly, if the report is unfavourable to the party who commissioned the report, the opposing party could call the therapist to give evidence or rely on the content of the report.

In certain civil cases, known as 'fast track cases', unless there is a direction to the contrary, an expert will not be called to give evidence at all. Therefore the court will rely entirely on the written content of the report. Once an expert's report has been served on another party, the latter may serve written questions about it on its proponent within 28 days of service. This situation will be uncommon.

Reports in criminal proceedings

In criminal cases, the duties of an expert are similar to civil cases, and were set out in *The Ikarian Reefer* [1993] by Cresswell, J. This is a frequently quoted passage, which is set out below in full. This is because, where there are no set rules or guidance forthcoming from a tribunal, these rules provide the anticipated standard.

(a) Expert evidence presented to the Court should be and should be seen to be, the independent product of the expert uninfluenced as to form or content or the exigencies of litigation.

(b) An expert witness should provide independent assistance to the Court by way of objective unbiased opinion in relation to matters within his expertise. An expert witness in the High court should never assume the role of advocate.

(c) An expert witness should state facts or assumptions on which his opinion is based. He should not omit to consider material facts which could detract from his concluded opinion.

(d) An expert witness should make it clear when a particular question or issue falls outside his expertise.

(e) If an expert's opinion is not properly researched because he considers that insufficient data is available, then this must be stated with an indication that the opinion is no more than a provisional one. In cases where an expert witness who has prepared a report could not assert that the report contained the truth the whole truth and nothing but the truth without some qualification, that qualification should be stated in the report.

(f) If, after exchange of reports, an expert witness changes his view on a material matter having read the other side's expert's report or for any other reason, such change of view should be communicated (through legal representatives) to the other side without delay and when appropriate to the Court.

(g) Where expert evidence refers to photographs, plans, calculations, analyses, measurements, survey reports or to other similar documents, these must be provided to the opposite party at the same time as the exchange of reports.

Notwithstanding the sentiments expressed in (a), an expert must address the issues in the case. Defining expertise in (d) is particularly interesting for therapists, as a detailed explanation of expertise should be made. If a practitioner specialises in relationship counselling, an opinion on a post traumatic stress victim, even if he is the counsellor's client, would have to be highly qualified. This is because a broadly based counselling qualification and expertise may cover this area, but any actual experience and standard of non textbook knowledge may be very limited.

It is important to note that in criminal proceedings certain psychiatric evidence is inadmissible. For example psychiatric evidence is inadmissible in order to establish whether the accused was likely to have been provoked (*R v Turner* [1975]). In this case, evidence that the accused had a deep emotional relationship with the victim, that produced both blind rage after a confession of infidelity and profound grief after the killing was presented. This was, however, considered a matter within human experience requiring no expert assistance. As such it is worth asking instructing solicitors in criminal proceedings about those matters that a therapist may give an expert opinion on and those which will not be admissible.

Reports in children's and family proceedings

When the therapist is asked to give evidence regarding children, unless he or she has previous experience or training in this area, then it is advisable to seek full guidance from those instructing. In family proceedings, reports are commonly requested by solicitors and the court regarding:

- the suitability of a child for therapy
- the effect on a child of reduced or increased contact with an absent parent
- the effect of a child being placed in care

This is to determine whether a proposed order concerning the child's future under the Children Act 1989 is in the best interests of the child. The expert owes a duty to the court *and* to the child. Usually these reports are requested by the court from well known child therapy or Family Centres. However, if a counsellor or psychotherapist is already working with the child, the court or the parents' solicitor may request a report from them.

No person may, without leave of the court, cause a child to be medically or psychiatrically examined or otherwise assessed for the purpose of preparation of expert evidence for use in proceedings (FPR r 4.18 (1)). Please note that, where the child is of sufficient understanding, the child may refuse to submit to such examination. Various guidelines regarding expert evidence in children's cases have been laid down. In *Re R (A Minor: Expert's Evidence (Note))* [1991] 1 FLR 291 per Cazalet J the following guidance was given:

The expert should not mislead by omissions

(1)   He should consider all material facts which could detract from his concluded opinion:
(2)   If experts look for and report on factors which tend to support a particular proposition or case, their reports should still:

(a)   provide a straightforward, not a misleading opinion,
(b)   be objective and not omit factors which do not support their opinion and
(c)   be properly researched.

(3)   If an expert's opinion is not properly researched because he believes there is insufficient data available, then he must say so and indicate his opinion is a provisional one:

(4)   In certain circumstances an expert may find that he has to give an opinion adverse to his client. Alternatively, if contrary to the appropriate practice, an expert does provide a report which is other than wholly objective – that is that it seeks to promote a particular case – the report must make this clear.

One area where (4) above is apposite is when a therapist has developed a longstanding relationship before any report was ever envisaged by the court. If the therapist has already formed their own views of what is best for the child, based largely on uncorroborated anecdotal evidence of the child, this must be put forward with caution. A detailed explanation should be given regarding any relevant information which is not provided. For example, there may have been only brief or limited interviews with parents or, perhaps, no interviews with parents were possible at all. If the therapist's expertise is in relationship or family counselling, but not necessarily in child psychology, this should be highlighted in the report. The courts are cautious, when, for example, testimony from adult psychiatrists is called on behalf of patients, and where the professional concerned may be unused to the child focussed approach of the court.

If a therapist is advancing a hypothesis in a Children Act case in order to explain a set of facts, they are duty-bound to explain to the court that it *is* a hypothesis and whether it is controversial. The therapist must also place before the court any material tending to contradict this hypothesis.

A good expert should always address the limitations of their expertise. The courts are sceptical of expert evidence, but the more open the report regarding the parameters of the therapist's expertise, the more credibility the report has in respect of those areas where the latter is demonstrably qualified.

In criminal proceedings, the report by Lord Justice Butler-Sloss on child abuse in Cleveland (1988) made a number of recommendations about the investigation of alleged offences against children and the conduct of interviews. The Butler-Sloss Report recommended that all interviews should be undertaken only by those with training experience and an aptitude for talking to children. An additional recommendation was made that, save in wholly exceptional circumstances, no one should undertake a video recorded interview with a child witness for the purposes of criminal proceedings unless they are familiar with the *Memorandum of Good Practice on Video Recorded Interviews with Child*

Witnesses In Criminal Proceedings (Home Office, 1992). It has been said that the full *Cleveland Report* should be required reading for everyone involved in the investigation of whether children have been sexually abused (Butler-Sloss, 1988).

Under the provisions made by the Criminal Justice Act 1991, a child will not be allowed to be examined in chief on any matter which, in the opinion of the court, has been dealt with in his or her recorded testimony. The recording therefore takes the place of the first stage of a child's evidence. Cross examination and re-examination both take place at the trial, but via live television link, saving the child the need to attend court.

The *Memorandum* gives guidance at every stage regarding planning setting up the interview and conducting the interview. Guidance can be obtained from Children Act Advisory Committee *Handbook of Best Practice in Children Act Cases* (CAAC 1997) and an *Expert Witness Pack* is also available (EWG, 1997). All instructions in children's cases should:

(a) define the context in which the opinion is sought
(b) set out specific questions for the expert to address
(c) identify any relevant issues of fact that enable each expert to give an opinion on each of the competing issues
(d) specify any examinations to be permitted
(e) list the documents to be sent to the expert
(f) require, as a condition of appointment, that the expert must, in advance of the hearing, hold discussions with other experts appointed in the same field of expertise, and produce a statement of agreement and disagreement on issues by a specific date.

This extract from the *Handbook of Best Practice in Children Act Cases* should provide the reader with some insight into how considered the area of expert reports has become in Family Law.

Family lawyers rely on experts' reports for guidance in numerous public law and private law cases, which is why there is so much guidance in the field available. It is not the purpose of this article to recite all the guidance. Those instructing the therapist should provide on request such guidance as is necessary, although they may assume that a knowledge of procedure is within the latter's expertise.

Guidelines on report writing

The art of report writing is well documented. There are many books on the subject and the Judicial Committee of the Academy of Experts has produced a model form of expert's report, reproduced as an appendix to this book. Following this model would be useful with regard to reports for

Criminal Injury Compensation Claim cases. However, it is important always to refer to the instructing solicitor regarding the most appropriate format, before writing the report.

Basic rules when writing an expert report

1 Obtain detailed instructions from those requesting the report.
2 Know your limitations, define your area of expertise and stick to it.
3 Make sure those instructing you know your area of expertise – set out what you can and cannot give an opinion about.
4 Make sure you have seen all the evidence.
5 Write out a factual chronology first, as it is invaluable in ordering matters.
6 Don't be scared to ask for more information.
7 State the facts or assumptions on which your opinions are based, as:

   (a) facts set out in evidence
   (b) facts reported to you
   (c) facts observed
   (d) evidence of a statistical nature or from research
   (e) where evidence is insufficient to reach a conclusion
   (f) facts assumed
   (g) the opinions of others.

8 Be objective and unbiased.
9 Include and identify points that detract from your opinion.
10 If you change your opinion, say so.
11 Provide an opinion that helps rather than hinders the court.
12 Do not offer any unnecessary opinion.
13 Don't forget that a good report should have a good narrative element – a beginning, a middle and an end!
14 Never hesitate to review the evidence.
15 Consider the opposite stance and challenge the report, consider which areas of the report would be most important to anyone holding the contrary view and consider their argument.

Therapists may encounter a problem concerning the extent to which opinion can be expressed (12). This is because so much information regarding the client is of a subjective nature. A starting point is to ask what is the question to be resolved and to discount the evidence that is not relevant. Often the therapist will have to see the client on more than one occasion to prepare for the report. It is worth preparing beforehand the questions to be asked and ensuring that they are proportionate and appropriate for writing the report. Furthermore, the therapist should clearly avoid any attempt to provide counselling when preparing the report, beyond using those counselling skills that may be deployed in obtaining an appropriate response from the client.

It is crucial that the counsellor or psychotherapist maintain their independence. In one instance, a counsellor under joint instructions met the subject of the report and, during the first session, tentatively agreed to become the client's counsellor *after* the report was written. This caused no end of concern regarding the independence of the report. While the report was not challenged, it was on any view open to such challenge.

Confidentiality should not raise a problem if the subject of the report is the therapist's client and consent has been obtained for the report to be written. In other circumstances, it may be that the therapist has been threatened that if they do not give evidence, he or she will be *compelled* to attend court. However, the courts have an inherent jurisdiction to disallow a *subpoena ad testificandum* i.e. a witness summons. The courts will not, as a rule, *compel* the attendance of an expert to give expert evidence 'against his wishes in a case where he has no connection with the facts or history of the matter in issue.' (*Seyfang v Searle* [1973]). Accordingly, if the therapist has not submitted a report, an application could be made for any summons to be set aside. However if a therapist is called as a witness of fact, the court may still compel attendance.

Appearing in court as a witness

With regard to an appearance at court, it is best to remember that there is no 'dress down' code practised by the judiciary (except in Family Courts, where judges do not wear wigs and gowns). It is best to dress smartly and sedately for the occasion. This includes a lack of ostentatious jewellery. Often barristers and solicitors wear loud ties or flamboyant blouses under smart suits, but these small symbols of professional confidence should be avoided by experts. Experts, unlike solicitors, are not advocates of their client's case. An expert is at court to present findings to the court and will be more authoritative if a sombre approach is adopted. However, there is nothing more irrating to a court than an expert who cannot explain his subject in plain English, except by using jargon. In giving oral evidence, any sociological or psychological terms should be explained or avoided altogether if incapable of brief explanation.

Social workers often appear before Magistrates' Courts to obtain Emergency Protection Orders dressed in jeans, baggy jumpers or dungarees, or whatever clothes are appropriate for their social work role. This never lends itself to giving the social worker authority. If time permits, they should change into clothes more suited to the court room.

It is worth noting here that the word oral means *spoken*, whereas the word verbal means something that may be *written or spoken*. It is now recognised that a verbal agreement universally means an oral agreement. However, if asked to name a source of spoken evidence, it is better to say, it was *oral* (i.e. someone *told* the story) as opposed to *verbal*.

Many people are scared of appearing as a witness and it can be a challenging process. However, if the therapist's report is comprehensive, then the therapist is free to refer to the report as an expert witness when giving evidence. The expert witness will be led through the evidence by the advocate who called the expert witness. This is known as examination-in-chief, and this is usually a matter of confirming the veracity and conclusions of the report. The opposing advocate will then have an opportunity to ask questions. These questions will be to challenge the report. Such questions may challenge the method in which the report has been compiled or the conclusions drawn. Please note that the 'all guns blazing' style of advocacy is no longer as common, and most advocates tend to use a quieter, more persistent approach, where they chip away at the evidence.

The traditional areas of challenging evidence concern the expert's qualifications, suitability, and the thoroughness of the expert's investigation. Such tactics as taking a drink of water while thinking about the answer tend to make the expert look less than frank. Asking the advocate to repeat the question is also not a favourable approach for the same reason. It is best to say that the answer needs to be considered, and for the therapist to take their time. If there is no right answer, then the therapist should make this clear. The advocate probably knows that this is actually the case. Some questions are designed to test the expert's probity and character, so that the court is satisfied as to the authority of the report. The advocate and court have the advantage of seeing many experts' reports and can judge whether a report is fundamentally sound. It is important to accept that a challenge in respect of certain conclusions or recommendations is not in itself a criticism of the report and not to become defensive.

An example might be a short medical report regarding a depressed client, which concludes that the latter is unlikely to 'hold down a job'. Clearly any lawyer would need to clarify whether the client will be able to work again, and, if so, for what duration. The report should be concise, well written and should display a sound knowledge of the client. Despite this, the precise ability of the client to work is crucial to his settlement, so the doctor will be questioned in this regard in detail. This would not be a criticism of an otherwise concise report.

When giving evidence, it is the Judge who should be addressed. Often the Judge is making a note of the expert's answer. It is important, there-fore, to speak no more quickly than the judge can write. The therapist should aim to be friendly and warm. It also helps if the therapist is help-ful and fairly down to earth. It is important not to assume superiority in manner or style, to avoid being brisk and always to be polite.

Conclusion

To conclude, advocates are often approached by counsellors and psycho-therapists who express concern about writing expert reports and giving evidence. If, however, a therapist is willing to research the demands of the particular court and is well instructed, the form of the report and issues are soon clarified. The writing of such reports can be remunerative and personally rewarding. The information provided here is not exhaus-tive, but it should allow the therapist to approach report writing with greater understanding. As this chapter shows, while different courts have different approaches, the intention is that the therapist should be better equipped to find out the rules of the particular court. What all courts have in common is the need for honest, impartial and learned expert opinion.

References

Butler-Sloss, E. (1988) *Report of the Inquiry into Child Abuse in Cleveland 1987*. Cm 412. London: HMSO.
Children Act Advisory Committee (1997) *Handbook of Best Practice in Children Act Cases*, London: CAAC.
Civil Procedure Rules (The White Book) (2000) London: Sweet and Maxwell.
Expert Witness Group (1997) *Expert Witness Pack for Use in Children Proceedings*, London: Jordan.
Home Office/Department of Health (1992) *Memorandum of Good Practice on Video Recorded Interviews with Child Witnesses in Criminal Proceedings*. London: HMSO.
Woolf, Lord (1996) *Access to Justice: Final Report*, London: HMSO.

Family Proceedings Rules (FPR) (1991) SI 1991/1247.

Legal references

Bolam v Friern HMC [1957] 2 All ER 118; 1 WLR 853
Bolitho v City and Hackney HA [1997] 3 WLR 1151, 4 All ER 771

Phelps v Hillingdon LBC [1997] 3 FCR 621
R v Turner [1975] AC QB 834
Re R (A Minor: Expert's Evidence (Note)) [1991] 1 FLR 291
Seyfang v GD Searle [1973] QB 148
The Ikarian Reefer [1993] 2 Lloyds Rep 68
Werner v Landau (1961) TLR 8/3/1961, 23/11/1961, Sol Jo (1961) 105, 1008

Part Two

LEGAL CHALLENGES
FOR THERAPY

7

Regulating Counselling and Psychotherapy: Lessons from Complementary Medicine

Julie Stone

Introduction

In recent years a huge increase in the popularity of alternative approaches to health and healing has been witnessed. The reasons for this are complex, but need to be seen in the context of a population suffering from an increased level of social and environmental stresses manifested in a variety of longer term, chronic ill-health problems which conventional medicine has been less than successful in treating.[1] Doctors have been criticised for regarding patients as a collection of their physical symptoms rather than treating them in a holistic context. At the same time, there has been a shift in the culture away from the materialistic excesses of late twentieth-century capitalism in search of some form of spirituality felt to be missing from many people's lives. As hi-tech medicine has become ever more reductionist and drug-based in its approach, many patients have turned to both counselling and psychotherapy, and complementary and alternative medicine (CAM) to alleviate their suffering.

Why regulation? Why now?

In an era of increased consumer sophistication, access to information and choice within health care, the role of the health professional has come under increasing scrutiny. Whereas in the past patients were more prepared both to accept the opinions of doctors without question, and to tolerate a more paternalistic style of health care, the dynamics of health care relationships have changed with the times and more and more patients want to be active participants in their own healing process.

Patients over the last 30 years have begun to challenge medical paternalism and the attitude that 'doctors know best'. Indeed, the conduct of the medical profession has been scrutinised like never before. Rather than being able to cover up blunders and poor professional performance, the whole question of self-regulation within health care has been put under the spotlight, fuelled by a catalogue of high-profile cases in which health professionals have physically or emotionally harmed their patients. Moreover, this current interest in self-regulation and accountability extends beyond medicine to all health professionals. To that end, the self-regulatory mechanisms of nurses, midwives, health visitors, social workers and professions supplementary to medicine have all been radically overhauled to bring these professions into line with current best practice. In each profession, disciplinary mechanisms have been made more accountable, notably by substantially increasing the proportion of lay representation involved in all stages of complaints procedures, and by defining what constitutes professional misconduct sufficiently broadly to allow a range of unacceptable conduct to fall within its remit.

The same regulation debates have been raging within counselling and psychotherapy, and complementary and alternative medicine, for some years. The major difference between these spheres of activity and orthodox medicine is that whereas only registered practitioners may practice medicine, nursing and the other professions listed above, the law in the UK currently permits *anyone* to set him or herself up in practice and call themself a counsellor, psychotherapist or complementary therapist. Within complementary and alternative medicine the only exceptions to this common law freedom to practise are osteopathy and chiropractic, both of which are now statutorily regulated[2] (although several other therapies are actively considering statutory regulation). While this obviously allows for diversity and maximum consumer choice, it also allows unscrupulous, poorly trained practitioners to exploit the vulnerabilities of people who may be emotionally or physically in need.

The primary purpose of regulation is to protect the public. Patients need to know that when they consult a health practitioner, whatever his or her therapeutic modality, that person will have had appropriate training, will be competent to practise and will be working to the highest ethical standards. Regulation is one means through which this can be ensured. In most health care professions, the public expects there to be a register of practitioners accountable to a professional body, which sets both standards for training and professional practice and disciplines errant practitioners, if necessary, by removing their licence to practise. Notably, many of the cases which require punitive action to be taken involve unprofessional conduct which is *unrelated to the practitioner's technical competence*. Examples of unethical conduct resulting in disciplinary action include sexual relationships with patients, charging patients for unnecessary treatment, treating patients without their consent and unauthorised disclosures of confidential information.

Should counselling and psychotherapy be regulated?

The general consensus is that anyone offering to treat patients should be accountable via some form of regulation. Several self-regulating bodies, notably the United Kingdom Council for Psychotherapy (UKCP), the British Confederation of Psychotherapists (BCP) and the British Association for Counselling and Psychotherapy (BACP) have made enormous progress in raising the standards and status of counselling and psychotherapy. Better standards of training and accountability have done much to raise the status of counselling and psychotherapy in the UK. This, together with an increased willingness to subject psychological interventions to research, has seen a greater willingness on the part of the medical profession to recommend psychotherapeutic interventions to their patients. Nonetheless, the current regulatory system still allows for counsellors or psychotherapists with little or no training to call themselves counsellors or psychotherapists and to charge clients on that basis. The most dangerous aspect of a voluntarily self-regulating activity is, of course, the fact that practitioners do not have to join a register and can choose to work quite independently of any professional body.

The testing question facing counselling and psychotherapy is whether now is the appropriate time to consider the transition from *voluntary self-regulation* to *statutory regulation*. Notwithstanding the impact this question would have on their common law freedom to practise, many therapists do not take any interest in the politics of their profession and may not even appreciate the difference between these two regulatory options. This is a somewhat short-sighted approach, since the outcome of any regulatory initiative will impact substantially on how therapists act and, indeed, whether they will even be allowed to continue to practise.

Differences between statutory regulation and voluntary self-regulation

The key difference between the two is that statutory regulation usually protects title.[3] This would mean, for example in the case of psychotherapy, that only a therapist registered with the statutory body would be entitled to describe themself as a psychotherapist. Any therapist who continued to describe him or herself as a psychotherapist who did not belong to the statutory register would be committing a criminal offence. Similarly, a therapist who was erased or suspended from the register would, theoretically, be unable to practise, as he or she could be prosecuted for continuing to call themself a psychotherapist. By way of comparison, a therapist who is currently censured by one of the existing voluntary self-regulating bodies can continue to practise and use the name psychotherapist, and could, quite conceivably, join an alternative registering body to achieve some credibility. With the exception of osteopathy and chiropractic, all CAM therapies are regulated through varying levels of voluntary self-regulation. The major stumbling block to protecting title is that it requires there to be a consensus, within the given profession, as to what constitutes the activity to be regulated. The question then, is whether the activities of counselling and psychotherapy can be sufficiently delineated to say both what they are and what competencies are required in order to be a suitably trained counsellor or psychotherapist.

Apart from this one major difference, voluntary and self-regulating bodies may share many of the same features. Highly evolved voluntary bodies, like the British Acupuncture Council, may operate along very similar lines to a statutory body. Working with an Accreditation Board, which accredits training establishments, the Council has a single professional register of members, a preliminary investigating committee, a professional misconduct committee and mechanisms for dealing with practitioners whose practice is adversely affected by ill-health. Critically, an effective voluntary self-regulating body may achieve similar standing in the public's eye as a statutory body. When this becomes the case, there is a stronger level of public protection afforded, provided that potential members ensure that their practitioner is in fact a member of that professional body.

Voluntary self-regulating bodies will also usually demand evidence of a suitable level of training, agreement by its members to be bound by its code of ethics or code of practice, and a disciplinary mechanism through which members of the public may bring a complaint. They may (but do not uniformly) require evidence that the registered member has appropriate professional indemnity. When a profession is united under a single regulatory framework, there will be a *register of individual members* rather than therapeutic organisations. This allows for greater accountability, since it will facilitate the process of ascertaining whether an individual practitioner is or is not a registered member of the profession. Both voluntary and statutory self-regulating bodies fund their activities through their members' subscriptions. The cost of membership to a statutory body is likely to considerably exceed subscriptions to a voluntary body and many therapists regard this as a major factor against pursuing statutory regulation.

A major argument in favour of statutory regulation is that it would consolidate the current array of registering bodies, each of which operates to different standards. A single statutory body per profession would be able to create national standards of training and competence which all therapists would have to adhere to, whatever their therapeutic leaning. Currently, patients have little way of distinguishing between a therapist or complementary practitioner with appropriate qualifications from a self-trained power seeker who 'needs to be needed'. This, of course, begs the question of what counselling and psychotherapy are and whether a prescribed training is a necessary precondition for being a 'good' therapist.

Are counselling and psychotherapy amenable to regulation?

Some therapists vigorously maintain that the psychotherapeutic relationship does not need to be regulated. Others would go so far as to say that statutory controls are impractical because this relationship cannot be regulated. Indeed, a major stumbling block to pursuing statutory regulation in the past has been this question of whether counselling and psychotherapy are even *amenable* to regulation. Opponents would argue that the activity of helping people to become better integrated or autonomous need not be regulated in the same way as say, surgery or obstetrics. On closer inspection, this argument has at least two components, each of which needs to be considered separately.

The first point implicit in the comparison is that counselling and psychotherapy are inherently less dangerous than other 'medical' interventions. A patient might die from a septic wound or from complications in childbirth, but will suffer no lasting harm if psychotherapy fails to foster greater autonomy. The second argument is that because counselling and psychotherapy do not require the same level of technical competencies as certain medical specialties, they do not require explicit, external regulation. Each contention is deeply flawed and needs to be explored further.

Any intervention which is able to help can also, in the wrong hands, cause harm. To suggest that incompetent or abusive therapy cannot cause harm to a patient is ludicrous, since it would belittle the very sort of suffering that counselling and psychotherapy is intended to alleviate. Emotional harm can be as devastating to a patient as physical harm, especially when a counsellor or psychotherapist has raised the patient's hopes and created false expectations. The impact of abuse within therapy can be particularly devastating. The suggestion that only mechanical skills require a determined level of competency is equally absurd. While an element of good counselling and psychotherapy requires intuition and ordinary human qualities (as is the case in all good health care encounters), providing counselling or therapy requires technical skills which can be taught and learned. Moreover, as has already been mentioned, disciplinary proceedings may relate to a therapist's unprofessional or unethical conduct, rather than his or her lack of technical expertise *qua* therapist. Indeed, in the case of counselling and psychotherapy, it might be uniquely difficult (except in exceptionally extreme cases) to show that the therapist's technical conduct was unacceptable.

A further argument against the regulation of counselling and psychotherapy and CAM, is that if a patient has a bad experience, he or she can always sue the practitioner through the courts. As with market forces, this is an inadequate means of ensuring patient protection.[4] In the first place, litigation operates retrospectively so that by the time a patient sues a practitioner, the damage has already been done, and the practitioner may already have harmed many other patients. Second, the virtual absence of litigation against CAM therapists in the UK and the USA indicates that it may be very difficult for patients to sue therapists. In part, this is because of the lack of standardisation within CAM therapies of psychotherapy, whereby it may be difficult for the patient even to ascertain what amounts to a reasonable standard of conduct against which the practitioner can be judged. The intense one-to-one relationship established in therapy or CAM might also dissuade a patient from suing, especially if the therapist has exerted an undue amount of influence over the patient or heightened their sense of dependency or vulnerability. Furthermore, few patients are likely to be able to afford the financial or emotional burden of bringing litigation, and even for those patients who are brave enough to mount a legal action, the courts are notoriously poor at compensating patients who have suffered emotional, rather than quantifiable, measurable, physical harm.[5]

Comparisons between counselling, psychotherapy, and complementary and alternative medicine

An obvious feature linking counselling and psychotherapy on the one hand, and complementary and alternative medicine on the other, is that each has, at various times and to varying degrees, been marginalised by and excluded from the medical orthodoxy. Although considerably fewer doctors would now refer to either as complete quackery, the absence of hard scientific proof as to the efficacy of counselling and psychotherapy or CAM has kept these activities largely in the private sector and outside state-funded health systems, which are increasingly bound by the twin demands of cost efficiency and clinical effectiveness. Another similarity is that, each, to varying degrees, has sought to devise appropriate research methodologies by which therapeutic outcomes of these interventions might be measured. Proving that counselling and psychotherapy or CAM 'work' inevitably requires far greater attention to be paid to the subjective experience of the patient or client than in therapeutic interventions which can be evaluated using more objective, external measures.

Therapeutically speaking, counsellors and psychotherapists, like CAM practitioners, are concerned with their patients' psychological wellbeing, rather than merely their physical problems. This is not to suggest that all doctors overlook the psychological dimensions of ill-health, or that all CAM therapists, counsellors or psychotherapists are necessarily holistic in their outlook. To the extent, however, that each works with aspects of the human condition which are not physical, problems of measurability and assessment of outcome abound. Who determines when a psychotherapy patient is 'better'? How can an acupuncturist know that the patient's chi is flowing evenly? Hopefully, to a large extent, patients themselves will be the best arbiter of when they feel that they have benefited from therapy, but in the hands of an unscrupulous therapist, therapy could be spun out over a longer period of time than is therapeutically necessary.

Yet another problem is whether people consulting such therapists should necessarily be regarded as patients or in any sense 'ill'. Many counselling, psychotherapy or CAM patients are highly accomplished, articulate individuals who are merely seeking to enhance their quality of life, rather than to rectify a significant health problem.[6] The reason that this matters for regulatory purposes is that in liberal democracies it is not generally thought to be the business of the state to intervene in matters of private choice (unless individual choice impinges on the freedoms of others). Adults should be allowed to pursue whatever activities they choose (including getting in touch with their inner child) free from external restraint. Moreover, should they choose to pursue such an activity, it is again up to them how much they are prepared to pay someone for providing this service. Arguably, in a free market economy, therapists can charge whatever patients are prepared to pay. Similarly, market forces could be said to exert a form of regulatory control in that clients will not return to poor practitioners, who will, eventually, go out of business and cease to practise.

While one would not seek to cast all patients in the same light, most people consult a therapist, be they counsellor or psychotherapist or CAM practitioner, because they feel that they have a problem which might be amenable to therapy. Not all patients are needy or vulnerable, but many will experience a temporary level of dependency on their therapist and experience feelings of transference towards their therapist or practitioner. Essentially, patients are thought, by reason of whatever ails them, to be less able to negotiate on a contractual basis than others seeking services and to be in need of protection from unscrupulous therapists who may exploit their sense of vulnerability and dependency. The relationship between any health practitioner and their client is a *fiduciary* one. Patients or clients trust that they will impart highly personal information in confidence, and that anything that is done to them will be in their best interests and that the practitioner has a reasonable basis for making an offer to treat. In both counselling and psychotherapy and CAM, the therapeutic relationship demands that the patient be an active participant in the process. Patients have to help themselves for most psychological interventions to be of any benefit. However, this does not shift the responsibility from the therapist, who must at all times act professionally and in the client's best interests.

A common factor for the purposes of regulation is that both counselling and psychotherapy and CAM, are characterised by hundreds of competing forms of therapy, underpinned by wildly different philosophies and schools of thought. Although each term is loosely used as an umbrella term, therapies and therapists lumped together under these broad headings may have little in common in terms of therapeutic style, belief systems or modes of intervention. Some therapists may have undergone an extensive, externally accredited training lasting many years, whereas others may have received a minimal training with limited access to continuing professional development (CPD) or supervision. The diversity in therapeutic orientation is matched by the level of professional diversity and fragmentation. A therapist may have a string of qualifications after his or her name but have had little or no practical experience in working with patients. Other than by word of mouth, a patient may have as much difficulty finding the right counsellor or psychotherapist as finding an appropriate CAM therapist. Should anything go wrong in the therapeutic encounter, a patient may have recourse to a speedy, accessible, responsive complaints system, or to none at all. Appropriate regulation, it is hoped, would remove this lack of consistency and ensure that patients were protected whichever therapist they consulted.

Ethical issues common to counselling and psychotherapy and CAM

In terms of patient protection, counselling and psychotherapy raise many similar ethical issues to CAM. Although most therapists prefer to concentrate on the technical aspects of their work rather than on ethical dilemmas which may arise, the very nature of the health care relationship gives rise to ethical tensions. The trust upon which the therapeutic relationship is based, and the disequilibrium between the therapist and their patient means that all therapists, whatever their therapeutic orientation, need to be sure that they are working in the best interests of their clients and not motivated by their own objectives. In the absence of obvious major side-effects as a direct result of therapy, most of the ethical issues arise out of the contours and dynamics of the therapeutic relationship itself. These include:

Competence
Ensuring that the therapist has undergone suitable training and recognises his or her limits of competence. Usually, but not always, this will require substantial training at an externally accredited training establishment. Competent practice also requires therapists to be in sound physical and mental health. Counsellors and psychotherapists, as well as

CAM therapists, must be able to recognise when a patient is in need of urgent conventional treatment, which will require a level of awareness of conventional medicine and the maintenance of open, trusting relationships with local GPs. Good record keeping is vital not just for competent, safe practice, but in the event of any subsequent legal or disciplinary action.

Research
In an increasingly evidence-based culture, being prepared to submit one's therapeutic endeavour to well-designed clinical research is critical to establish, if nothing else, that the therapy is capable of providing more good than harm. The absence of research skills amongst many therapists and CAM practitioners is an ethical issue in itself. The lack of expertise on the part of many research ethics committees to evaluate qualitative research protocols also requires attention.

Continuing professional development (CPD)
Recognising that professional knowledge, skills and attitudes can and should be learned throughout one's professional career, rather than as a means to satisfying entrance requirements to a professional register. CPD may be less attractive to therapists who are having to pay for additional training themselves, in time that could be spent seeing fee-paying clients. The quality of much CPD training is also dubious.

Negotiating contracts with patients
In particular the need to build regular reviews into the therapeutic encounter so that the patient and therapist can monitor how therapy is progressing, and to elucidate the therapist and the patient's responsibilities from the outset. This is even more important where the patient is expected to be an active participant in his or her own healing process.

Respect for autonomy and consent
Enhancing autonomy will be a goal of most therapists within counselling and psychotherapy and CAM. Although most therapists would assume that they are respecting patient autonomy in a client-centred therapy, this may not always be the case.[7] Therapists need to determine with patients the balance that needs to be struck between sacrificing some autonomy in the short term for longer term therapeutic gains. Therapists must avoid patients becoming unduly dependent upon them, or being seduced by their own need to be needed and prolonging therapy beyond what is necessary to benefit the patient. Consent to therapy should always be sought and is in no sense implied by virtue of the patient showing up for therapy. Part of respecting a patient's autonomy involves

acting as the patient's advocate, which may have implications if a therapist becomes aware that the patient has been treated inappropriately by a fellow therapist.

Respecting confidentiality

Therapists must respect the confidentiality of personal health information imparted in circumstances which the patient has good reason to expect will lead to a duty of confidentiality. If the therapist cannot offer complete confidentiality (in circumstances where the client represents a danger to him- or herself, or a danger to third parties, for example), this should be explained to the patient at the outset of the therapeutic encounter. Disclosure of sexual abuse within a therapeutic session may present particular dilemmas for therapists.[8] In order to maximise autonomy, a patient should usually be informed if the therapist intends to divulge confidential information prior to the disclosure.

Maintenance of professional boundaries

The creation and maintenance of appropriate professional boundaries is the therapist's responsibility. Sexual, emotional and financial abuses are known to occur in both counselling and psychotherapy and CAM.[9] Therapists must be sufficiently self-aware to recognise how counter-transference affects dealing with their patients and should always discuss potential issues with a supervisor.

To the extent that CAM therapists use psychotherapeutic techniques as part of their holistic practice, they will face similar dilemmas to psychotherapists as to how much they should disclose to the patient about the therapeutic process itself before this undermines any possible therapeutic benefit.[10] There may also be ethical issues concerning patients' access to their clinical notes, particularly where the therapist feels that seeing the therapist's interpretation may cause the patient undue distress. The use of deception and paradoxical interventions also raises particular ethical issues, since these appear to be inimical to respecting the patient's autonomy.[11]

Learning lessons from complementary and alternative medicine

If the regulatory experiences of CAM reveal anything at all, it is that each type of therapy has its own unique issues which will ultimately determine whether statutory regulation is the right course of action for them to pursue. It may well be, for example, that the regulatory questions facing counselling are very different to those facing psychotherapy. However, it is not the function of this chapter to discuss the substantive issues upon which this decision will depend. This is an issue which only the members of the counselling and psychotherapy professions can resolve. Nonetheless, the politics of CAM regulation may provide some useful food for thought for therapists who wish to make an informed decision about statutory regulation and how it might affect them. While some of these issues may be more pertinent to counselling and psychotherapy than others, it is instructive to consider how CAM has approached the regulation question. The following points represent a summary of the major points to have surfaced in the CAM regulation debate in recent years:

- The government is unlikely to intervene in the regulation of counselling or psychotherapy, or CAM, leaving it up to each individual profession to decide if and when it is ready to pursue statutory regulation.
- The recent Health Act 1999 allows professions to seek statutory regulation via an Order in Council, which is a speedier and probably less costly mechanism than pursuing autonomous statutory regulation using usual parliamentary means.
- The common law freedom to practise is unlikely to be revoked at the present time, notwithstanding fears about European harmonisation.
- A single professional register of members is desirable to allow patients and purchasers to determine who is, and who is not, appropriately qualified and to minimise confusion.
- Therapies which are capable of causing direct, physical harm are most in need of vigorous, external regulation. Psychological and spiritual interventions are considered less of a risk to the public than physically invasive therapies such as acupuncture, herbalism, homoeopathy, osteopathy and chiropractic.
- Even therapies which cause no obvious benefit are capable, in the wrong hands, of causing a patient harm and require some form of regulation.
- All therapists, whatever their sphere of activity, should carry professional indemnity insurance.
- Regulation may be a means to achieving enhanced respect from the orthodox medical profession although this will vary from therapy to therapy, the amount of evidence available regarding effectiveness, and the extent to which the therapy represents direct competition to allopathic medicine.
- Regulation may be a means to achieve enhanced public respect.
- Regulation may be a helpful precursor to NHS integration, and it is certainly easier for the NHS to negotiate with a single professional body rather than a number of competing bodies.
- Statutory regulation is more likely to ensure high uniform standards of training and practice.

- Statutory regulation can protect the public, but only if the professional body is prepared to censure its members appropriately.
- Statutory regulation has more effective sanctions than does voluntary self-regulation, although it remains to be seen what would happen if a significant number of professionals refused to join a statutory register.
- Statutory regulation is costly for members of a profession (the smaller the profession, the higher the costs to be shared).
- Research and development is much harder when there is lack of professional cohesion and fragmentation.
- Statutory regulation may lead to a loss of diversity within a profession and a gravitation towards dominant (and possibly more conservative) schools of thought.

Conclusion

At the time of writing, Lord Alderdice's Psychotherapy Bill was being presented to Parliament. The response by the government has been to open the door to statutory regulation of (potentially both) counselling and psychotherapy via the use of the Health Act 1999.[12] How rapidly this step will be taken, remains to be seen, but the progress of the Bill is indicative of the willingness of psychotherapists to put aside their differences and come together for the benefit of their patients and their profession.[13] Whether counsellors and psychotherapists decide to pursue statutory regulation or not, most therapists are now convinced of the advantages of a more unified profession. There are sufficient parallels between the practice of counselling and psychotherapy, and complementary and alternative medicine, for therapists to review the regulatory experiences of CAM therapists with interest. Ultimately, however, counselling and psychotherapy raise distinct issues which may make statutory regulation impossible or undesirable. Moreover, therapists should realise that external regulation is not a panacea. Whether voluntarily or statutorily regulated, the final responsibility not to abuse the professional relationship rests with the individual practitioner. Without ethical practitioners the therapeutic potential and high standing of the profession as a whole will be called into question.

Notes

1 For a discussion of the reasons people are seeking unconventional approaches to healing see Stone, J. (2002) *An Ethical Framework for Complementary and Alternative Therapists*. London and New York: Routledge.

2   Although it has been some years since the passing of the Osteopaths Act 1993 and the Chiropractors Act 1994, the respective statutory registers have only recently come into operation. The transition from voluntary self-regulation to statutory regulation is slow as well as costly and involves hard questions, particularly around the question of who is a competent practitioner? And which schools ought to be accredited to allow entrance onto a statutory register?

3   Rarely, statute may protect function as well as title, but this is unlikely in the case of counselling and psychotherapy, since many occupational groups use counselling-based approaches in their work and protection of function would bring them within the remit of any such legislation.

4   For a detailed discussion of the shortcomings of litigation as a means of resolving problems within the therapeutic encounter see Stone, J. and Matthews, J. (1996). *Complementary Medicine and the Law*. Oxford University Press: Oxford.

5   When a patient sues a therapist, he or she must satisfy the burden of proof, on a balance of probabilities, that the practitioner caused the harm in question. The major difficulty in establishing causation is that the courts may be inclined to assume that if the patient was psychologically disturbed at the outset of therapy, then any subsequent emotional problems are as likely to be due to the patient's underlying condition as they are to the negligence of the practitioner.

6   Certainly this argument has been used as a reason for why these therapies should not be provided on the NHS.

7   Johnston, M. (1999) 'On becoming non-judgmental: some difficulties for an ethics of counselling'. *Journal of Medical Ethics*, 25: 487–491.

8   See Lindsay, G. and Clarkson, P. (1999). 'Ethical dilemmas of psychotherapists', *The Psychologist*. 12(4): 182–185.

9   For a discussion of sexual abuse within psychology, see: Garrett, T. (1998). 'Sexual contact between patients and psychologists'. *The Psychologist*, 11(5): 227–230.

10   Holmes, J. and Lindley, R. (1998) *The Values of Psychotherapy*. Karnac Books (revised edition): London.

11   Foreman, D.M. (1990) 'The ethical use of paradoxical interventions in psychotherapy'. *Journal of Medical Ethics*, 16: 200–205.

12   For the full Hansard debate and government response, see: *http://www.parliament. the-stationery-office.co.uk/pa/ld199697/ldhansrd/pdvn/lds01/text/10119-05.htm# 10110.05_head0*

13   Browne, S. (2001) 'Regulation coming soon', *Counselling and Psychotherapy Journal*, March, pp. 4–5.

8

Legal Issues in Therapeutic Work with Adult Survivors of Sexual Abuse

Annabell Bell-Boulé and Très Roche

> Because of the clash of perspectives between psychotherapy and the law, mental health professionals often find their interactions with legal systems confusing, frustrating or even frightening. Given the broad range of conditions that are now addressed by the law, such interactions are inevitable for practising professionals, particularly psychotherapists (Meyer et al., 1988:3).

This statement was made more than a decade ago in the USA, before the major increase in recourse to the law by litigants, and serves to remind us that it is essential not to demonise the law or ignore its increasing importance to the practitioner in the UK. Similarly, two decades ago Mason and McCall Smith said that in the UK 'Medical jurisprudence is something of a growth industry. The ethical issues raised by new medical techniques, fanned by rapidly changing public values, are matched in interest by the intense legal problems they provoke' (1983: vii). Despite their differences, law and psychotherapy have something important in common: they both aim to change behaviour in beneficial ways. Furthermore, psychotherapy must inevitably take place within a broader social, political and legal context.

The differences between the legal and medical ethos in the UK and the USA make comparisons in relation to medical negligence tentative. The USA has a higher rate of medical negligence claims, 30 per thousand of the population, compared to only 8 per thousand in the UK (Ham et al., 1988: 20). In addition, because health care costs are met by insurance claims in the USA, actions are more likely to be commenced, since the litigant does not have to pay for a lawyer personally to begin an action. Consequently, it is easier to commence and continue legal action in the USA. In the UK it is now common for medical negligence lawyers to offer a 'no win, no fee' arrangement for clients. This copies the US system, making it easier in this country to commence, and continue legal action.

In the 1980s, between 10% and 15% of Americans utilised some form of psychotherapy (Austin et al., 1990: 7). As the number of clients in the USA has increased, so too have clients' knowledge and expectations about psychotherapy increased. With more clients of psychotherapy and greater client knowledge about psychotherapy, clients expect more from the experience and are more willing to protest when expectations are not met. In the USA, this has led to an increasing number of complaints against psychotherapists in the form of malpractice suits and complaints filed with ethics committees and licensing boards (Austin et al., 1990: 8). Similarly, in the UK, health carers claim that patients are now more demanding, informed and less deferential. In 1993 the Health Service Commissioner (or Ombudsman) stated:

> In the National Health Service there are clear signs of an increase in the volume of complaints. I regard that as an indication of a public service, which is increasing the knowledge of those, who use or seek to use it of how to complain and to whom. If patients and their families feel that the service provided has been below the level it should be attaining, the Patient's Charter documents and similar leaflets produced locally should help them to seek redress. (HSC, 1993: 1)

Whilst the medical and legal cultures are different in the UK and USA, the similarity between UK and US medical and legal cultures is an increase in the professional and legal accountability of health carers. This can be witnessed in other professions, including psychotherapy. It is also important to regard the situation in the USA as an example of the possible state of psychotherapy and the law in years to come in the UK.

Increasingly, consumers of health services are turning to the law to settle their disputes. Clare Dyer, the legal correspondent for the *British Medical Journal*, wrote that 'Medical litigation faces British revolution' (1996: 330). Her discussion focussed on the proposals to revolutionise the way medical negligence litigation works, in which the system would be led less by lawyers and less adversarial, and would therefore lead to the civil justice system being viewed as simpler, cheaper, and more accessible. In other words, medical disputes would be easier to litigate. As Otto and Schmidt averred: 'Insofar as litigation addresses wrongs that have been committed by professionals and deters others from behaving in similar ways, it has the potential to increase the accountability of mental health professionals' (1991: 309). This has been seen in the past few years in the field of public enquiries into sexual abuse in children's homes in England and Wales, and the increasing public awareness of the prevalence of sexual abuse. In the context of psychotherapy and counselling becoming more clearly regulated as professions under the Psychotherapy

Bill, and therefore more open to litigation, the authors of this chapter aim to look at the legal implications for counsellors and psychotherapists, particularly those working in the private sector with survivors of sexual abuse. Any therapist working with adult survivors of sexual abuse is guided by four major premises:

- the theoretical orientation within which she works,
- the ethical guidelines to which she adheres,
- the requisite legal framework, and finally
- her own ethical/moral stance or integrity which she brings to bear when balancing ethics, professional practice and the law.

Theoretical orientation

The theoretical orientation of the therapist obviously impacts upon her approach to working with clients who have been sexually abused. However, for most therapists it is crucial to respect the client's integrity and through respect, kindness and compassion to establish an interpersonal relationship that provides affirmation of such integrity. In furtherance of this the therapist becomes the client's ally by placing all the resources of her knowledge, skill and experience at the client's disposal. It may be that in the initial assessment of the client DSM IV (American Psychiatric Association, 1994) is used as an aid to understanding rather than as a diagnostic tool. However first assessment sessions are undertaken, it is important for the therapist to be aware of the likely impact the experience of childhood sexual abuse has had on the client's mental health.

Judith Herman states that 'people who have endured horrible events suffer predictable psychological harm'. As a consequence, 'the child trapped in an abusive environment is faced with formidable tasks of adaptation' (1992: 96). The final ethical/professional stance, which is therefore adopted, is that the core experiences of psychological trauma are disempowerment and disconnection from others. In conclusion, the role of the therapist is both intellectual and relational, fostering both insight and empathic connection.

All therapists are expected, in law, to keep abreast of current thinking in their particular discipline, to read the requisite journals and to be cognisant of current professional practice.

Ethical Guidelines

The United Kingdom Council for Psychotherapy (UKCP) *Ethical Requirements for Member Organisations* (1998) and the Sherwood

Psychotherapy Training Institute (SPTI) *Code of Ethics and Professional Practice* (1996) reflect the content of many professional codes in that the pertinent parts are those relating to competence and client safety and include *inter alia*;

UKCP:

2.8   Psychotherapists are required to maintain their ability to perform competently and to take the necessary steps to do so.

SPTI:

5.1   Members must take all reasonable steps to protect clients from physical or psychological harm during therapy.
7.1   Members accept clients commensurate with their training, skill and supervision arrangements.
7.2   Members should pay attention to the limits of their competence. Where a Member recognises they are reaching their limit then consultation with a colleague and/or supervisor is essential. It may be appropriate to refer the client to someone else.
7.3   Members have a responsibility to maintain their own effectiveness and ability to practise. Members should not work with clients when their capacity is impaired because of emotional problems, illness, alcohol or any other reason.
7.6   Members should have appropriate therapeutic and supervisory support to maintain ethical and professional practice.
13.1   Members should be reasonably conversant with the legal implications of their work as counsellors/psychotherapists and have access to legal advice.
13.3   Members, who become aware of a specific crime in the course of their clinical practice, whether current or past, should seek supervisory and legal advice immediately.

The British Association for Counselling and Psychotherapy (BACP, 2002: 6) refers to counsellor competence as following;

7.   All counsellors, psychotherapists, trainers and supervisors are required to have regular and ongoing supervision/consultative support for their work in accordance with professional requirements. Managers, researchers and providers of counselling skills are strongly encouraged to review their need for professional and personal support and to obtain appropriate services for themselves.
8.   Regularly monitoring and reviewing one's work in essential to maintaining good practice. It is important to be open to, and conscientious in considering, feedback from colleagues, appraisals and assessments. Responding constructively to feedback helps to advance practice.
9.   A commitment to good practice requires practitioners to keep up to date with the latest knowledge and respond to changing circumstances. They

should consider carefully their own need for continuing professional development and engage in appropriate educational activities.

Professional practice involves the theoretical orientation of the therapist as well as the code of ethics to which they adhere. In addition, the concept of ethics also includes, according to Stephen Pattison, 'using one's critical reason, making up one's own mind, freely adopting a particular principle or course of action, and then being able to account for this publicly using words and arguments that other rational beings will be able to understand and evaluate' (1999: 374–5). In other words a therapist must understand and take seriously the rules and conventions that govern society generally and their professional practice in particular, and make their own judgements accordingly.

Working with survivors of sexual abuse involves a myriad of issues professional, ethical and legal of which the therapist needs to be cognisant. In the USA, and increasingly in the UK, working with survivors of sexual abuse is regarded as trauma treatment and consequently understood in terms of the concept of Post Traumatic Stress Disorder, (PTSD). Judith Herman asserts that 'There is a spectrum of traumatic disorders, ranging from the effects of a single overwhelming event to the more complicated effects of prolonged and repeated abuse' (1992: 3). Whatever her orientation, the therapist is bound, both ethically and legally, to be aware of these complicated effects and to judge whether she is competent enough to deal with them.

The therapist in the public sector may have more constraints put upon them when working in this area; however these restraints are in place to protect them and their clients. The therapist in private practice has a code of ethics and supervisory support and in the final analysis, professional indemnity insurance. However, the most effective support is knowledge, which includes knowledge of current theoretical thinking and knowledge of the existence and content of the codes of practice to which they must adhere. Finally a therapist must have a personal stance which incorporates her views and understanding of the two aforementioned areas.

Legal Framework

The British Association for Counselling and Psychotherapy (BACP, 2002: 6) states that:

10.   Practitioners should be aware of and understand any legal requirements concerning their work, consider these conscientiously and be legally accountable for their practice.

Most codes of ethics for psychotherapists include a similar phrase to that used in the Sherwood Psychotherapy Training Institute (SPTI) (1996) which provides, inter alia:

13.1 Members should be reasonably conversant with the legal implications of their work as counsellors/psychotherapists and have access to legal advice, and

13.3 Members who become aware of a specific crime in the course of their clinical practice, whether current or past, should seek supervisory and legal advice immediately.

The law is seen as a 'crucial cornerstone of safe, ethical and competent therapeutic practice (Bond, 1993: 103).

The definition of sexual abuse varies from author to author and between therapeutic traditions. Hall and Lloyd (1997: 2) leave the definition to survivors themselves, which has been adopted by campaigning groups. Their definition is: 'The sexual molestation of a child by an older person perceived as a figure of trust or authority – parents, relatives (whether natural or adoptive), family friends, youth leaders and teachers, etc.' Michelle Elliot, Director of Kidscape provides a broader definition:

… when a child is forced, coerced or manipulated into either doing or having things done, to their body by a person, male or female, who is in a position of control, care or power over that child. I include the child being made/asked to watch other people engaging in sexual acts whether by force or agreement. Or being exposed in any way to sexual activity, talk, picture etc, which are way beyond the child's sexual and psychological development'.

Definitions are, however, changing.

There is no single criminal offence of abusing a child, although major changes to the law in this respect are currently under discussion (see below). As Cathy Cobley (1995: 5) says 'legal definitions of criminal offences that may be committed when a child is abused are of limited assistance in defining a social problem'.

However, there are a number of criminal offences which may be used against an abuser, a summary of these and the maximum penalties follow.

Sexual Abuse: Sentences available to the courts

Rape
Maximum penalty: life imprisonment

Intercourse with a girl under 13
Maximum penalty: life imprisonment

Intercourse with a girl under 16
Maximum penalty: 2 years imprisonment

Incest by a man
Maximum penalty: 7 years imprisonment
Life imprisonment if with a girl under 13

Incest by a woman
Maximum penalty: 7 years imprisonment

Buggery
Maximum penalty: life imprisonment if with a person under 16 years or an animal.
5 years imprisonment if the accused is of or over the age of 21 and the other person is under the age of 18: otherwise 2 years imprisonment

Assault with intent to commit buggery
Maximum penalty: 10 years imprisonment

Gross indecency between men
Maximum penalty: 5 years imprisonment if by a man of, or over, the age of 21 years and the other person is under the age of 18 years: 2 years imprisonment in all other situations

Indecent assault on a woman
Maximum penalty: 10 years imprisonment

Indecent assault on a man
Maximum penalty: 10 years imprisonment

Indecency with children
Maximum penalty: 2 years imprisonment

Inciting a girl under 16 to have incestuous sexual intercourse
Maximum penalty: 2 years imprisonment

Indecent photographs of children
Maximum penalty: 3 years imprisonment

Indecent exposure
Maximum penalty: 14 days imprisonment

Most, though not all, of the above offences come within the Sexual Offences Act 1956, (for more details see Cobley, 1995).

The law of incest (Sexual Offences Act 1956 Sections 10 & 11) prohibits sexual intercourse between parent and child, grandfather and grand-daughter, and brother and sister. The relationships are restricted to blood relations, and incest is therefore inapplicable to cases of abuse involving step-parents or more distant relatives. (Such abuse will, of course, fall within the definition of other sexual offences previously mentioned).

It has been proposed that a new crime of 'sexual abuse within families' is expected as part of the first major overhaul of the law on sexual offences in England and Wales for nearly 50 years. The new offence would bring together existing crimes such as incest, rape and indecent assault but at the same time would make clear that the law no longer regarded such crimes as private matters. Other recommendations listed in the Home Office Report *Setting the Boundaries: Reforming the Law on Sex Offences* (2000) include a redefinition of the offence of rape, which has been extended to include oral penetration. Proposed new offences include, *inter alia*:

- sexual assault, to cover sexual touching without the victim's consent
- trespass with intent to commit a serious sex offence
- compelling another to perform sexual acts
- persistent sexual abuse of a child
- buying the sexual services of a child
- recruiting, inducing or compelling a child into commercial sexual exploitation

This report, stated Jack Straw, 'is only the beginning of a debate on the way forward' (Home Office, 2000: i). Consequently there is still some time to await the introduction of legislation to change the present archaic laws.

It may be important for therapists to know these different offences and their sanctions in order to assist a client to balance the risks and trauma involved in taking legal action against the abuser, against an outcome, which, in some cases, may be seen by the client as an inadequate sanction.

Balancing ethics, professional practice and the law

The main components of professional negligence will be briefly stated here. These are:

- the existence of a duty of care (from therapist to client)
- a breach of that duty
- subsequent damage as a result of that breach.

The therapist owes a duty of care to her client. At issue is whether there has been a breach of that duty to take care. The standard of care required must meet the ordinary and reasonable standards of those who practise in the same field. This is regarded as the standard of *a competent respected professional*, i.e. the 'Bolam test'.

The *standard of care* owed by all psychotherapists and counsellors whether working in the public or private sector, whether paid or volunteers, is that of a reasonably competent professional. *This is the standard if the therapist is an experienced full time mental health professional or a trainee with no experience working as a volunteer ... the courts will apply the same standard to both.* Where a counsellor or psychotherapist is employed in this capacity they are governed by their contract of employment. The employer/employee relationship, in law, means that the employer is liable for the negligence of the employee committed during the course of their employment. This is known as vicarious liability. There will also be a contract between the two parties and part of the contract will detail the procedure to be adopted in certain cases when seeing clients, for example assessing the risk of self-harm.

The therapist is not only expected to know, have interpreted, understood and come to her own conclusions about the code of ethics and her own stance, but also that of her theoretical orientation. In addition to this the law expects that the *reasonably competent* professional also know the legal implications of her work.

In the authors' experience, a client is usually aware of having been sexually abused and comes into therapy with this awareness. This is particularly the case when working with survivors in counselling/therapy groups, which have been publicly funded and advertised as counselling for survivors of sexual abuse. The first contact with the client is usually at an assessment session. This may be carried out by the therapist herself or by a case manager or other person. It is crucial that when working with a client who has been sexually abused the therapist works within her competence. This is an ethical requirement under most codes of practice and it is also a legal one, under the *Bolam* test.

It is important at the outset to have some insight into how the presenting issues may be manifested in a therapeutic framework and to understand the complex interactions between psychology, behaviour and thinking. This understanding of the phenomenological field of the client is not intended to pathologise the client but rather refers to symptomatic behaviours that initially may have been considered adaptive and creative ways of surviving trauma, but may have become contextually inappropriate components of the person's adult personality. The long term health implications of childhood sexual abuse are varied and can include depression, anxiety, suicidal thoughts, relationship problems and eating disorders. Hall and Lloyd (1997: 91) summarise the long-term consequences of sexual abuse with a cautionary note: 'not all the problems are present in every survivor and their severity varies ....'

The severity of *some* consequences should put the therapist on alert (particularly the novice) that she could be regarded as 'beyond her competence'. Were she to see such a client, with, for example, eating disorders, dissociative problems, dissociative identity disorder, abuse of self, substance abuse or certain sexual problems, then she should have a knowledge of these specialist areas and be aware of current literature and articles. It is a daunting task to begin to help the survivor with the long term effects that she is experiencing. The therapist is helped by knowing her code of ethics, having the knowledge and insight to be aware of the likely impact, through traumatic countertransference, of this work. As Judith Herman (1992: 140) succinctly asserts: 'Trauma is contagious ... the therapist may begin to experience symptoms of post-traumatic stress disorder.'

Awareness of some of the themes in therapeutic work with survivors is paramount. These include: retraumatisation, regression, anger, disclosure, handling confidentiality and supporting a client in court, and will require clinical competence in all these areas. The issue of recovered memories may also be a theme with some clients; the legal implications of recovered memories are dealt with in Chapter 11.

Retraumatisation, regression and *anger* are issues in this particular work which frequently arise in the therapy room. A therapist must be aware of current professional practice with regard to keeping the client safe and the importance of boundaries in order to provide a competent standard of care.

Disclosure of the abuse can have a devastating effect on the survivor. It may be appropriate to enlist support from other agencies such as community or health agencies, rape crisis groups, community psychiatric teams, health visitors and so on. Not all disclosures require this level of support but the therapist needs to be aware that even a small disclosure can produce a very significant emotional reaction in the survivor.

Those psychotherapists working in the public sector have clear guidelines as to the circumstances when they are required to break *confidentiality*. In the private sector this is not so clear. Some codes of ethics give guidance, however some state that confidentiality is absolute (Phillips, 1991). However this may conflict with a code of ethics which also states that any knowledge of a criminal offence must be disclosed to a supervisor or other person. Consequently if the survivor knows, believes, or suspects that her abuser is continuing to abuse others a dilemma in some cases presents itself. It is assumed that before breaking confidentiality the therapist would have discussed this with the client; however, if the client does not give her permission this is a dilemma for the therapist.

The view of the court is that it is in the public interest that confidences should be maintained and protected by the law. This was established in the case of A-G. v Guardian Newspapers (No.2) [1988]. However this aspect of the public interest may be outweighed by another competing public interest. The greater the risk to the public, the stronger is the public interest in disclosing the perceived source of danger. There is no doubt that suspected child abuse is such an area. In Gillick v West Norfolk and Wisbech Area Health Authority [1986], it was said that 'there is no law of confidentiality, which would command silence when the welfare of the child is concerned' (at 149). The dilemma is that if the client does not give permission for disclosure, this breach of confidence may be met by an injunction and an action for damages by the client.

It is accepted practice in most areas of the profession that therapists require supervision. It might be regarded as substandard care were a therapist to be working without supervision, particularly when working with adult survivors. Those who seek consultation or supervision are most likely to fulfil the standard of care whereas those who work in isolation from their peers and whose treatment is markedly different from that of their peers are more at risk than the average practitioner is. The standard by which the court will judge is probably the medical model where supervision is mandatory.

Additionally the courts have accepted the concept of transference as a powerful and accepted part of analytic treatment. It follows from this perspective that failure to abide by the accepted safeguards in its use, would amount to substandard care (see Werner v Landau (1961)).

Substandard treatment may be seen to be one or a number of the following.

- failing to secure supervision or consultation
- practice in isolation; the quality of which significantly departs from the quality of service generally accepted by the professional community
- failure to adequately document the treatment
- failure to demonstrate knowledge of, and adherence to, mental health law and ethical principles
- failure to demonstrate knowledge of, or inability to utilise, authoritative clinical and scientific literature on sexual abuse and trauma treatment

---

To summarise, standard of care is objectively based, on reasonably competent behaviour, and not simply on the personal approach taken by a particular therapist. However, if the therapist is seen as possessing specialist skills then a higher duty of care exists. There is no such lowering of the 'reasonably competent' practitioner for those therapists who are in training or who are new to the profession.

Finally, the person taking action against the therapist has to show that she has suffered damage as a result of the breach of a duty to take care. In the case of an adult survivor who is alleging negligent therapy this may be the psychological effect of the therapy, and perhaps economic loss if she was unable to work. In the *Ramona* case in the USA, there was an allegation that a third party, a father, had suffered financial loss. The allegation was that his daughter had recovered memories of his sexual abuse after being given sodium amytal by her psychiatrist. As a result of these allegations he lost business and in addition to claiming psychological damage he claimed economic loss (see Jenkins, Chapter 12).

Legal remedies available to a client who has been sexually abused:

Criminal Proceedings—Taken by the police or Crown Prosecution Service against the alleged abuser. There are no time limits in determining whether to prosecute; however, despite recent changes, if the client is now an adult and the abuse happened many years ago the authorities may decide that the offence is too archaic and therefore will not prosecute.

Civil Action—The client may be entitled to sue someone for personal injuries she has suffered as a result of the abuse. The client has to show someone is to blame, she has to show negligence, or sue the abuser for the assault. The client has to show that the negligence caused the injury.

The time limits for bringing this type of action (i.e. for personal injuries) are within three years from the date on which the cause of action accrued or the date of knowledge (if later) under the Limitation Act 1980. All the client can receive from the court is compensation. The court has no power to punish the abuser. The case may take a long time, usually between 2 and 5 years.

Criminal Injuries Compensation—This is available for abuse committed after 1964 where it can be regarded as an act of violence.

Public Enquiry—A solicitor may help the survivor and representation is usually free in this case. (For example the North Wales

Tribunal in 1998 which was an inquiry into abuse in residential care run by the local authority).

Local Enquiry—The difference between a local enquiry and a public enquiry is that a local enquiry is organised by a local authority and a public enquiry by central government.

Access to Records—A client is entitled to see her personal social services file if it came into existence after 1989, or medical records and independent therapy records from 1991 (the Access to Health Records Act 1990, now consolidated in the Data Protection Act 1998).

Tribunals—Sometimes a solicitor can advise the client and represent her at the Tribunals of Enquiry, where there is a hearing to clarify an issue. Legal Aid may be available.

Supporting a client in court needs careful consideration. If a therapist is called as a witness then she may be disqualified from having contact with the client during the court proceedings. If she is not being called then she has to be aware that criminal proceedings are held in public and may be quite lengthy, the trial may involve the client in a considerable degree of stress, and possibly retraumatisation. It may be seen as unethical *not* to support the client through court, however the therapist must only offer the support she can realistically give. In this case therapists have to be aware of whether the client has enough self support to go through the proceedings. It may also be useful for the therapists to be aware of the possible pitfalls of taking the alleged abuser to court. Unfortunately, the dynamics of child sexual abuse can be replicated during the legal process, which can exacerbate the devastating damage caused by the original abuse.

The Home Office Justice & Victims Unit issued, in April 2000, a consultation document entitled 'Pre-trial therapy for vulnerable and intimidated witnesses'. This proposed a good practice guide, which is intended, amongst others, for therapists and those who commission or arrange therapy. It provided that 'agencies providing or commissioning pre-trial therapy should ensure that those directly providing this should have appropriate training or supervision and are aware of the potential criminal justice implications of their work' (2000: 2). This draft document and the ensuing Practice Guidance should be required reading for those psychotherapists involved with clients who have been sexually abused and who may be contemplating legal action against the abuser (Home Office, 2002).

In response to concerns that victims of abuse were unable to find lawyers to take on their cases or who were experiencing poor standards of advice, the Association of Child Abuse Lawyers (ACAL) was established, which aims to improve standards and provide resources to solicitors in this rapidly expanding area of practice. Uninformed lawyers who work with sexually abused clients are running very real risks of retraumatising their clients and exposing themselves to the symptoms of secondary trauma. So it is important for the client to find an informed lawyer who understands about this type of abuse, how to deal with claims sensitively without retraumatising them and who knows how to stay healthy while so doing, and therefore is able to provide a crucial service. There can be a real therapeutic value to justice and properly trained lawyers will facilitate it.

Human Rights Act 1998

The above Act came into force on 2 October 2000 and incorporated the European Convention on Human Rights (ECHR) into English Law (see Chapter 13). The Act is directed at *public authorities* which has been interpreted quite broadly to include bodies which are performing a public function, and includes National Health Service hospitals, local authorities such as privatised prison services and quasi-public bodies. This means that an individual who feels that a public authority has breached any of the Articles may take action against that authority. The Articles, which might be used, include those relating to cruel and inhuman treatment. This could be the case of a person who was sexually abused whilst in the care of a local authority.

The key issues for health care providers therefore are covered in Article 3, which concerns inhuman and degrading treatment. This is likely to cover sexual abuse, both of adults and children. Article 8 examines the right to privacy, which includes the information kept by therapists and others and states that:

> Everyone has the right to respect for his private and family life, his home and his correspondence

However, this is not an absolute right, there are limitations. It is qualified by the 'interests of the public'; this means that public authorities can interfere with this right 'in accordance with the law' and if 'necessary ... in the interests of [for example] public safety or ... for the protection of health or ... of the rights and freedoms of others.' What is probably required is that *explicit* consent is necessary for disclosure. This would be interpreted to mean a signature by the client. It would probably be in the best interests of the therapist and the client were a signature on a contract obtained at the outset of therapy, making clear the situations when disclosure by the therapist might happen.

This enshrinement of the client's right to privacy means, according to Hardy and Hill (1999: 372), that this will 'increase the likelihood of litigation in the event of breach of confidentiality. In the light of such developments counsellors should exercise caution in the management of confidentiality and keep abreast of changes to the law which affect counselling'.

Conclusion

Psychotherapists must be aware of the law, and the implications for their psychotherapy practice, and also report infractions of the criminal law to an appropriate person, usually a supervisor. This may involve contacting the psychotherapist's insurance company. However, Sandy Murray, Manager of the Psychologists Protection Society has stated 'I would like to give you some warnings. It is a common belief that insurance will protect you. This is not necessarily true. It would be a mistake to have insurance as your only protection' (1995: 7). Therefore counsellors and psychotherapists must acquire a thorough knowledge of the law as part of their training. Also this must be part of their continuing professional education. The necessity for supervisors of psychotherapists to have advanced knowledge of the legal implications for practice is particularly pertinent in both private practice and within an organisational setting. Vicarious liability for wrongful or negligent supervision is an untested area in the UK; however, the likelihood of supervisor liability is probably rather limited. This leaves the onus on individual psychotherapists, not only to have adequate insurance cover, but, more importantly to keep themselves informed of the legal implications for their practice, and not to rely on their supervisors to do this for them.

The idea that psychotherapists need to have a reasonable knowledge of the law is a fairly new one in the UK. This is indicated by the dearth of material in counselling and psychotherapy literature and legal journals. By contrast, the plethora of material in legal/medical journals and psychotherapy literature in the USA, and even the existence of a website dealing with legal and ethical issues for therapists, is indicative of their more advanced knowledge in response to litigation.

Just as psychotherapists must respond to and practise within the law, law likewise should reflect the theoretical and clinical issues raised in psychotherapy. Codes of practice for psychotherapists are for their information and support, and concomitantly for the benefit of their clients. The law, too, may be seen in this way, as underpinning and strengthening the practice of psychotherapy, not restraining, but liberating.

References

American Psychiatric Association (1994) *Diagnostic and Statistical Manual of Mental Disorders*. Fourth edition. Washington, DC: APA.

Austin, K., Moline, M. and Williams, G. (1990) *Confronting Malpractice:Legal and Ethical Dilemmas in Psychotherapy*. London: Sage.

Bond, T. (1993) *Standards & Ethics for Counselling in Action (First edition)*. London: Sage.

British Association for Counselling and Psychotherapy (2002) *Ethical Framework for Good Practice in Counselling and Psychotherapy*. Rugby: BACP.

Cobley, C. (1995) *Child Abuse and the Law*, London: Cavendish Publishing.

Dyer, C. (1996). 'Medical litigation faces British revolution', *British Medical Journal, 312:330*.

Hall, L. and Lloyd, S. (1997) *Surviving Sexual Abuse*. London: Falmer Press.

Ham, C., Dingwell, R., Fenn, P. and Harris, D., (1988) 'Medical negligence'. *Briefing Paper No.6, Centre for Socio-Legal Studies*. Oxford, London: Kings Fund Institute.

Hardy, S. and Hill, A. (1999) 'Human rights in counselling practice. *Counselling*, December 10(5) pp. 371–373.

Health Service Commiisioner (HSC) (1993). *Annual Report for 1992–93*. London: HMSO.

Herman, J. (1992) *Trauma and Recovery*. London, New York: Basic Books.

Home Office Justice and Victims Unit (2000) *Pre-Trial Therapy for Vulnerable and Intimidated Witnesses, Current Good Practice Guidance: Consultation Document*. London: Home Office.

Home Office (2000) *Setting the Boundaries: Reforming the Law on Sex Offences: Summary Report and Recommendations*. London: Home Office.

Home Office (2002) *Provision of Therapy for Vulnerable or Intimidated Adult Witnesses Prior to a Criminal Trial: Practice Guidance*. London: Home Office.

Jenkins, P. (1992) 'Counselling and the Law' *Counselling*, August 3(3) 165–7.

Jenkins, P. (1997) *Counselling, Psychotherapy and the Law*. London: Sage.

Meyer, G., Landis, E. and Hays, J. (1988) *Law for the Psychotherapist*. New York: Norton.

Mason, J.K. and McCall Smith, R.A. (1983) *Law and Medical Ethics*. London: Butterworth.

Murray, S. (1995) *The Law and the Training of Counsellors and Psychotherapists*, Crowborough: Wealden College.

Otto, R. and Schmidt, W., (1991) 'Malpractice in verbal psychotherapy: problems and some solutions', *Forensic Reports*. 4: 309–36.

Pattison, S. (1999) 'Are professional codes ethical?' *Counselling*, December. 10(5) pp. 374–380.

Phillips, M. (1991) 'Violations of the ground rule of confidentiality in a counselling centre: the contribution of Langs' *Counselling* 2(3): 92–4.

Sherwood Psychotherapy Training Institute (1996) *Code of Ethics and Professional Practice*. Nottingham: SPTI.

United Kingdom Council for Psychotherapy (1998) *Ethical Requirements for Member Organisations*. London: UKCP.

Legal references (UK)

AG v Guardian Newspapers No. 2 [1988] 2 All ER 545
Bolam v Friern HMC [1957] 2 All ER 118
Gillick v West Norfolk and Wisbech Area Health Authority [1986] AC.112
Werner v Landau [1961] TLR 8/3/1961, 23/11/1961, Sol Jo [1961] 105, 1008

Legal references (US)

Ramona v Isabella, Rose, M.D. and Western Medical Center, Anaheim [1994] C61898
   California Supreme Court Napa County

9

Counselling in Legal Settings: Provision for Jury Members, Vulnerable Witnesses and Victims of Crime

Brian Williams

It might be reasonable to expect that the criminal justice system would generally aim to avoid making things worse for the victims and witnesses of crime and for those who serve on juries. In practice, despite attempts made to protect them from unnecessary distress, many victims believe their involvement with criminal justice agencies to be a form of secondary victimisation. In other words, contact with the system makes them feel worse, not better. Jurors and witnesses also complain of traumatic experiences at the hands of professionals and courts. There is a growing recognition in England and Wales that the system needs to become more victim-focused, and that in most instances, secondary victimisation is avoidable. This chapter considers the nature of the problems faced by victims, witnesses and jurors, and describes the current arrangements for protecting their interests in England and Wales. Some recent reforms aimed at protecting the court users regarded by the authorities as vulnerable are reviewed.

Secondary Victimisation

Many victims of crime find themselves marginalised by the way the criminal justice system is organised. Their first contact with the system is usually with the police, whose prime concern is often to secure a conviction. They tend to view victims, their family members and witnesses in an instrumental way: they may be treated primarily as people with relevant information, rather than being seen as aggrieved parties with their own needs and vulnerabilities. With certain types of offence, they are likely to be treated with suspicion, either in the belief that they might have been involved in the offence in some way, or because it is thought that they may be withholding information. Murders, for example, are often committed by people close to the victim, and the bereaved relatives often fall initially under suspicion. Police officers operate in a culture of mistrust, and some find it difficult to switch from a doubting attitude towards suspects to a more reassuring approach to victims.

Victim status is more easily conferred upon certain types of people than others (see the section on vulnerable victims below). Even once they are recognised as such, victims may have other obstacles to surmount. The police do not always keep them informed as they should (Williams, 1999b). When cases go to court, victims and witnesses also have difficulty obtaining information, and their time is often wasted with court appearances which lead only to adjournments (Mawby and Walklate, 1994). Where there are trials, lawyers' questioning can be experienced as aggressive, and cross-examination can be gruelling or even oppressive to victims and witnesses (Temkin, 1997). Offenders may do deals and obtain more lenient sentences by plea-bargaining, they may be sentenced in ways that victims and their families regard as insufficiently punitive, or they may not be convicted at all. Very often, these processes occur without any discussion or consultation with victims (CPS, 2000, Para 6.7–8; Home Office, 1998; Walklate, 1989). In more serious cases, the probation service may eventually contact the victim or surviving relatives to discuss the offender's release from prison, which is understandably unwelcome in many cases, especially when it is unexpected (Crawford and Enterkin, 1999).

However, the criminal justice process can also have a therapeutic value for victims of crime. When the system works well, it can provide a cathartic experience, for example by relieving any feelings of guilt experienced by victims, by collecting compensation or by punishing the offender (Zedner, 1997). In certain cases, direct or indirect reparation is arranged, and victims can be reassured that they have nothing further to fear from the offender (Warner, 1992). In practice, though, things do not always go so well.

In extreme cases, victims and witnesses may bitterly regret having become involved with the criminal justice system. The impact of feeling that their word has been doubted by the police, the prosecution service, lawyers or a judge and jury can be profound and disillusioning. People who have always assumed that the criminal justice system was there to protect them sometimes find that this is not its primary purpose, and feel understandably aggrieved. They have not volunteered to become involved, except to the extent that they have made a complaint about or witnessed a crime, and they may find themselves responding to events over which they have little control. In many cases, they feel that they have been treated insensitively and denied information, and this increases their distress. Similarly (although not usually to the same extent), jurors can find the experience difficult, distressing, and less easy to put behind them than they might have expected. In what follows, each of these groups is considered, along with the services currently provided in an attempt to reduce the distress their involvement with the system may cause. Some of the more general issues are then discussed, along with recent and proposed changes to accommodate the needs and concerns of victims, witnesses and other participants in the criminal justice process.

Witness Protection

The first criminal justice agency with which most victims and witnesses come into contact is the police. The attitudes, training and occupational culture of the police have an important impact on the impression people gain of the criminal justice system at this early stage. While, in most cases, the initial response of the police is satisfactory, levels of victim satisfaction tend to decrease with lengthier contact (Zedner, 1997). The police have good reasons for providing a high level of service to victims and witnesses: successful prosecutions often depend upon the quality of the evidence given in court. In police forces which recognise this link, the initial service offered is correspondingly good. However, this is not always the case at every stage of criminal proceedings, and police contact and support often tail off as a case progresses. The instrumental view of victims and witnesses as people who can help to ensure a successful prosecution is unfortunate: what is needed is a consistent service which provides information and support when it is requested, and few police services have yet committed the resources necessary to achieve this.

In response to criticism of the treatment of women reporting rapes, police practice in this area has begun to change. Trained investigating officers and victim liaison officers, dedicated interview suites, and a generally increased emphasis on witness care, have led to improved levels of satisfaction with the police response to this type of offence (Zedner, 1997). This is not to say that these changes go far enough: women reporting sexual offences are still often examined by male doctors without being given any choice, and then asked questions which have already been asked by police officers without being told why this is necessary. The experience of reporting rape is still degrading and demoralising for many women (Temkin, 1997), and dedicated interview facilities are not available in all areas. In many cases the police fail to keep women informed of the progress of investigations, and prosecutions are dropped or charges downgraded without consultation (Williams, 1999b). The police in some areas take the view that investigating and liaison officers of either sex are equally well qualified, and therefore women who prefer to discuss an offence with a female officer may not have any choice. Only a small proportion of reported rapes result in successful prosecutions (Lees, 1997). As a result, many women decide not to report offences, and the burden of supporting rape survivors falls upon voluntary agencies rather than the police.[1]

The policy in some police services of appointing a female officer with specific responsibility for liaison with survivors has been successful in those cases where sufficient evidence is available to mount a prosecution. Often, the liaison officers feel that, given more time, they could provide an even better service (Temkin, 1997). Some display worrying signs of secondary victimisation themselves: they have nightmares and become so involved in cases that they work on them in their own time (Nuttall and Morrison, 1997). Workloads can be large, and the existence of liaison officers does not guarantee that victims and witnesses receive a satisfactory service if these officers are overworked. Clearly, they need proper support and supervision, and realistic caseloads. The appointment of liaison officers may provide an appropriate model for supporting witnesses more generally, if ways can be found to ensure that the officers themselves are appropriately supported.

In those areas where the needs of victims and witnesses are recognised, the police provide sophisticated services to victims and witnesses of serious crimes of all kinds. These range from providing leaflets telling people what to expect (such as Home Office, 1997), to escorting people to court and following up cases with home visits (Williams, 1999b). Large metropolitan police services have Witness Protection Schemes, and some have a more comprehensive witness care department (as in Staffordshire). These areas have found it much easier to comply with the recommendations in 'Speaking Up for Justice' (discussed below) than the police in areas with less well-developed arrangements.[2] They automatically treat all victims of racist and homophobic offences as 'vulnerable', which triggers the provision of additional services.

Where witnesses or victims are in danger of intimidation, this is taken very seriously. The police have the resources to provide physical protection and in most areas they will also prosecute offenders. Their ability to provide reassurance and advice varies from one area to another. Some police services are able to draw upon specialist witness care units. Such units not only provide direct support to individual victims, they also inform police training and policy by drawing attention to victims' needs internally (Williams, 1999b). They may also refer people to Victim Support, Rape Crisis, racial harassment projects and other voluntary agencies for peer support.

Witness protection might be defined to include the provision of appropriate pre-trial therapy to those witnesses and victims who are traumatised by their experiences. Because of the complexity of the law relating to such counselling, this is discussed in the sections on the role of counselling and on ethical and legal dilemmas below.

Victim Services

The services available to victims from non-statutory agencies range from practical advice to long-term counselling. While Victim Support is generally keen to emphasise that its volunteers do not offer counselling, some are in fact trained to do so. The organisation mainly exists to provide short-term advice and neighbourly support in the immediate aftermath of victimisation. In more serious cases, a proportion of volunteers who have received extra training can offer longer-term involvement. Often, however, people with more serious difficulties will be referred elsewhere. Some Rape Crisis groups, on the other hand, require all their volunteers to train as counsellors, and provide appropriate supervision. There is a range of other victim service agencies, often involving some volunteers with counselling qualifications and some reference to counselling skills in volunteers' initial training. Projects with paid staff tend to allocate them the most complex cases, and provide them with some sort of supervision (for example, from the probation or social services representative on the group's committee). Formal affiliation to professional counselling organisations is increasing, but not many voluntary victim support agencies can meet the requirements of (for example) the British Association for Counselling and Psychotherapy. Some, however, have such high standards that they are recognised as placement providers by educational establishments with counselling courses, as in the case of some Rape Crisis schemes.

The voluntary nature of the self-help victims' organisations is important for a number of reasons. Despite the tendency of some professionals to believe that voluntary organisations are by nature amateurish, many victims value voluntary offers of help. In some cases this is because help is given by people with personal experience of victimisation. They are presumed to know more about the experience than professional agency staff do, and can offer a genuinely empathetic response. The voluntary nature of the offer may also be valued because the element of altruism is recognised. Local volunteers can offer a genuinely neighbourly response to victimisation. However, some people have reservations about this model of providing support for victims.

Confidentiality can clearly be an issue. While the agencies concerned all stress the need to respect client confidentiality in their volunteer training, some potential clients may be put off by the knowledge that a service is provided by local people. Particularly where sensitive issues are involved, as with sexual offences, anonymous telephone contact may be preferred to direct personal meetings. Agencies are aware of this need, and Rape Crisis centres in particular are organised in such a way as to facilitate it. Many clients are concerned about sensitive information being added to their medical records, and the independence of the voluntary agencies is reassuring in this respect. Only a minority of Rape Crisis clients disclose their abuse to anyone else.

Another concern is the extent to which volunteers receive appropriate support and supervision. Most voluntary victim support agencies encourage their volunteers to attend regular support group meetings, and they also offer individual supervision on an ad hoc basis where it seems appropriate. Those agencies which use trained counsellors also make arrangements for formal supervision in the counselling sense of the term. However, some smaller agencies do appear to risk over-involvement by volunteers who have suffered severe traumatic experiences of victimisation themselves. Nevertheless, no matter how professionalised the victim support agencies may become, the fact remains that many service users prefer volunteer support. It is important that the choice remains available to them.

State-provided services to victims have quite a long history in the UK, dating back to the establishment of the victim compensation scheme in 1964, but policy on victims is politically sensitive. The British state has tended to treat victims of crime as consumers of criminal justice services – a status they do not seek and a political approach which makes it hard for the views of victims to be heard (Williams, 1999a). As a result, change has been relatively slow. When the government department predominantly concerned with these issues, the Home Office, has attempted to ascertain victims' views, it has (at least until recently) mainly consulted one organisation, Victim Support. When a wider consultation exercise was undertaken in 1998, many other groups became involved (Home Office, 1998), and the government began to consider more radical change. The resulting legislation and further proposed changes are discussed below.

In 1996 the decision was taken to set up two experimental projects: the 'One Stop Shop' initiative and the pilot projects compiling Victim Statements giving information about crime victims to the courts. Both innovations responded to research findings about the wishes and needs of victims of crime. Victim Statements (VS) drew upon experience in a number of other countries where victims are encouraged to provide information which may influence criminal justice decisions. Projects of this kind in the USA and Australia had been thoroughly researched, and the evidence from these studies (although contradictory and confusing) was taken into account in designing the UK experiment (Mawby and Walklate, 1994; Ashworth, 1993). The One Stop Shop was designed to ensure that the police share information with victims in the cases where offenders are identified and proceedings are initiated against them. Again, previous research had identified a need for such information to be shared more systematically (Mawby and Walklate, 1994; Wemmers, 1996; Lees, 1997).

The projects showed that most victims welcomed the opportunity to make a statement about the impact that the crime had on them, but a significant minority expressed dissatisfaction about the process of making such a statement. This seems to have arisen largely because the existence of the VS procedure raised unrealistic expectations about the extent to which victims' views would influence decisions (Hoyle et al., 1998). Similarly, the One Stop Shop experiment made most victims feel more in control of the criminal justice process and helped to reduce some people's levels of anxiety. Many felt, however, that they received information too late and that some information excluded from the scheme should have been included (such as notifying victims of decisions about granting defendants bail – and the reasons for such decisions). These problems would need to be resolved before it would be feasible to widen the availability of these projects (Hoyle et al., 1998). Nevertheless, the pilot projects demonstrated a new commitment on the part of central government to explore the best way of meeting the known, unmet needs of victims of crime. More recent innovations are described in the penultimate section of this chapter, below.

Child Victims and Witnesses

There is a growing recognition that children who become involved in the criminal justice system, either as victims or witnesses, have special needs which should be met wherever possible. The criminal justice system has had to adapt to the increasing involvement of children in the roles of victim and witness, recognising both their comparative vulnerability and the likelihood that questions may be raised about their competence to testify (Murray, 1997).

Child victims and witnesses are more likely than adults to be seen as needing to be protected from the accused. Given that they are also more likely to be unfamiliar with legal conventions, their probable need for some form of preparation for involvement in criminal trials is also generally recognised. This tallies with a concern to ensure that they are enabled to give good evidence, and is not wholly motivated by concern for the child's welfare. The child's interests are not seen as paramount, because of the need to protect the rights of the accused, but they are increasingly taken into account. Specifically, the law in England and Wales recognises:

• that children suffer additional stress in taking part in court proceedings
• that such stress may affect the way they give their evidence
• but that there is nevertheless a need to bring to justice people who offend against children (see Ball et al., 1995: 83–6)

The Youth Justice and Criminal Evidence Act 1999 allows courts to apply a range of special measures when it is believed that these will improve the quality of the evidence given by vulnerable victims or witnesses, including anyone under the age of 17. These arrangements include giving evidence by video recording or live video link, the removal of judges' and barristers' wigs and gowns while evidence is given, and the use of screens protecting witnesses from being 'eye-balled' by defendants (Baird, 1999). The law came into force in October 1999, but the Home Office has indicated that further changes may be needed, and a consultation exercise in relation to child witnesses may lead to further legislation (Home Office, 1999).

In addition to these changes to court procedures, criminal justice agencies have also altered pre-trial arrangements in recognition of children's particular needs. The Crown Prosecution Service (CPS) has arranged to bring cases involving child witnesses to court more quickly, provided special training for the prosecutors who work with children, and established detailed policies aimed at protecting the interests of child victims and witnesses.

Unfortunately, these policies are not being consistently implemented in practice. For example, courts are not being kept informed about which child victims and witnesses are receiving therapy prior to cases coming to court, which means that the issues of 'coaching' and 'contamination' may be raised inappropriately by defence counsel during trials (see the section on ethical and legal dilemmas below). Despite the general agreement that young people should be offered familiarisation visits to courts prior to giving evidence, these are not always provided when needed, and it is not clear which agency is responsible for ensuring that this is done. Children are also still being kept waiting at court when it would be appropriate to use 'stand-by' or 'deferred attendance' arrangements which have been agreed in principle, allowing them to wait elsewhere until required. (New arrangements for the use of telephone pagers to call witnesses who are standing by to give evidence should improve this situation; see Home Office, 1999). The Crown Prosecution Service is also failing to collect the necessary information about individual child witnesses' capability as witnesses and about their preferences in relation to the method of giving evidence (CPSI, 1998). Clearly, more needs to be done to ensure that crown prosecutors both understand and implement the policies which are designed to protect children. A staff training programme is being designed at the time of writing, and should be in place within a matter of months (see Home Office, 1999).

The CPS policy on the provision of pre-court therapy to child witnesses and victims is a child-centred one. It states that:

> the best interests of the child are the primary consideration, and that the CPS does not have any authority to prevent therapy taking place (CPSI, 1998: 20).

This principle is reiterated in more recent guidance in respect of vulnerable and intimidated witnesses: all witnesses under 17 are by definition vulnerable (CPS, DoH and Home Office, 2002).

Sadly, the very next paragraph of the Inspectorate report points out that not all the lawyers interviewed were aware of this policy, and some were still attempting to discourage therapists from working with young people before court proceedings had been concluded. The CPS clearly has a responsibility to put its house in order, but social workers and therapists will also need to be vigilant to ensure that young people's right to receive appropriate therapy is respected by local prosecutors (CPS, DoH and HO, 2001).

Other 'vulnerable' victims and witnesses

While it is undoubtedly true that some people cope better with criminal victimisation than others, it is unfortunate that the concept of a 'vulnerable' victim has taken such hold on the discourse of victim support. People's responses to crime are individual and unpredictable. It does not necessarily follow that because someone is defined as belonging to a vulnerable group, they will respond particularly badly to being victimised. The groups sometimes defined as vulnerable are huge, covering the majority of the population: they include women, black people, children, older people, and those living alone. Clearly not everyone who happens to belong to one or more of these groups will react adversely to becoming a victim of crime. The police and the victim support agencies use the notion of vulnerability to prioritise the provision of services, but there is a danger that in doing so, they are stereotyping people and allocating resources incorrectly.

The criminological literature refers repeatedly to the 'ideal' victim who is seen as deserving of help. Such a victim is a member of a vulnerable group, engaged in respectable activities in a public place at the time of the offence, has no personal relationship with the offender, suffers unprovoked physical harm at the hands of someone stronger, and cooperates with the police investigation (Williams, 1999b: 126). Clearly, only a small proportion of real victims conform to this ideal type. But the concept of the ideal victim serves to legitimise the failure to provide universal services. For example, a prostitute who reports a 'john' for assault may not receive the same service from the police as a man who alleges that she has taken his wallet. Both are victims, but one fits the stereotype of a deserving victim more readily, even though the assault is more serious than the theft. Victim support agencies are increasingly sensitive to such stereotyping, and in the case described, the woman will probably be offered contact with Victim Support and the man not. However, if it is left to the police to refer victims for help, as in many areas it is, she might not be referred in the first place.

Greater understanding of the politics of victimisation is required by those with decision making powers. The police, for example, define some people as victims and others as witnesses, as if the two categories were mutually exclusive. The treatment of Duwayne Brooks, who saw his friend Stephen Lawrence killed in a racial attack, illustrates the dangers of this lack of sophistication (particularly when combined, as in this case, with institutional racism). Although he was diagnosed as suffering from post-traumatic stress disorder (PTSD), Brooks was prosecuted for an offence of criminal damage committed during a demonstration about the police handling of the Lawrence murder, and he was treated extremely insensitively during the murder enquiries (Macpherson, 1999). Criminal justice officials often fail to recognise that offenders may themselves have been victimised, or that in some cases the police may mistakenly allocate victims to the category of offender. In any event, there is known to be a considerable overlap between the two groups: many offenders have previously been victimised in a variety of ways (Boswell, 1999).

The law has begun to change in recognition of the needs of new groups of victims and witnesses. There is no space here to go into detail, but the particular needs of people with learning difficulties are increasingly being recognised (Sanders et al., 1997). The law has also been changed to take account of the need to protect racial minorities from abuse and violence by increasing the penalties for racially-motivated damage to property and harassment or assault.[3]

Jurors

There is very little research on juries, and the literature that does exist is mostly American. When it comes to the health effects of jury service, there is only a handful of studies. Academic interest in juries has mainly focused on the decision-making process and on the issues which influence jurors' deliberations, and this area of research has been circumscribed by concern to avoid interfering with the judicial process. In the UK, there is considerable secrecy about juries, although some anecdotal information about the experience of serving on juries in particularly notorious criminal trials has emerged.

In this section, the literature on the health risks to jurors is briefly reviewed, mainly with a view to informing the discussion on the role of counselling in the next section of the chapter. Some of the anecdotal accounts of the risks involved for jurors in extreme cases are also used for illustrative purposes.

The literature on the health effects of jury service is difficult to interpret. There is no doubt that serving on a jury is stressful for a minority of jurors, but the severity of the effects observed differs substantially between research reports. One small study found that a majority of jurors reported one or more physical or psychological ill-effects, including a minority who became ill as a result. 4 of the 40 jurors reported symptoms consistent with post traumatic stress disorder (Kaplan and Winget, 1992). Two other small studies reported jurors' reactions to particularly traumatic and high-profile cases, and found that they were shocked and agitated by the gruesome evidence presented. The instructions they received, to avoid discussing the case with anyone else during the trial, seemed to aggravate matters. All of them showed signs of stress during and after the trials. For some jurors, this was extreme (Feldman and Bell, 1991; Hafemeister and Ventis, 1992, cited by Shuman et al., 1994).

These studies relied on self-reported data, and they neither used control groups, nor did they attempt to control for extraneous sources of stress which may have affected jurors' symptoms.

A larger and more rigorous study was conducted by Shuman et al. (1994), who followed up 312 individuals who had served on 26 juries in Dallas, Texas, five or six months previously. About half of the respondents had served on juries in less stressful cases, and they formed a control group. All respondents were asked about other stress factors in their lives, as well as a battery of questions about their health. The researchers looked for signs of depression as well as symptoms of post-traumatic stress disorder (PTSD).

Shuman and his colleagues found that only one juror showed symptoms consistent with PTSD, and he had not been involved in a traumatic case. However, a significant minority of the jurors reported symptoms of depression during the trials, and for 12% of those involved in traumatic trials this persisted five or six months later (compared with 4–5% of the general US population). The authors suggested that jurors' (mistaken) belief that they were not allowed to discuss their feelings about jury service (as opposed to the details of the case) with anyone else may have aggravated their distress. The process of decision-making was also experienced as stressful by some jurors, whose views were perhaps marginalised in the interests of reaching an agreed verdict. The authors observed that:

> While consensus may benefit judicial efficiency, jurors who profess agreement with a verdict, but who harbor private misgivings, may suffer stress from that compliance (Shuman et al., 1994: 279).

The authors' recommendations include giving jurors more information in advance about what to expect and strategies for dealing with stress. They also suggest greater clarity about what jurors may discuss and with whom. In particular, guidance about how the jury should conduct its deliberations might be helpful. For our present purposes, the first two issues may be particularly important.

The Role of Counselling

Where jurors are concerned, the secrecy surrounding jury service makes it unlikely that counsellors will be allowed to offer preventive help. Indeed, there is some research evidence that this very secrecy can aggravate jurors' distress (see above). The advice given to jurors by judges, and in the form of preparatory leaflets and videos, could clearly be improved with a view to preventing the distress that arises from taking the rules on secrecy too literally. People need to be encouraged to talk about their feelings regarding serving on a jury with those close to them, while avoiding breaches of confidentiality. Research carried out for the Law Commission in New Zealand makes useful recommendations in this respect (Young et al., 1999).

Counsellors are more likely to become involved after the period of jury service has ended. The possible link between jury service and depression needs further research, but it is a factor to look out for. The much rarer association between involvement in sensational or gory cases and post traumatic stress disorder will also lead to some calls upon the expertise of counsellors. In these cases, the needs of people who have served on juries are likely to be similar to those of anyone else with post traumatic stress symptoms. It should be relatively easy to make the link in such cases between the traumatic experience and the subsequent distress.

This link may be much less obvious, however, where witnesses to and victims of crime are concerned. Although some will present with intrusive thoughts, hyper-arousal and flashbacks which clearly relate to the offence, other people will disclose signs of distress without having made a link between a past event and their present feelings. Counsellors therefore need to be aware that depression and stress may arise from the experiences of initial victimisation, being a witness to a crime, or subsequent distressing contact with the criminal justice system.

Intervention can be constrained by legal rules on the contamination of evidence. A case can sometimes be made for giving the client's welfare priority over the need to collect and preserve legal evidence (see the next section). Professional intervention is likely to be influential in such cases. Often, however, it may be necessary to wait until the legal process has been concluded. While this may seem unfair, the stress which would be caused to a victim or witness by an unsuccessful prosecution also has to be borne in mind. Pre-trial counselling can be interpreted as 'coaching', leading charges to be dropped.

Most victims and witnesses need reassurance that they are not to blame for what happened, and that their reactions are not unusual or a sign of mental illness (see Williams, 1996; 1999b). Many will already be in contact with victim support agencies, and counsellors may benefit from collaboration with the staff of such agencies. If they have been involved with the client over a lengthy period, there is likely to be a strong and trusting relationship on which to build. The agencies may also welcome consultation, given their specialist experience and their knowledge of the individual client's circumstances. In many cases, they will have encouraged the client to seek outside help.

Ethical and Legal Dilemmas

Lawyers have great difficulty in distinguishing therapy from 'coaching'. According to legal ideology, barristers should never discuss cases with non-expert witnesses outside the court, for fear that evidence might thereby be 'contaminated' (Hailsham, 1989: 380; Code of Conduct for the Bar, 1989, para. 23.4; Rock, 1993). In the UK, this convention has been taken to apply also to contact between potential expert witnesses and victims who will be giving evidence. Thus, a professional person who might be required to give evidence about the trauma suffered by a victim has to take great care not to provide help to the victim: assessment for the court's purposes has to be kept separate from therapy. Of course, this is not always possible in practice. Counsellors have to take scrupulous care to avoid discussion of the actual offence, even where such discussion might assist the victim. Although these rules are under review (both where the Bar is concerned: see Royal Commission, 1993, and with reference to therapists: see Home Office, 1998[4]), they currently remain in force.

With appropriate training, counsellors and other therapists have found ways to avoid being accused of 'coaching' witnesses or contaminating evidence (Bond, 1998; Sanders et al., 1997), while providing appropriate help. It would clearly be much more satisfactory, though, if the legal obstacles to providing the help people need could be removed, as in some parts of the USA (Spungen, 1998).

Guidance recently issued by the Crown Prosecution Service, the Department of Health and the Home Office goes some way towards clarifying these issues in respect of vulnerable and intimidated witnesses (CPS, DoH and Home Office, 2002) and in respect of child witnesses (CPS et al., 2001). The guidance on vulnerable witnesses is specifically intended for the use of counsellors working with them, and the introduction makes clear that it is susceptible to revision in the light of experience. It accepts that some witnesses will need pre-trial therapy, and preparation for giving evidence, and clarifies the circumstances in which this might interfere with the subsequent legal case and how this can be avoided.

Operating under these guidelines is unlikely to be straighforward, however: for example, there are real constraints upon confidentiality and it is stated that new offences disclosed during therapy must be reported. Records of therapy can in some circumstances be required by the courts. Proper professional supervision may not always be available for volunteer counsellors or for statutory agency staff undertaking counselling roles. As a consequence, they may make mistakes or experience distress themselves. Some such cases may come to the attention of professional counsellors, and they will need to take appropriate action. Some voluntary agencies may wish to engage outside professionals for supervision or consultation. Others will find it hard to see the need, and unless they are affiliated to the relevant professional association, it may be difficult to bring any pressure to bear upon them. In some cases, however, legal action is accelerating change.

For example, police officers acting as family liaison officers in murder cases, and those actively involved in disasters or individual cases, are owed a duty of care by their employers (Jenkins, 1999). In recent years, such workers have increasingly taken legal action in an attempt to gain compensation for the stress experienced, as have, in a few cases, people more peripherally involved with the criminal justice system, such as the volunteer advocate who sat in on police interviews with mass murderer Frederick West (*Leach v Chief Constable of Gloucestershire* [1999]). The current state of our knowledge is such that lawyers are likely to recruit rival experts to help them argue the merits of compensation in individual cases, and those involved in counselling parties to such cases may find themselves involuntarily drawn into the legal arena.

The controversy about the effectiveness of different treatments for PTSD also has implications for professionals working with those claiming to be damaged by their contact with the criminal justice system. Counsellors need to keep abreast of developments in this field in order to avoid using inappropriate methods and making matters worse (Jenkins, 1999). The Health and Safety Executive's website offers a useful source of information.[5]

Recent and proposed legal and policy changes

As noted earlier, increasing attention is being paid to the support and information needs of victims and witnesses. Victims of crime have become a social issue – some would say a social movement – in recent decades, and it is increasingly difficult for politicians and policy-makers to ignore their concerns (Rock, 1999; Williams, 1999a). After the election of the Labour government in 1997, the pace of change accelerated. The market ideology which treated victims as consumers of services (despite their involuntary involvement with the system) has remained in place, but it has been complemented by a greatly increased awareness of some of the particular factors which can help to turn people into victims of crime. The report of the Macpherson Inquiry into the murder of Stephen Lawrence made it clear that much violent crime is motivated by racism, and included recommendations aimed at improving the support provided for victims and their families. The report of a working group on the needs of vulnerable and intimidated witnesses summarised the available evidence and drew attention to the relevance of a number of other factors such as gender, age and disability. Between them, these two reports made it easier to locate victim policies within a *politics* of criminal victimisation (Rock, 1999). They also made it much more difficult for politicians to ignore the need for change. Indeed, substantial changes are currently being made to the system (Home Office, 1999).

The Stephen Lawrence Inquiry report analysed a racially-motivated murder in great detail, and made clear recommendations about witness care, methods of keeping victims informed of the progress of investigations, police training and recruitment, the Victim's Charter and race relations legislation which are mostly being implemented (Macpherson, 1999). The outcome should be that victims and witnesses in the case of racially-motivated offences, but also victims and witnesses more generally, are treated with greater sensitivity by the police and the Crown Prosecution Service in the future. Local criminal justice forums have set up inter-agency implementation groups in some areas (see Staffordshire Criminal Justice Forum, undated).

The Youth Justice and Criminal Evidence Act (1999), as we have seen, made far-reaching changes to the procedures for giving evidence in court. Its provisions are part of a process which seems to have accelerated since 1997: of victim and witness needs being kept under review and changes being made to the system at a greater momentum.

The programme of work outlined in 'Action for Justice' (Home Office, 1999) involves implementing almost all the recommendations of the 'Speaking up for Justice' report (Home Office, 1998) by 2003. The substantial expenditure involved in making these changes suggests that the issues discussed in this chapter are being taken increasingly seriously.

Conclusions

A new version of the *Victim's Charter* (as recommended by the Stephen Lawrence Inquiry report) and legislation promised for the 2003/4 session of Parliament (Dominey, 2002) will codify the rights of victims and witnesses, and one hopes that it will reflect many of the concerns raised in this chapter. Change may be slower in the case of protecting the interests of jurors, and more research is needed to ascertain their needs, but the existing literature suggests that there are issues which need to be addressed.

Counsellors have a part to play both in helping individuals and in drawing attention to the failings of existing processes and systems. Whether individually or through their professional organisations, they have played a part in influencing the current programme of change in criminal justice. This can only be beneficial.

Notes

1 The term 'survivor' is here used to refer to women who have been raped, and also to the surviving relatives of murder victims. The word survivor is preferred to 'victim' in rape cases both because it acknowledges the life-threatening seriousness of many rapes, and because it has fewer derogatory connotations (but see Williams, 1999b: 21, for further discussion of this question).

2 Staffordshire Police and their partner agencies were already complying with 29 of the 78 recommendations of the report when the Home Office conducted a survey early in 2000. Of the 78 recommendations, 20 apply directly to local police services (Hood & Lawlor, 2000).

3 In sections 28–33 and 96 of the Crime and Disorder Act 1998.

4 The report 'Speaking up for Justice' recommended that 'vulnerable or intimidated witnesses should not be denied the emotional support and counselling they may need both before and after the trial' (Home Office, 1998: 10). The Crown Prosecution Service has issued guidance on pre-trial therapy (CPS, DoH and HO, 2001; CPS 2002).

5 www.open.gov.uk/hse/hsehome.htm

References

Ashworth, A. (1993) 'Victim impact statements and sentencing', Criminal Law Review, July: 498–509.

Baird, V. (1999) 'Youth justice and criminal evidence act 1999: Part 2', Legal Action, December, 15–16.

Ball, C., McCormac, K. and Stone, N. (1995) Young Offenders: Law, Policy and Practice. London: Sweet & Maxwell.

Bond, H. (1998) 'Support in evidence', Community Care 1217, 9–15.

Boswell, G. (1999) 'Young offenders who commit grave crimes: the criminal justice response', in Kemshall, H. & Pritchard, J. (eds.) Good Practice in Working with Violence. London: Jessica Kingsley.

Chisholm, I. (1999) 'Pleas in mitigation', in Home Office, The Role of Victims in the Criminal Justice Process: Conference Report. Liverpool: Home Office Special Conferences Unit.

Code of Conduct for the Bar of England and Wales (1989) (4th edn) Cited in Hailsham, Lord (ed.) (1989) Halsbury's Laws of England, Vol. 3 (1) London: Butterworths.

Crawford, A. and Enterkin, J. (1999) Victim Contact Work and the Probation Service: a Study of Service Delivery and Impact. Leeds: University of Leeds Centre for Criminal Justice Studies.

Crown Prosecution Service (2000) The Code for Prosecutors, London: CPS.

Crown Prosecution Service, Department of Health and Home Office (2001) *Provision of Therapy for Child Witnesses Prior to a Criminal Trial: Practice Guidance*, London: CPS. http://www.homeoffice.gov.uk/cpd/pvn therapy book. pdf.

Crown Prosecution Service, Department of Health and Home Office (2002) *Provision of Therapy for Vulnerable or Intimidated Witnesses Prior to a Criminal Trial: Practice Guidance*. London: Home Office. http://www.homeoffice.gov.uk/cpd/pvn/provision of therapy.pdf.

Crown Prosecution Service Inspectorate (1998) *The Inspectorate's Report on Cases Involving Child Witnesses*. London: CPS Inspectorate.

Dominey, J. (2002) 'Community Justice Files' section, *British Journal of Community Justice*, Vol. I No.2.

Erez, E. (1999) 'Who's afraid of the big bad victim? Victim impact statements as victim empowerment and enhancement of justice', *Criminal Law Review* July 545–56.

Feldman, T.B. and Bell, R.A. (1991) 'Crisis debriefing of a jury after a murder trial', *Hospital and Community Psychiatry* 42, 79–81.

Hailsham, Lord (ed.) (1989) *Halsbury's Laws of England*, Vol. 3 (1) (4th edn, reissue) London: Butterworths.

Home Office (1997) *Witness in Court (This leaflet tells you what to expect)*. London: Home Office Communications Directorate.

Home Office (1998) *Speaking Up for Justice: Report of the Interdepartmental Working Group on the Treatment of Vulnerable or Intimidated Witnesses in the Criminal Justice System*. London: Home Office.

Home Office (1999) *Action for Justice: Implementing the Speaking up for Justice Report*. London: Home Office Justice and Victims Unit.

Hood, T. and Lawlor, J. (2000) Personal interview, 21 February, with Inspector Hood and Acting Sergeant Lawlor of Staffordshire Police.

Hoyle, C., Cape, E., Morgan, R. and Sanders, A. (1998) *Evaluation of the 'One Stop Shop' and Victim Impact Statement Pilot Projects*. London: Home Office.

Jenkins, P. (1999) 'Stress at work: the creaking of floodgates', *Counselling at Work* Autumn, 26, 3–4.

Kaplan, S.M. and Winget, C. (1992) 'The occupational hazards of jury duty', *Bulletin of the American Academy of Psychiatry* 20, 325–33.

Lees, S. (1997) *Ruling Passions: Sexual Violence, Reputation and the Law*. Buckingham: Open University Press.

Macpherson, W. (1999) *The Stephen Lawrence Inquiry: Report of an Inquiry by Sir William Macpherson of Cluny*. Cm. 4262-I. London: Stationery Office.

Mawby, R.I. and Walklate, S. (1994) *Critical Victimology: International Perspectives*. London: Sage.

Murray, K. (1997) *Preparing Child Witnesses for Court: A Review of Literature and Research*. Edinburgh: Scottish Office Home Department Central Research Unit.

Nuttall, M. and Morrison, S. (1997) *It Could Have Been You*. London: Virago.

Rock, P. (1993) *The Social World of an English Crown Court*. Oxford: Clarendon Press.

Rock, P. (1999) 'What should the victim's role be? England and Wales', in Home Office, *The Role of Victims in the Criminal Justice Process: Conference Report*. Liverpool: Home Office Special Conferences Unit.

Royal Commission (1993) *The Royal Commission on Criminal Justice: A Report*. CM 2263. London: HMSO.

Sanders, A., Creaton, J., Bird, S. and Weber, L. (1997) *Victims with Learning Disabilities: Negotiating the Criminal Justice System*. Oxford: University of Oxford Centre for Criminological Research.

Shuman, D.W., Hamilton, J.A. and Daley, C.E. et al. (1994) 'The health effects of jury service', *Law and Psychology Review* 18, 267–307.

Spungen, D. (1998) *Homicide: The Hidden Victims, a Guide for Professionals.* London: Sage.

Staffordshire Criminal Justice Forum (undated) *Towards Equality for Ethnic Minorities in the Criminal Justice System.* Stafford: Staffordshire Police.

Stead, M., MacFadyen, L., Hastings, G. and Eadie, D. (1997) *Information Needs of Scottish Jurors: An Evaluation of the Scottish Courts Service Leaflet.* Edinburgh: Scottish Office Home Department Central Research Unit.

Temkin, J. (1997) 'Plus ça change: reporting rape in the 1990s', *British Journal of Criminology* 37 (4) 507–28.

Walklate, S. (1989) *Victimology: The Victim and the Criminal Justice Process.* London: Unwin Hyman.

Warner, S. (1992) *Making Amends: Justice for Victims and Offenders.* Aldershot: Avebury.

Wemmers, J-A. (1996) *Victims in the Criminal Justice System.* Amsterdam: Kugler.

Williams, B. (1996) *Counselling in Criminal Justice.* Buckingham: Open University Press.

Williams, B. (1999a) 'The victim's charter: citizens as consumers of criminal justice services', *Howard Journal of Criminal Justice* 38 (4) 384–396.

Williams, B. (1999b) *Working with Victims of Crime: Policies, Politics and Practice.* London: Jessica Kingsley.

Young, W., Cameron, N. and Tinsley, Y. (1999) *Juries in Criminal Trials Part Two: A Summary of the Research Findings.* Wellington, New Zealand: Law Commission.

Zedner, L. (1997) 'Victims', in Maguire, M., Morgan, R. and Reiner, R. (eds.) *The Oxford Handbook of Criminology.* 2nd edn. Oxford: Clarendon Press.

Legal references

Leach v Chief Constable of Gloucestershire Constabulary [1999] 1 All ER 215
Youth Justice and Criminal Evidence Act 1999.

Acknowledgements

The contributions of those who read earlier versions of this chapter, and those who agreed to be interviewed in the course of its preparation, are gratefully acknowledged.

10

The Law of Confidentiality – A Solution or Part of the Problem?

Tim Bond

In my experience few issues produce as much concern and are a source of such difficulty for therapists as the management of confidentiality. It touches on many different aspects of therapy. Confidentiality concerns protecting information as secret. It marks the boundary between the realms of what is considered public and therefore communicable to people about the client and matters that are private to the person concerned. This raises potentially contentious and sometimes difficult questions concerning who should decide what falls within the public or private realms. Should it be the therapist or the client? To what extent should these decisions be determined by people or authorities less directly involved such as agencies providing therapeutic services, professional bodies, the courts or the government through legislation? The management of confidentiality also entails issues of trust. The Latin roots of 'confidence' and 'confidentiality' are *confidere*, meaning 'to have full trust'. All of the talking therapies require the disclosure of personally sensitive information to the therapist, which is only likely to occur when there is sufficient trust between the client and the therapist and if the therapist actively seeks to attain a high level of trustworthiness. At the heart of many of the challenges experienced by therapists concerning the management of confidentiality are difficulties in determining what should be kept secret and issues of trustworthiness. There is clearly an ethical dimension to this challenge but it is also an area of practice where there is a growing body of law. Indeed the law of confidentiality is one of the most rapidly developing areas of law both within the British Isles and internationally.

The rapidity of development of law on this topic has the potential for compounding differences between local legal systems. The British Isles is a surprising mixture of legal jurisdictions with significant differences between them. The legal systems in Eire and Scotland are based on Roman law in contrast to the common law traditions of England, Wales and Northern Ireland. The Isle of Man also has its own law-making powers independent of Parliament and the English legal system. All jurisdictions have developed legal protection of confidences, but not necessarily in the same way, so local legal advice may be required. Much of this chapter applies primarily to England, Wales and Northern Ireland. I recently had an opportunity to gain some insight into the Scottish approach as a result of the British Association for Counselling and Psychotherapy (BACP) commissioning a Scottish edition of an information sheet on 'Confidentiality: counselling, psychotherapy and the law in Scotland' (Bond et al., 2001). My overall impression is how similar the two approaches to confidentiality are in their general approach. For example it has been stated in the House of Lords that the basis of the law of confidentiality may differ to some extent between Scotland and England, but the substance of the law in both countries is the same (*Lord Advocate v The Scotsman Publications Limited* [1989]). English cases have persuasive authority in Scotland and English courts may consider parallel judgments in Scotland and other jurisdictions. In many cases, where statutes passed in London do not apply in Scotland, there is parallel Scottish legislation in most instances. Apparent differences between the rights of young people aged between 16 and 18 in England and Scotland generally result in very similar outcomes (Bond et al., 2001). This common ground in the law concerning confidentiality would not necessarily apply to other areas of law where there are considerably greater differences.

Regardless of local variations the fundamental challenges posed by confidentiality remain the same. It is, in the first instance, about trust and secrecy between practitioner and client but cannot be considered adequately from this perspective alone. There are additional layers of potential difficulty concerning the practitioner's (and client's) wider social responsibilities and thus the relationship between law and professional ethics. In this chapter I want to explore the nature of these challenges and examine the extent to which the legal framework that applies primarily in England, Wales and Northern Ireland eases or compounds the difficulties. My starting point is one of open-mindedness as to whether the current legal framework is a help or a hindrance to practitioners. Logically it is quite possible for law and ethics to coincide and support each other. Where this is the case, good practice is both reasonably easily identifiable and supported by an adequate social infrastructure. On the other hand, the law and ethical considerations may point in different directions. What is ethical may not be legal. What is legal may be unethical. It will become apparent that there are examples of both situations where ethical practice is supported by the legal framework and others where the relationship is more problematic. At the end of the chapter I will consider some strategies to resolve the more problematic aspects of the law of confidentiality.

The main sources of the law concerning confidentiality

It is one of the strange features of the law of confidence, that its existence and applicability to counselling, counselling psychology and psychotherapy is accepted by the courts without any clear authorities for this legal development. The extension of the law of confidence, from state and trade secrets to protecting personally sensitive information, is a relatively recent development, starting with the protection of royal bedroom secrets (*Prince Albert v Strange* (1849)). From contentious origins, the law has continued to develop in the courts through a system of precedence by which the judgments of senior courts influence the outcome of subsequent cases. These developments in common law and equity have been extended and sometimes supplanted by statutory law. As a general principle statutory law overrides common law. There are also differences in aspects of the law of confidence between that which operates in England and Wales and elsewhere in the United Kingdom. I will consider some of these differences separately. Already it will be apparent that the multiple sources of law and the way the law is continually developing makes this an area where it is inappropriate to be too doctrinaire or definitive about the law of confidence. Francis Gurry (1984), in a seminal work that is frequently cited in current legal texts on this topic, recommends 'being tentative and devoid of dogmatism' in attempting to understand this area of law. He also points out that the courts have tended to be pragmatic and flexible in how they seek to respond to the circumstances of each case. This pragmatic approach to the circumstances of each case works against high levels of certainty about the application of general principles in any particular instance.

Nonetheless, it is possible to set out some of the general principles of confidentiality. I will start by considering the three areas of law that are particularly applicable to therapists. These are the general law of confidence derived from a combination of common and statutory law, the legal requirements concerning human rights and those concerning data protection. Recent developments in the procedures by which the courts obtain and manage evidence have proved to be one of the more problematic issues for therapists. I will consider each of these in turn with some hypothetical examples loosely based on actual incidents of how the law is likely to work in practice.

The general law of confidence

The law starts with a general assumption in favour of the free exchange of information. This assumption is considered fundamental to ensuring a democratic and open society. Legally protected confidences are therefore exceptional and require justification. There needs to be a balance of benefit to the public in protecting confidences that outweighs the benefit derived from the free exchange of information. This balance of benefit requires that the talking therapies are viewed as a beneficial service; that the provision of therapy depends on fostering the free exchange of information between the people concerned; and, that a fear of disclosure to others might inhibit frankness in the exchange of information. The application of the law of confidence to the talking therapies is probably best viewed as an extension of the confidentiality developed in law applicable to medicine and health care.

A duty to protect confidences may arise by statute or as a contractual term, for example in a contract of employment or an agreement to provide confidential services. Even where there is no statutory requirement or clear contractual term, the courts will enforce confidences concerning 'personal information'. 'Personal information' has been defined as 'consisting of those facts, communications or opinions which relate to the individual which it would be reasonable to expect him or her to regard as intimate or sensitive and therefore to want to withhold or at least to resist their collection, use or circulation' (Wacks, 1989: 26). It is reasonably well established that the law of confidence is not applicable to the protection of information that is either adequately anonymised to prevent the identification of the person concerned or adequately generalised and depersonalised, for example by the use of statistics. The emphasis is on 'adequately' and this can be a demanding standard when applied to people who know the person concerned if the anonymisation or generalisation is to be sufficient to prevent the deduction of that person's identity.

The courts will protect confidences about personal information when:

(a) information is disclosed by someone who explicitly states that the communication should be treated confidentially; or
(b) someone accepts a communication in confidence; and
(c) it would be just in all the circumstances to prevent disclosure of that information. (A-G v Guardian Newspapers (No 2) [1988]) at 658 per Lord Goff

Therapy creates the circumstances in which it would usually be appropriate to prevent disclosure of personal information. This presumption about the importance of protecting information disclosed in therapy is sufficiently strong for the courts to imply a term of confidentiality unless there is clear evidence of a contractual term between the practitioner and client that limits confidentiality. This is particularly important for counsellors providing services for a fee as this falls within the scope of the law of contract. An example illustrates the potentially serious consequences over lack of clarity concerning any limitations to confidentiality.

A young adult seeks counselling from someone working in private practice. The only information offered prior to counselling is that it is confidential. The client wants to discuss a situation that has worried her so much that she has begun to develop suicidal feelings although at this stage she is determined not act on these feelings and is hoping to find a way of alleviating her high levels of anxiety. The counsellor is sufficiently concerned to suggest that she see her general practitioner. The client rejects this suggestion and explains that she has chosen to come to a service that has no connection with her health care as she will require medical references and reports in order to pursue her career. She also states that she is confident that she is not at any immediate risk of committing suicide. Nonetheless the counsellor insists that if the client will not consult her doctor the counsellor will contact him on her behalf. The counsellor does contact the doctor with the consequence that the client's future career is adversely affected. The client sues for breach of confidence and substantial damages for loss of earnings.

In such circumstances a court would be very likely to uphold the confidentiality of the counselling relationship and that the counsellor acted in breach of this obligation. This would be a relatively easy and cheap action for a client to bring. The counsellor would be hard pressed to defend her actions unless she could establish:

(a) The existence of a clear contractual term, for example included in the pre-counselling information leaflet or a letter setting out the terms on which counselling is offered prior to the counselling commencing. The following form of words or similar might be used, 'counselling is confidential except when the client is considered to be at risk of causing serious harm to him or herself or to others. In such circumstances the counsellor may seek appropriate additional assistance on a confidential basis'. However, the mere existence of such a form of words would probably be inadequate in these circumstances, unless the counsellor could establish reasonable grounds for her concerns that the client was sufficiently at risk of self harm to justify notification of the doctor against the client's express wishes. Even if the counsellor had reasonable and well-founded concerns, she might have been wiser to have considered alternative sources of medical assistance, such as private medical consultation with someone other than the client's GP, in view of the client's specific concerns about avoiding entries on her medical records. Overriding an adult client's refusal of consent or acting contrary to their explicit wishes is a serious matter that requires substantial legal grounds for doing so and adequate justification on the basis of the circumstances.

(b) The client explicitly consented to the disclosure to the doctor even though she held reservations about giving this consent. One of the options for the counsellor in these circumstances would have been to seek to persuade the client of the advantages of her proposed course of action and to encourage her consent.

(c) The client implied consent to the disclosure. Reliance on implied consent is always less satisfactory and more risky in law than explicit consent. In order to establish implied consent, the counsellor would need to be able to establish that (i) the client knew of the proposed course of action; (ii) the client had an opportunity to object and did not do so; and (iii) it is reasonable to imply consent from the client's actions. This would not be possible on the facts as presented in the example but might be successful if the client had not forbidden informing her GP and had provided details of how to contact her GP, especially if this occurred after the counsellor stated her intention to contact him.

I will return to the issue of suicide later under defensible breaches of confidence as this is a potentially complicating factor in this scenario.

A further, more straightforward example would be:

> A therapist working in an employee assistance scheme promotes the service as totally confidential but unknown to her clients provides reports to their employer. One client detects a change in his employer's attitude towards him following counselling. When challenged the employer states that his therapist had had several conversations with him and had submitted a written report giving a very negative assessment of the employee's emotional state.

In this case a court would be very likely to find that an obligation of confidentiality was owed to the client and that the counsellor acted in breach of this obligation. In the circumstances described in this example the therapist would have no grounds for claiming a valid contractual limitation on confidentiality, or either explicit or implied consent to the disclosures.

In this example, the client is paying fees directly to the practitioner. However, it is increasingly commonplace for therapy to be provided on the basis of a third party employing the therapist to provide the service to others, for example in employee counselling services funded by their employer. This raises the question of whether a contractual term between therapist and employer requiring that the therapist provide reports would be consistent with a duty of confidentiality to the client. There is no clear legal authority on this point.

The English Law Commission (Law Commission, 1981: 52) considered these circumstances.

A doctor or a psychologist employed in industry is faced with a demand by his employer for the disclosure of medical records relating to other employees of the firm who have frankly discussed their personal problems with him on a confidential basis and without any express or implied understanding that the information would be made available to the employer.

The Law Commission decided that provided that no question of public interest (for example, the health and safety of other employees) was at stake, the practitioner must preserve the confidences. Only an express or implied term limiting confidentiality in the agreement reached between the practitioner and the client would permit the disclosure required by the employer.

Remedies for breach of confidence

When breach of confidence is established the court has a range of options open to it. It may make an order to prevent further breaches of confidence. It may award damages for losses. The damages may be substantial if it can be shown that there was damage to social reputation, severe injury to feelings, job loss, or reduced prospects of promotion. Damages may be awarded even if the client cannot show any losses because there may be no better way of acknowledging the harm that had been done. In serious cases judges have speculated that imprisonment would be an appropriate penalty, for example for a health worker who leaked the name of doctors infected with HIV to the press (X v Y [1988]).

These remedies would not apply where either the breach of confidence is legally defensible or there is a legal obligation to disclose confidential information.

Defensible disclosure of confidences

Consent for disclosure has been obtained: Obtaining the client's consent is often the best way of resolving legal and ethical dilemmas about confidentiality (Cohen, 1992: 19). A client's consent to disclosure has the effect that the practitioner is released from an obligation of confidentiality. The release may be limited by agreement about the content, the timing or to whom disclosure may be made. These conditions are legally enforceable and if breached remove the protection of a defensible disclosure. An implied disclosure would have the same effect but is more vulnerable to being challenged because of potential uncertainty about what exactly is being implied. Oral consent is legally sufficient but a written consent provides better legal evidence in the event of a dispute.

Information is already in the public domain: Information that is already in the public domain cannot usually be protected by confidentiality. To do so would create a legal absurdity. However, few practitioners of talking therapies would wish to rely on this as legitimating the communication of information disclosed by clients. The ethical priority of maintaining client trust makes disclosing any information about clients highly sensitive, even if that information is already known by other people.

Balance of public interest in favour of disclosure: The concept of balancing conflicting interests runs throughout the law of confidentiality. Legal protection of confidentiality is not absolute but is contingent on consideration of the circumstances in the legal approaches adopted in the United Kingdom. This approach requires that the practitioner decides at what point the usual expectation of confidentiality for this type of activity changes in favour of disclosure. The decision is based upon an exercise of weighing the public benefits of preserving confidences against the benefits of disclosure. This exercise is rather misleadingly called 'a balance of public interest', which does not mean satisfying the public appetite for salacious news, but an assessment of the balance of what is for the good of the public. This places a considerable responsibility on the person making the decision which cannot be devolved to others and requires the exercise of as careful consideration as the circumstances allow. The advantage is the possibility of using one's professional judgement in order to respond to the circumstances rather than being required to comply with strict rules determined by the authorities. The price is a degree of uncertainty about whether the decision will withstand scrutiny in a court of law. The courts are influenced by evidence of the care with which a decision has been made and the quality of the reasoning that justifies the decision.

In a leading case, a psychiatrist not only breached the common law expectation of confidentiality, but an explicit contractual term of confidentiality in order to prevent the release of a mental patient from a secure hospital into the community that he considered to be dangerous. In ordinary circumstances the expectation of confidentiality would have been extremely high. However, the court upheld his decision that the degree of risk to others and the public interest in prevention of harm in the circumstances of this case justified warning the authorities of his concerns, and his breach was therefore judged to be defensible (W v Egdell [1990]). It is worth noting that the reasoning and legal framework in an English court is significantly different from the well known American case, Tarasoff v Regents of the University of California (1976), which created an obligation to warn of significant dangers posed to others. The English legal tradition stops short of creating an equivalent obligation as there is no general obligation to rescue (McCall Smith, 1993: 55). However the law will offer protection against actions for breach of confidence where the person concerned acts in the balance of public interest. Satisfying the following tests increases the probability of such a finding if:

- the disclosure is based on an assessment of the balance of public interest, that is public benefit or for the public good; and
- the assessment is made in good faith and based on evidence which the person making the decision has reasonable grounds to believe to be true; and
- the matters disclosed are restricted to that required to protect the public interest, which would sometimes be only part of what has been confided; and
- any disclosures are restricted to people able to act in the public interest, usually the relevant authorities in the first instance (rather than the press) or by warning the person at risk of harm directly; and
- any disclosures are protected from further disclosure other than to further the public interest by a condition of confidentiality.

The balance of public interest may be more easily determined in the case of protecting others from harm than in the case of someone posing a serious threat of harm to him or herself perhaps by attempting or committing suicide. If the method chosen poses a threat to others' safety such as jumping off a bridge into traffic or pedestrians, the issue of preventing self harm may be overridden by preventing harm to others. However, if the client is an adult and only poses a threat to themself there is no general obligation to rescue. There are legal risks in going against a clear instruction from the client that forbids notifying other professionals, friends or family in order to obtain assistance for them. Patience and persuasion in order to obtain consent are the safest ways of responding to minimise legal liability. Consent will usually be implied to obtaining life saving treatment for someone who is unconscious or so ill to be incapable of consent.

However, the anxiety experienced by many practitioners is compounded by a degree of ambiguity about the intentions of the person who is threatening self harm, especially with regard to their expectations of the practitioner. For example what should one do if someone discloses that they have recently taken an overdose of paracetamol for which there is a window of opportunity to administer an antidote before the effects become irreversible? This is a fairly commonplace situation, which, if left untreated, is sometimes followed by a period of apparent recovery, before progressive and unstoppable deterioration commences. The combination of apparent recovery followed by irreversible deterioration usually becomes increasingly distressing for everyone concerned and typically much regretted by the person who took the overdose. If the person concerned refuses to permit the seeking of medical assistance and leaves the premises there is clear refusal of treatment. What if the person verbally refuses treatment but stays on the premises? The issue has been extensively discussed in the *British Medical Journal* (Hassan et al., 1999; Hewson, 1999). The intentions are much more ambiguous because of the contradiction between the words and actions. In a discussion that I attended between doctors, one medical practitioner summarised his dilemma as being faced with a choice between being excessively respectful of individual autonomy and the requirement of consent or overzealous in seeking to preserve life and risking being sued for assault for unauthorised treatment. The practitioner of talking therapies faces an analogous choice because, although she is unlikely to be able to administer the treatment herself, she is choosing between a possibly over strict interpretation of consent in ambiguous circumstances and risking breach of confidence in seeking to preserve life. This is perhaps the ultimate example of where the scope for professional discretion in the English approach to confidentiality creates a significant dilemma. In my view it is probably more desirable to be faced with this dilemma than to lose the discretion to make decisions according to the circumstances. It is certainly a situation where it is important to have access to good professional support and legal advice when required. Professional liability insurance provides an additional safety net.

With the exception of Northern Ireland there is no general obligation to disclose crime. However, the public interest in the prevention and detection of serious crime will usually make disclosures to the appropriate authorities defensible. Some crimes have been considered so serious by government that there are specific statutory obligations to disclose. I will consider some of the more commonly occurring situations in the next section.

Legal requirements to disclose

Any legal obligation to inform the authorities about fellow citizens sits uneasily in a liberal democratic society. For this reason the obligation is exceptional and usually tightly defined in terms of what is required to be disclosed, by whom and to whom. Any disclosure that is authorised or required by statute is legally defensible against breach of confidence. I am aware of three types of situation in which practitioners have found themselves within the scope of legislation requiring disclosure of confidences. The first has been the subject of considerable misunderstanding.

The Children Act 1989 represents a major step in child care legislation for England, Wales and Northern Ireland in asserting and protecting the rights of children, especially with regard to the responsibilities of public authorities for the upbringing of children. The Act requires that 'the child's welfare shall be the paramount consideration' (s. 1.1). One of the aspects of the law that has impacted on therapists of all kinds has been provision to prevent and detect child abuse. Some therapists remain under the misapprehension that the law requires them to take the initiative in reporting all suspected child abuse. This is not the case. There is a strong moral case for doing so but this is not a legal requirement. The creation of a general mandatory requirement to report suspected child abuse was considered in a preparatory review prior to the legislation but was rejected (Bainham, 1990: 144). Instead an existing obligation on local authorities to investigate any suspicion of children at risk of harm was widened and strengthened. Section 47 imposes a qualified duty on staff working in specified public bodies to reply to written requests for information about named individuals by offering advice and information in order to assist any investigation. It is now regarded as good practice to include information about whether the young person concerned has consented to the request for any information about them. The aim of this provision is to promote co-operation between organisations likely to hold relevant information arising from their involvement with families and children. The specified 'persons' with an obligation to respond are another local authority, any local education authority, any local housing authority, any health authority and 'any person authorised by the Secretary of State for the purposes of this section' (s. 47(11)). The obligation to respond is qualified by the unusually worded clause 'except where it would be unreasonable in all the circumstances of the case'. The interpretation of this exception is uncertain but would probably apply in circumstances where the response would compromise an existing relationship with a young person in ways that are inconsistent with that young person's welfare, perhaps by placing him or her in additional danger. Based on a misunderstanding of this section of the Act, counsellors have sometimes been pressured into various forms of mandatory reporting. For example, legal opinion obtained by the British Association for Counselling and Psychotherapy, found that principals of colleges of further education were acting outside their powers by attempting to require that student counsellors inform the colleges of all instances of allegations of child abuse made by clients (Friel, 1998). The legal opinion advised that the decision about whether to take the initiative in reporting suspected children at risk of harm rested with the counsellor and this could not be overruled without statutory authority. The college principals lacked the statutory authority to enforce disclosure by counsellors. It follows that the issue of how to respond to suspected child abuse remains primarily an ethical and moral dilemma for all professionals working outside the immediate scope of the Act. The public interest in the prevention and detection of child abuse is so strong that any disclosure consistent with the criteria outlined above would usually be regarded as defensible.

While there is no general obligation to report crime to the authorities, two issues have been the cause of such concern that statutory obligations have been created. The importation and manufacture of illicit drugs is a major if well concealed industry that has a destabilising effect on society and is a major cause of crime by those seeking to fund their drug addiction. Similarly the sectarian disputes in Northern Ireland and associated terrorism throughout the UK have had terrible consequences for many communities and individuals. The Drug Trafficking Act 1994 addresses the first social problem by creating an obligation to inform the authorities about information gained during one's trade or profession about the proceeds of drug trafficking. Although primarily directed at bankers and accountants, it is deliberately worded to apply more widely. It is a separate offence to inform the person concerned that you have informed the authorities. A similar approach has been adopted towards the prevention and detection of terrorism. The Terrorism Act 2000 (s 19) requires the disclosure of information to the appropriate authorities where a person believes or suspects that another person has committed a terrorist offence; and this belief or suspicion is based on information which comes to his or her attention in the course of a trade, profession, business or employment. Failure to do so may constitute a criminal offence. The Act also provides legal protection for the disclosure of information concerning money or property associated with terrorism (s 20). If in doubt about your obligations under these Acts which apply throughout the United Kingdom, it is best to seek legal advice as the potential penalties include substantial fines and imprisonment.

Not all legislation is concerned with overriding a duty of confidentiality. There are examples of strengthening the right to confidentiality. Two recent Acts of Parliament have the effect of creating obligations to confidentiality and form new points of growth in the expanding law of confidentiality.

Data Protection Act 1998

The scope of data protection has been widened considerably in recent years. It includes records held on computer and paper. This is a complex piece of legislation with wider implications than confidentiality which are discussed at greater length in Chapter 5 by Peter Jenkins. One of the potential outcomes of this legislation is to provide an alternative route for clients and others to challenge poor practice over confidentiality of records or the communication of inaccurate information. This may be particularly useful to clients, trainees or supervisees who are not paying for their services directly and therefore are faced with higher financial and practical barriers to seeking remedies through the courts than someone seeking to enforce a contract. The absence of a legally enforceable contract means that any enforcement through the courts would need to be through the High Court. This is considerably more expensive and requires potentially more preparation than bringing a case in the local County Court, which is the obvious option for the fee paying client. Instead the data subject may prefer to seek enforcement through the Data Protection Act. The type of data that is most likely to be of concern is classified under the Act as 'sensitive personal data'. This includes information about 'physical or mental health or condition' and 'sexual life'. This is data for which there are additional safeguards and specific provision for 'confidential counselling'. Generally the recording of personally sensitive data and any communications of this data to third parties requires explicit consent. As with other aspects of confidentiality, obtaining a client's 'explicit consent' is usually the best basis for ensuring that the therapist is working ethically and legally. The Act also permits 'processing' (for example, the recording and communication of data) which:

... must be in the **substantial** public interest and:

(a) necessary for the discharge of any function which is designed for the provision of confidential counselling, advice, support or any other service; and

(b) carried out without explicit consent of the data subject because the processing –

    (i) is necessary in a case where consent cannot be given by a data subject,

    (ii) is necessary in a case where the data controller cannot reasonably be expected to obtain the explicit consent of the data subject, or

    (iii) must necessarily be carried out without the explicit consent of the data subject being sought so as not to prejudice the provision of that counselling, advice, support or other service. (The Data Protection (Processing of Sensitive Personal Data) Order 2000 (SI 2000 No. 417) Article 2 s. 4) (Emphasis added)

The inclusion of the term 'substantial' indicates that there is no routine exemption from the requirement to obtain explicit consent. Peter Jenkins has discussed the interpretation of 'substantial' with the Information Commissioner's staff, who have indicated that a substantial public interest requires a high level of justification. A possible example includes responding to emergency situations following a disaster where the level of distress and the circumstances of providing the service in the immediate aftermath make attention to matters like consent secondary to ensuring that the service is provided. Advice about other types of situation that would satisfy the test of a 'substantial public interest' may be obtained from the Information Commissioner.

The Act also provides for a wide range of ways by which a data subject can check the accuracy of any records and that they are being lawfully processed. A full description of these can be found in specialist guides to the legislation. This legislation was originally inspired by potential threat to personal privacy by the increasing use of computers but has now expanded its scope to provide much wider protection in terms of the accuracy and use of any personal information (Carey, 2000).

Human Rights Act 1998

The European Convention on Human Rights and Fundamental Freedoms has been incorporated into UK legislation by the Human Rights Act 1998. Article 8 of the Convention establishes a right to privacy. It states:

(1) Everyone has the right to respect for his private and family life, his home and his correspondence.

(2) There shall be no interference by a public authority with the exercise of this right except such as is in accordance with the law and is necessary in a democratic society in the interests of national security, public safety or the economic well-being of the country, for the prevention of disorder or

crime, for the protection of health or morals, or for the protection of the rights and freedoms of others.

You will note that the Act concerns the behaviour of 'public authorities' rather than individuals acting independently of any public authority. Public authorities include government departments, education authorities, local government and the National Health Service. The work of a therapist employed by a public authority would be covered by the Convention but not when the therapist is working for a commercial organisation or in private practice. If the legislation is applicable, it may be used to protect privacy, for example to protect the publication of sensitive medical information concerning the HIV status of someone who has been recklessly or knowingly infected by the defendant in a case of attempted manslaughter. In Z v Finland (1998) an appeal court was found to have acted contrary to a victim's rights to privacy by disclosing her health status (Kennedy and Grubb, 2000: 1048). On the other hand in (MS v Sweden 1999), Article 8(2) has been held to justify disclosure of medical records to a government department in order to determine the validity of a claim for industrial injury benefits. This judgment was based on grounds of protecting the 'economic well-being of the country' (Kennedy and Grubb, 2000: 1056). One of the consequences of the incorporation of the Convention into UK law is that matters can be raised and considered in local courts without the inconvenience and expense of mounting a case in a European court. Experts disagree about the implications of this Act and the scale of changes that it will effect in the activities of public bodies. This will become clearer over time as the courts consider cases relating to privacy and other aspects of the legislation (see Chapter 12).

Disclosure required during court proceedings

Lawyers have discovered the potential value of therapeutic notes as a source of evidence in a variety of cases. One of the most frequent queries that I receive concerns therapists who have been required to disclose their records to a court or to appear as a witness. It is too early to be confident of the scale of the problem that this poses for therapists, but it appears to be quite commonplace involving therapists working in a wide variety of voluntary, statutory and commercial organisations and in private practice. The types of cases involved seem to fall into three broad categories and awareness of these may be the best protection available to therapists. To be forewarned eliminates the element of surprise and enhances the therapist's ability to take precautionary measures. I will consider each of the three types of cases in turn.

The first concerns criminal prosecutions for sexual assault and rape. The courts have taken the view that the seriousness of the crime, the difficulty of establishing what occurred, and the seriousness of the consequences of the verdict for both the alleged perpetrator and the victim require that all the available evidence ought to be available to the court. Courts have taken this view following a series of convictions being overturned on appeal. Frequently the original verdict has been overturned because of the discovery of new evidence that ought to have been available at the time of the original trial and after the alleged perpetrator has served a substantial period of time in prison. The prolonging of litigation by the appeals process usually increases the trauma of the victim. In these circumstances there is a strong case for arguing that the public benefit in ensuring justice at the first trial is greater than the benefit of preserving confidentiality, even when that involves intruding on the victim's privacy. The usual procedure starts when a police officer acting on behalf of the Crown Prosecution Service approaches the therapist with a request for any records. The therapist will be shown a general consent to their release signed by the client. This consent may have been signed at the end of prolonged interviews and medical examinations. The client is very likely to have been told that no prosecution will be considered without her consent to the release of her records. In these circumstances the therapist may have justifiable concerns about the validity of the consent and may wish to consult the client before releasing the records. The records may form a central part of the prosecution's evidence if the first account of the traumatic event was given in therapy and especially if this precedes the version given to the police. In any event the defence will pick over the records in search of any inconsistency in accounts or to find permitted ways of discrediting the victim. Inconsistencies over the day of the week that an assault occurred or other material facts have been sufficient to have the case dismissed. It is quite possible that information from the records will be discussed in open court and may be reported in the media.

The second type of case arises in a variety of civil actions, where a claimant is seeking damages for emotional and psychological distress. The most frequent cases that I am aware of concern trauma arising from road accidents and stress-related illnesses originating in the workplace. These cases have become much more frequent with the introduction of American-style litigation in which lawyers advertise for cases to be conducted on a 'no win, no fee' basis. The therapist is usually approached by the client's solicitor with a request for a copy of any records and possibly to appear as a witness. Again the records will be seen by both sides and used to strengthen their respective cases. These cases are seldom reported in the media.

The third type of case arises in the Family Court when consideration of the care or custody of children, typically as a consequence of the separation of adults with parental responsibility, is made. We have already seen that the child's welfare is the paramount concern in these types of hearing. It is of such concern that the courts have been willing to insist on disclosure of information that would otherwise have been protected by higher levels of confidentiality than that available to therapists. For example the Family Court has insisted on disclosure of communications between lawyers and their clients that would be protected from disclosure in any other type of case. The Family Court has almost unlimited powers to order disclosure in the interest of child welfare.

I am often asked what types of records are required to be disclosed? For example, some therapists believe that their process notes are not required. Others have considered keeping two sets of records, one for the courts and another for therapeutic purposes. Neither of these strategies will work and any attempt to conceal records runs the risk of being regarded as a serious contempt of court or as a criminal offence. The courts require the production of all records. These include the complete file, any correspondence, notes written for training or supervision or any other evidence. Courts particularly value spontaneous notes written at the time such as any notes made during the session that you may have to help with writing the record for the file. It is increasingly commonplace to find that references to the existence of other related records that may be held by a supervisor, manager or trainer are followed up and required for consideration by the court.

Elsewhere in this book are accounts of how therapists have sought to resist disclosure of their records. When considered chronologically these accounts point to a legal trend in favour of disclosure of records. The courageous and well-argued stance taken by Anne Hayman in Chapter 2 might be less successful. Judges are much more likely to order disclosure of records for consideration by the lawyers representing the parties involved in the case. The current assessment of the balance of public benefit has tilted in favour of disclosure in the interests of justice rather than preserving the privacy of clients or of the therapeutic relationship. Most therapists who have been required to disclose records have serious reservations about doing so as there is considerable potential for misinterpretation and misapplication of material created for therapeutic aims being used for forensic purposes. The forensic process undermines the usually carefully constructed therapeutic relationship and often destroys any benefits gained from this work. I consider that there is an accumulation of cases that point to the impossibility of individual therapists resisting disclosure by legal means in the types of cases outlined above. Medical practitioners have had much longer exposure to legal scrutiny than practitioners of the talking therapies. It may be that we can learn from their experience and revise how we keep records until the relevant professional bodies negotiate a more satisfactory state of affairs.

Sensible practice concerning record keeping that is vulnerable to disclosure would include:

- Keep records as brief as possible and purposeful.
- Include only undisputed facts or restrict the record to facts that have been confirmed by the client, if litigation is a foreseeable possibility.
- Avoid or limit descriptions of a client's emotions or relationships to matters that will not cause undue distress if disclosed in the context of a legal dispute.
- Avoid speculation.
- Avoid process notes or references to counter-transference unless you are prepared to sacrifice a corresponding degree of your own privacy.
- Destroy supplementary materials such as correspondence and return any client-produced material when retaining it ceases to serve any useful purpose.
- Avoid the use of client names or abbreviations in other personal records for supervision, training case studies, analysis of therapeutic process or relationship, personal diaries or other records in order to minimise the risk that they will be required to be disclosed.

It is tempting to consider using abbreviations, codes, genograms, or other diagrammatic representations as means of encrypting your notes. However this is unlikely to be successful with regard to the client, who has the right under the Data Protection Act 1998 (s. 7) to have personal data 'communicated to him in intelligible form'. Similarly the courts may require a full explanation of the encryption.

The professional press produced for practitioners of the talking therapies contains a steady stream of articles expressing concern about use of therapeutic records in courts. This concern is probably widely supported by practitioners and within the profession there is growing pressure to campaign for changes in the law. However, it would be foolish to underestimate the degree of difficulty in changing the current practices of the courts. It would require the combined efforts of the relevant professional bodies and careful consideration of the desired outcome. Nonetheless, there are some grounds for optimism that a campaign would be successful. The American Counseling Association succeeded in extending the legal protection of records held by licensed social workers providing psychotherapy from disclosure in court proceedings (*Jaffee v Redmond* (1996)). However, there are significant differences between the legal system in the USA and this side of the Atlantic that might make finding a solution more difficult.

Conclusion

The complexity and changing nature of the law on confidentiality make it very difficult to distil the application of the law of confidentiality to a few principles that would apply widely to the diverse range of circumstances in which talking therapies are provided. Any practitioner who is concerned about the legal requirements applicable to their practice is wise to seek legal advice and to discuss their concerns with experienced practitioners. Additional information may be found elsewhere (Jenkins, 1997; Bond, 2000; Daniels and Jenkins, 2000). The following principles will usually form an adequate starting point for managing confidentiality in ways that satisfy most legal and ethical requirements.

(1)   Practitioners of the talking therapies are legally required to provide a high degree of confidentiality concerning personally identifiable and sensitive information about clients in most circumstances unless they have explicitly limited this obligation.

(2)   There is no legal right to absolute right to privacy or confidentiality. Practitioners can incur legal liability by being too lax over the protection of confidences as well as by being too doctrinaire or rigid in protecting confidences. The legal framework concerning the management of confidentiality is constructed in ways that usually require consideration of the circumstances and the exercise of personal and professional judgement in deciding the limitations of any requirement of confidentiality. In information given to clients, it is best to combine a simple assertion of the commitment to confidentiality with mention of any reasonably foreseeable limitations to the extent of confidentiality. The exact form of wording would vary according to the circumstances. Variations on the following wording are widely used:

> High standards of confidentiality will be maintained about information concerning clients. Confidential information about clients will usually only be communicated to others if the client concerned has given consent. In exceptional circumstances a practitioner may disclose confidences without consent in order to protect a client or others from serious harm or when legally required to do so.

The use of 'may' in the final sentence permits the practitioner to determine the appropriate response according to the circumstances.

This conforms closely to the usual legal and ethical requirements and provides an adequate indication to clients of the importance of confidentiality and its limitations. A concerned client has been given adequate information to alert them that they might need to discuss the limits of confidentiality with their therapist.

(3) Decisions about when to maintain or disclose confidences by therapists require as conscientious and careful consideration as the circumstances permit. The courts do not expect that all practitioners would make the same decisions in similar circumstances. They do appear to take into account the degree of care that the practitioner has taken in reaching a decision as well as the reasons that the practitioner gives for her actions concerning the protection and disclosure of confidences.

(4) A client's consent to disclosure is both ethically desirable and the best legal protection for the practitioner. It is good practice to obtain a signed consent. If this is not possible, writing a contemporaneous note in the case record that consent has been obtained is the next best line of legal protection.

(5) Responsibility for decisions about the protection and disclosure of confidences rests primarily on the practitioner who receives the confidence and cannot be devolved to others or to agencies.

(6) Practitioners should be cautious about any requirements to disclose personally identifiable information of a sensitive nature unless and until they are satisfied that the requirement is lawful. Reliance on terms in a contract of employment on its own would not amount to a lawful requirement unless there is additional legal authorisation, usually as resulting from legislation.

(7) The current practice with regard to obtaining and presenting evidence in courts does pose serious ethical difficulties for therapists. These will continue unless there is a successful campaign to change the law as has occurred in the USA. In the meantime practitioners should be mindful both of their clients' rights to inspect records concerning themselves and the possibility that their records may be required to be disclosed in open court. This has significant implications for the content of any records.

References

Bainham, A. (1990) Children: The New Law, the Children Act 1989. Bristol: Jordon and Sons.

Bond, T. (2000) Standards and Ethics for Counselling in Action. (Second edition) London: Sage.

Bond, T., Higgins, R.A. and Jamieson, A. (2001) Confidentiality: Counselling, Psychotherapy and the Law in Scotland. Rugby: British Association for Counselling and Psychotherapy.

Carey, P. (2000) *Data Protection in the UK*. London: Blackstone Press.

Cohen, K. (1992) Some legal issues in counselling and psychotherapy. *British Journal of Guidance and Counselling*, **20**, 10–25.

Daniels, D. and Jenkins, P. (2000) *Therapy with Children: Confidentiality, Children's Rights and the Law*. London: Sage.

Friel, J. (1998) *In the matter of the British Association for Counselling, the Association of Student Counselling and the Association of Colleges. (An unpublished legal opinion obtained by the British Association for Counselling).*, British Association for Counselling and Psychotherapy: Rugby.

Gurry, F. (1984) *Breach of Confidence*. London: Clarendon.

Hassan, T.B., MacNamara, A.F., Davy, A., Bing, A. and Bodiwala, G.G. (1999) Managing patients with deliberate self harm who refuse treatment in the accident and emergency department. *British Medical Journal*, **319**, 107–109.

Hewson, B. (1999) The law on managing patients who deliberately harm themselves and refuse treatment. *British Medical Journal*, **319**, 905–907.

Jenkins, P. (1997) *Counselling, Psychotherapy and the Law*. London: Sage.

Kennedy, I. and Grubb, A. (2000) *Medical Law*. London: Butterworths.

Law Commission (1981) *Breach of Confidence*. London: HMSO Cmnd 8388.

McCall Smith, A. (1993) The duty to rescue and the common law. In *The duty to Rescue: The Jurisprudence of Aid*. (Eds) Menlowe, M. and McCall Smith, A. Aldershot: Dartmouth Publishing, pp. 55–91.

Wacks, R. (1989) *Personal Information: Privacy and the Law*. Oxford: Clarendon Press.

Legal references (Europe)

MS v Sweden (1999) 28 EHRR 313
Z v Finland (1998) 25 EHRR 371

Legal references (UK)

A-G v Guardian Newspapers (No 2) [1988] 2 All ER 545
Lord Advocate v The Scotsman Publications Limited [1989] SLT 705, HL
Prince Albert v Strange (1849) 2 De Gex & Sm. 652 (on appeal) 1 Mac & G 25

Legal references (US)

Jaffee v Redmond (1996) 116 S Ct 1923
Tarasoff v Regents of the University of California (1976) CA 131 Cal Rptr 14 (Cal Sup Ct)
W v Egdell [1990] 1 All ER 835, (1989) BLMR 96 (CA)
X v Y [1988] 2 All ER 648

11

False Memories or Recovered Memories? Legal and Ethical Implications for Therapists

Peter Jenkins

A troubling phenomenon emerged in the early 1990s, with serious repercussions for therapeutic practice, and for its standing in society at large. Therapists, since the time of Freud and Breuer (1895/1991), have long accepted the validity of forgotten childhood trauma resurfacing via behavioural symptoms, or during therapy. This concept has even gained a wide measure of public or common-sense acceptance, for instance describing a person as being 'repressed'. The recent emphasis on investigating child sexual abuse in advanced industrial countries has promoted an atmosphere where medical, social work and counselling professionals have sought to explore the dimensions of abuse, and its devastating impact on individuals and families. However, there have been a number of cases where doubt has been thrown on the actual *truth* of memories of childhood abuse, and on the *validity* of the methods used to uncover such memories. In certain well-publicised cases, it was alleged that such memories were sometimes false, namely imagined or fantasised by the victim, or, worse, implanted in the victim's mind by their therapist. The implication was that it was the person *against whom* allegations were made who deserved support and recognition: it was *therapy* at fault. Therapists were alleged to be irresponsible, out of control, breaking up families, and giving voice to allegations without substance.

A typical scenario consisted of an adult daughter, with no previous declared history of childhood sexual abuse, who recovered memories of possible abuse only via receiving therapy. She (only a minority of cases concerned adult males) then made allegations of abuse against her parents, breaking off formerly cordial relations with them, and refused further contact except in the form of taking legal proceedings. Usually the allegations could not be confirmed, as the passage of time did not permit forensic evidence to be collected, and the alleged perpetrators continued to deny that the abuse had occurred.

Early indications of this development could be found in the changing media coverage and public attitudes towards the potent issue of child abuse. In the UK, an apparent 'backlash' against the rediscovery of, first, physical, and then sexual, abuse was initially expressed in the critical judgments of courts and enquiry reports accompanied by hostile publicity in the press about social workers (Asquith, 1993; Butler-Sloss,1988; Parton, 1985). In the USA, where the practice of private therapy was perhaps better established and more widely recognised, the public response to the focus on child sexual abuse took a different form (Levine et al., 1995). Then , in 1994, the *Ramona* case in California produced a judgment where a third party, a father, successfully sued his adult daughter's therapists, for damages of $475,000. His legal victory was widely taken by the media as endorsing the view that therapists 'implant' false memories of sexual abuse. The case had serious implications for therapists both in the USA and the UK. The court's decision suggested an area of legal vulnerability for practitioners involved in the therapeutic endeavour of uncovering childhood trauma. It raised a series of ethical and legal dilemmas for therapists about how to work with memories of childhood sexual abuse.

These issues provide the main focus for this chapter. The generic term 'therapist' is used to denote both counsellors and psychotherapists, while recognising the distinctions that may be otherwise drawn in terms of the respective focus and purpose of their work (Worden, 1991: 79). The purpose of the chapter is to explore issues which may increase therapists' vulnerability to legal challenge in the future. The debate about false memories of abuse will first be placed in its social context. Using the concept of the Drama Triangle, drawn from Transactional Analysis, some of the main ethical dilemmas for therapists will be identified. The widening range of legal consequences for therapists associated with work in this field will then be explored, and possible implications for future therapeutic practice examined.

The debate about false memory

The *Ramona* case (1994) was not unique. Other cases were reported in the US press where former clients had successfully sued therapists and clinics for damages consequent upon recovering unsubstantiated memories of abuse. The publicity in the US media on this issue steadily grew in the mid-1990s, and there was concern that a similar situation may develop in the UK. While the legal systems of the USA and the UK are significantly different, there are some broader parallels which are worth noting. The growing movement of adult children accusing parents of abuse in the USA brought about the formation of a self-help group for the accused, the False Memory Syndrome Foundation (FMSF) in Philadelphia. Consciously following the American model, a British False Memory Society (FMS) was also established. Both organisations sought to act as self-help groups, actively researching therapeutic practices, and lobbying for changes in the law to regulate therapy more closely. The activities of the False Memory Society were then challenged by counter-organisations such as Accuracy About Abuse (AAA) in the UK. Marjorie Orr, spokesperson of AAA, pointed to the paedophile links of former FMSF board members such as Dr Ralph Underwager (Orr, 1995), and the fact that allegations of abuse have been made against a FMSF founder, Peter Freyd, and against a previous FMS Chairman, Roger Scotford, by their adult daughters. In reply, the FMS pointed to Marjorie Orr's astrological interests as undermining her credibility in speaking on therapeutic issues (Aldridge-Morris, 1995: 16).

The British Psychological Society issued a critical report on false memory (BPS,1995a). The Royal College of Psychiatrists later produced its own, more distanced research, with the ensuing divisions in the medical literature accurately reflecting the sharply differing professional opinions held by practitioners on this topic (Brandon et al., 1997; Andrews et al., 1999). Therapists' organisations, the British Association for Counselling and Psychotherapy (BACP) and the United Kingdom Council for Psychotherapy (UKCP) both also issued statements in turn on this topic (McGuire, 1997; Murdin, 1997). Key features of the debate included the nature and accuracy of memory of childhood trauma, and the status of the Freudian concept of repression. The roles played by hypnosis and suggestibility in the therapeutic setting were also important areas to be explored. These aspects were clearly key elements in the debate, but deserve separate coverage as a topic in their own right, and are therefore not addressed in detail here (cf. Loftus & Ketcham, 1994; Nelson, 1990; Pope & Hudson, 1995; Rose, 1993; Terr, 1988, 1994; Webster, 1995; White & Pilemmer, 1979).

The terms 'false memory syndrome' and 'recovered memory' are themselves persuasive definitions, which may reflect the adoption of partisan positions in the debate. The terms are therefore used in this paper without judgement as to their appropriateness or validity, unless this is specifically referred to in the text. Confusingly, the concept of false memory is itself rarely defined with any precision. Terr has described false memory as 'a strongly imagined memory, a lie or a misconstrued impression' (1994: 159). The FMSF and Johns Hopkins Medical Institutions have jointly defined false memory as 'a condition in which a person's memory of a traumatic experience ... is objectively false but the person strongly believes it to be true' (Quirk & DePrince, 1995: 259). The memories are here held to be 'objectively false', but according to what criteria? Child sexual abuse consists of sexually inappropriate contact between a child and an adult, in a private situation where other independent witnesses are often unlikely to be forthcoming, forensic evidence is difficult to obtain after a passage of time, and confession by the perpetrator is all too rare. The concept of 'false memory' *assumes* as fact what is actually at issue here: in what circumstances can allegations of child sexual abuse be confidently assumed to be based on demonstrably false memories?

Rather than attempt a comprehensive definition, it is suggested that four key elements are commonly found in allegations of false memory, while leaving unresolved the problematic status of the memories as factual or fantasised. These aspects are:

1 Memories of abuse in childhood are discontinuous
2 Memories of abuse in childhood are recovered in a therapeutic setting
3 There is an absence of corroborative evidence (either forensic in nature, or by means of a confession without duress by the alleged perpetrator, or via confirmation by a third party with direct knowledge of the abuse)
4 Therapeutic retrieval of memories of childhood abuse is then followed by disclosure and confrontation with the alleged abusers, who deny the accusations.

A further common feature of allegedly false memories is the extremely traumatic nature of the abuse experienced, often in highly ritualised settings. Ritual or satanic abuse is a complex topic, deserving fuller treatment in its own right, and consequently will not be discussed in greater detail here (cf. Gomez, 1995; LaFontaine, 1994; Sinason, 1994; Wright, 1994).

The criteria suggested above thus help to distinguish between two scenarios of abuse memory recovery. In the first, an individual has, for example, been abused in childhood, has always retained a knowledge of that abuse, and has chosen not to disclose this until adulthood. In the second scenario, previously unknown memories of abuse are recovered in therapy. Cases where an individual's memories are corroborated by a valid confession by the alleged perpetrator would not be defined here as false memories. The contributory, indeed *confirmatory*, role of a therapist is claimed by the false memory movement to be essential to understanding the phenomenon of false memory (Prendergast, 1995; Sanderson, 1995). What is perhaps overlooked by critics such as Prendergast is that, in a proportion of cases, clients' recovery of discontinuous memories of abuse *precedes* their entry into therapy (Enns et al., 1995: 212). The BPS (1995b) suggests that up to one third of clients recovered memories of abuse independently of contact with the therapists in their research study. This would suggest that therapists' alleged primary responsibility for the retrieval of unsubstantiated memories is somewhat overstated by critics.

In the absence of corroborative evidence, the memory's legal status continues to be doubtful. Such recovered memories may be accurate, fantasised, or a mixture of both. Whether such memories are true in an actual historical sense, or part of a wider therapeutic narrative, may ultimately be a matter for the courts to decide. The conflicting perspectives on sexual abuse, on the value of memories as evidence, and on the relative status of the abuse survivor and alleged abuser, may be presented and heard in a judicial arena (Magner and Parkinson, 2001; Memon, 1998). However, the court itself may not be beyond the influence of current beliefs and prejudices concerning the issues in contest.

Child abuse

One such set of beliefs concerns the nature and causes of child sexual abuse. The rediscovery of child sexual abuse in the USA and in the UK in the 1980s has been shaped into a major feminist critique of the nature of family relationships, the oppressive power of men, and the neglected rights of children as the victims of abuse (Campbell, 1989). One detailed research study, for example, suggests that nearly one third of women experience unwanted sexual contact before the age of 16 (Anderson et al., 1993). While the full extent of sexual abuse in society cannot, by definition, be known with certainty, the debate over its scope has wider social and political implications. If abuse is rare, then it can be viewed as a problem only to be found in 'deviant' or 'abnormal' families; if it is widespread, then abuse is part of the actual fabric of family relationships, which by their nature are therefore oppressive and abusive to family members. Both defenders and critics of the nuclear family have an investment in the debate about the extent of childhood abuse, which goes well beyond a detached or scientific interest, and forms part of a wider social discourse.

The historical background to this debate about child abuse suggests that the process of its discovery is cyclical in nature. Previous discoveries of childhood abuse have been challenged by powerful social reactions. In the 1850s, advances in medical science permitted the description of unexplained childhood physical trauma. In the 1890s, Freud's initial theories posited the 'seduction' of children by parents. In both cases, changes in perception of sexual phenomena were met by powerful social responses, which challenged the accuracy of statements made by women and children against mainly male figures (Masson, 1985; Olafson & Corwin, 1993). The previous cycle at the turn of the twentieth century coincided with the rise of feminism, and furthered the growth of an implicit critique of the nature of the nuclear family. This process appears to have been repeated during the 1980s.

One of the most highly publicised consequences of false memory allegations concerned the break-up of what were apparently stable family units. The effects of false memory syndrome take various forms, including allegations of abuse against parents and caretakers, and subsequent legal proceedings, both civil and criminal, against alleged perpetrators. It may entail the break-up of family relationships, the termination of contact between adult children and parents, or between grandparents and grandchildren and the loss of reputation and livelihood of alleged perpetrators.

A second level of debate includes a wider agenda, based on respect for traditional nuclear family values, and a reaction to the growth of feminism. One supporter of the concept of false memory alleges that 'these therapists are generally angry women, many of whom are on a lifelong vendetta against men. Anything they can do to hurt men provides them with a sense of morbid gratification' (Gardner, 1992: 190). Research has noted that the FMSF, for example, concentrates its criticism largely on the practice of *female* therapists with their *female* clients (Enns et al., 1995: 196).

Ethical Dilemmas for Therapists

The preceding section has sought to put the debate about false memory in a social context. Moving on to the question of the ethical aspects of counselling abuse survivors, writers such as Dryden (1997) have pointed to a number of counselling dilemmas relevant here. These include issues of the therapist's role and responsibility towards clients, and the problematic issue of informed consent. Another approach has looked at ethical dilemmas arising in relation to three main areas: the survivor's relationship with the therapist, with other family members, and with the alleged abuser (Daniluk & Haverkamp, 1993).

The survivor's relationship with his or her alleged abuser, and with his or her therapist, will be looked at in some detail, particularly with regard to the legal aspects which can arise. The framework adopted for this will be the Drama Triangle (Karpman, 1968) (Figure 11.1). The basis of this model is that when one person intervenes in a conflict between two other persons, perhaps to help the one at a disadvantage, he or she enters into the dynamic relationship between the original parties, becoming embroiled in the drama, and in the emotions it has generated. The other parties involved can then turn upon him or her, and roles can rapidly reverse. The example of the media coverage of Cleveland in 1987 is illustrative, where 117 children were taken by social workers into local authority care, following the discovery of alleged widespread sexual abuse by parents, foster-parents and other adult care-takers (Butler-Sloss,

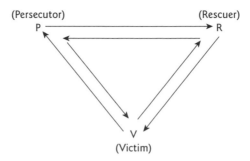

Figure 11.1   *The drama triangle (Karpman, 1968).*
The drama triangle was originally published in 'Fairy Tales and
Script Drama Analysis' bu Stephen B. Karpman, MD, in the
Transactional Analysis Bulletin, Vol. 7, No. 26, pp. 39–43, 1968.
Reprinted here with permission of Stephen B. Karpman and the
International Transactional Analysis Association.

1988). From the perspective of the Drama Triangle, the social worker initially intervenes to rescue children from alleged abuse. The parents and media portray this as persecution of innocent people. The social worker as *rescuer* quickly becomes seen as the *persecutor* of the family. The alleged persecuting parent then becomes seen as the *victim* of interference by professionals.

The Drama Triangle offers a way to understand some of the powerful emotions aroused by issues of exploring child sexual abuse, whether in the case of child protection, or in the case of false memory allegations. The model is outlined for its explanatory value in this context, and there is no intention to suggest that there is an automatic or inevitable progression for therapists towards assuming the different roles within the model. The model lays stress on *perception* rather than *intent*: therapists may be perceived by other parties as taking on the role of 'rescuer', 'persecutor' or 'victim', although this is not the therapist's *intention*. The use of the model is also not meant to imply that there are significant or increasing numbers of therapists seeking a wider social role as advocates for clients abused as children, but to try to clarify some of the dilemmas which confront practitioners in this complex area of work.

The Drama Triangle can be used to explore some of the main ethical and legal issues confronting therapists working with memories of abuse. Interest in the ethical aspects of therapy has received increasing attention (Bond, 2000; Dryden, 1997; Jones et al., 2000; Tjelveit, 1999). Daniluk & Haverkamp (1993) suggest six ethical principles which have a direct relevance to this area, in terms of interrogating and guiding practice.

- *Autonomy*—The promotion of the client's freedom of choice and action
- *Fidelity*—Faithfulness, loyalty, the keeping of trust
- *Justice*—Achieving equity, fairness, avoiding discrimination
- *Beneficence*—Doing good, promoting the client's welfare
- *Non-maleficence*—Avoiding harm or damage
- *Self-interest*—Promoting the self-knowledge, self-protection and self-development of the counsellor

Ethical principles are more easily stated than put into practice, particularly where the interests of therapist, client and third parties may conflict, as in the case of allegations of sexual abuse. Some of the potential conflicts are illustrated in Figure 11.2, viewed in the context of the changing roles for therapists which may be associated with the Drama Triangle.

There is a tension here between the perceived interests of the therapist, the client and potential third parties who could be affected by the outcomes of therapy, via what is an essentially *private* form of communication between client and therapist. The wider public interest in recovered memories accrues at the point where therapeutic activity is perceived by third parties as moving from the private to the public arena. For the small proportion of clients seeking legal redress, this may entail moving from the consulting room to the court room.

Legal Implications of Therapeutic Practice

Beginning with the client's relationship with the therapist, it is useful to look at research on patterns of disclosure of allegations of childhood abuse (Roesler & Wind, 1994). One survey of 228 women survivors of abuse found that disclosure to parents or family tended to happen at an average age of 15 years. Disclosure to friends often occurred later, at an average age of 26 years. A third of the sample made disclosure to a therapist, at an average age of 38 years; these women were also more likely (28% of sample) to have repressed memories of childhood abuse. So the therapist is often being entrusted with material which has not previously been disclosed, and which is, indeed, often not consciously known to the client her/himself. The therapeutic relationship could be explored here using the model of the Drama Triangle described above. The process of disclosure may offer the role of 'rescuer' to the therapist, in the triangular relationship between the therapist, client and alleged abuser (see Figure 11.3).

From a legal point of view, the steps that the therapist could take might include reporting the child abuse, whether past or current. Such reporting is mandatory in the USA, and required of most child care professionals in the UK who are working in a health or social work setting. Another step would be to assist the client in seeking compensation for

Ethical principles involved	Therapist's dilemmas
The therapist as potential 'rescuer'	
Fidelity versus Justice	Do I believe my clients' retrieved memories, or guard against the possibility of their fantasising abuse?
Beneficence versus Justice	Do I use open-ended techniques such as regression, visualisation, or dream work to explore material which is possibly linked to childhood abuse?
Beneficence versus Autonomy	Do I influence clients to reconstruct memories in accordance with my own assumptions, in ways which are possibly outside my own awareness?
The therapist as potential 'persecutor'	
Justice versus Non-Maleficence	Do I support clients in confronting their alleged abusers as part of the therapeutic process, or maintain neutrality regarding the alleged abuser?
Non-Maleficence versus Fidelity	Do I consider the possible effects on alleged abusers and their families of a false accusation, or determine my role as solely having responsibility to the client?
Fidelity versus Justice	Do I assume that all recovered abuse material is true in an actual historical sense, rather than part of a wider therapeutic narrative?
The therapist as potential 'victim'	
Justice versus Self-Interest	Do I involve myself in court proceedings in support of my client, or seek to distance myself from legal proceedings unless compelled to participate by the court?
Justice versus Autonomy	Do I avoid searching for possible childhood abuse, and concentrate on developing my client's survival skills geared to coping with the present?
Self-Interest versus Non-Maleficence	Do I use recording techniques to protect myself from possible litigation, but which are then potentially available to a court, to my client's possible detriment?

Figure 11.2 *Ethical dilemmas for therapists working with retrieved memories of childhood sexual abuse*

The therapist as 'rescuer' of the client

• In reporting child abuse to the authorities
• As 'McKenzie' or informal supporter in court
• As the supporter of a client in claiming compensation from the Criminal Injuries Compensation Authority

The therapist as 'persecutor' of the alleged abuser

• As the advocate of personal confrontation with the alleged abuser
• As the witness of fact for the client in civil or criminal proceedings against the alleged abuser
• As the expert witness for the client's case

The therapist as 'victim' of legal action

• Via forced disclosure of records of therapy through a court order
• As the subject of negligence action brought by a third party
• As the subject of 'retractor action' brought by a former client
• As the subject of hostile statutory registration and control measures

Figure 11.3 *Potential roles of the therapist in legal proceedings relating to allegations of abuse*

past abuse under the Criminal Injuries Compensation Scheme, whereby victims of abuse can receive compensation. However, the actual process of obtaining compensation may itself become arduous and prolonged for the abuse survivor, and is not an easy option to pursue without a strong network of support.

It is in the area of survivors' relationships with their alleged abusers, perhaps by making contact with them or even by confronting them with their new realisation, that a shift may occur. Here, it is necessary to consider the influence of the women's movement and the survivor self-help movement, as represented by the work of Bass & Davis. Their views on the validity of unclear or repressed memories are frequently cited by critics: 'if you are unable to remember any specific instances like the ones mentioned above but still have a feeling that something abusive happened to you, it probably did' (1991: 21). They quote one survivor who follows a familiar pattern:

> My first flood of memories came when I was 25. The memories I get now are like fine-tuning – more details, more textures. Even though there was more of a feeling of shock and catharsis at first, remembering is harder now. I believe them now. It hurts more. I have the emotions to feel the impact. I can see how it's affected my life (1991: 80).

The reasons suggested by Bass & Davis for confronting the alleged abusers include revenge, speaking out, financial compensation, or protecting others still at risk. They make the necessary and important point that confrontation is an *option*, but *not* an obligatory part of the healing process (1991: 34).

Therapist as rescuer

The critical part of the argument advances the role of the *therapist as rescuer* in this process, '*Support clients in speaking out.* This may include confronting abusers, disclosing to family members, taking legal action, or becoming an advocate for abused children' (1991: 349, emphasis in original). On the validity of recovered memories, Bass & Davis are adamant: 'You must believe that your client was sexually abused, even if she sometimes doubts it herself … If a client is unsure that she was abused but thinks that she might have been, work as though she was … *No one fantasises abuse*' (1991: 247, emphases in original).

Bass & Davis represent an influential trend in therapy with survivors. They are often heavily quoted by advocates of the false memory perspective (Prendergast, 1995), and there have also been unsuccessful attempts to sue them for damage allegedly caused by their writings (Slovenko, 1994). However, extensive quotation from a popular self-help manual for abuse survivors does not constitute proof of widespread malpractice by the majority of therapists who work with survivors.

On the issue of confrontation, another piece of research involved a longitudinal survey of 72 women (Cameron, 1994). A third of the women had been amnesic over their abuse and a fifth had repressed certain memories. Confrontation with their abusers was seen by the survivors as a step in their healing: 'their strong desire to confront the abuser arose largely from a need to have him validate and help them understand their returning memories' (1994: 13). This survey found that between 1986 and 1992, a third of the women were able to to confront their abuser, and the vast majority had in fact done so, some on several occasions. The benefits lay for the survivors in feeling able to carry out the confrontation, rather than in producing any specific outcomes. Mostly, they were met by denial by the alleged abuser, or more rarely by occasional partial admissions. These were then often followed later by denial on the part of the alleged abuser, by minimisation of the harm caused, or by claims of having been 'misunderstood'.

Therapist as persecutor

In supporting or advocating confrontation, the therapist may be in danger of being perceived by third parties, such as parents, as moving from a private, individual and therapeutic role into one that is public, political and accusatory. Starting with the role of rescuer, the drama triangle can embroil the therapist in a moral issue fought out in the courts and in the media on the terrain of the defence of family values, as appears to have happened in the *Ramona* (1994) case. Here we have the figure of the *therapist perceived as persecutor* by external interests such as third parties, and by the media.

The therapist's legal involvement with the client's case can take a number of forms, for example as an informal supporter of the survivor in court, or as an expert witness supporting the plaintiff or the prosecution case. A successful prosecution may be more likely if the abuse is ongoing with other family members. Often, evidence based on memory alone will be inadequate to sustain the case, with the Crown Prosecution Service (CPS) looking for a more than even chance of successfully proving the case in court. The alternative of a private prosecution is still fairly rare in criminal cases generally, but there are occasional examples of successful private prosecutions, in the absence of action by the CPS.

The most widely used route for clients is that of suing the alleged abuser for damages. In the USA, half of state legislatures amended the statute of limitations to permit civil action being brought within 3 to 6 years of the emergence of the repressed memory, rather than within 3 to 6 years of the actual abuse. In England and Wales, there is a 6 year time limit from the age of 18 for bringing actions in the case of deliberate injuries incurred in childhood. There is a 3 year time limit for victims of negligence, which runs from the date when the individual became aware of their right to sue, and which is extendable at the discretion of the court. This has been used as the grounds to sue the survivor's *mother*, not the abusing father, for negligence in failing to protect the survivor as a child, when the time limits for action against the father had run out. However, extending the statute of limitations can prove to be problematic, as events in the USA have suggested. There, former clients have used this change in the law to sue their therapist for negligence, with the benefit of a wider time-frame within which to initiate proceedings.

Therapist as victim

The final stance is that of the *therapist as victim*. This is suggested by the appeal of the False Memory Syndrome Foundation (USA) to litigation specialists, promoting this as a growing market for legal action against therapists. The conclusion of a FMSF conference organiser was that 'only one professional organization can stop [Recovered Memory Therapy] and that's the American Trial Lawyers' Association' (Golston, 1995: 29). This development seems, incidentally, to bear out the accuracy of a remark made by De Tocqueville in the 1830s, to the effect that 'scarcely any political question arises in the United States which is not resolved, sooner or later, into a judicial question' (De Tocqueville, 1840/1956, p. 126). The uncanny prescience of this comment now appears evident in the case of the false memory movement in the USA.

There have been few cases of successful litigation against therapists in the UK (*Werner v Landau* [1961]; *Phelps v Hillingdon LBC* [1997]. Negligence cases are difficult for clients to win, given the standard applied of the 'reasonably competent practitioner', for example in medical cases, such as *Bolam v Friern HMC* [1957] and *Maynard v West Midlands RHA* [1984] (Cohen, 1992) (for a fuller discussion of negligence law and therapy, see Jenkins, 1997). There is a much more extensive case law on this topic in the USA, though even there, successful cases have been fairly rare until recently (Kermani, 1989). What has developed in the USA, however, has been the use of *third party* actions for negligence. In the *Ramona* (1994) case, Holly Ramona recovered memories of childhood sexual abuse during therapy; her father's reputation and business interests allegedly suffered as a result. He then sued the therapists involved – a counsellor, Marche Isabella, and a psychiatrist, Richard Rose MD, plus the clinic involved, Western Medical Center of Anaheim, for $8 million. He was, however, awarded the significantly lower sum of $475,000, for loss of a year's earnings only, rather than for pain and suffering as claimed. The judgment held that the therapists were liable for damages caused to a third party as the result of their work with a client: i.e., 'by implanting or reinforcing false memories that (the) plaintiff had molested her as a child', according to the court record (*Ramona* (1994)). Holly Ramona's own attempt to bring a civil case against her father was later dismissed on the basis that the prior court's decision had demonstrated that abuse had been shown *not* to have taken place.

The complexity of the *Ramona* case has not been widely grasped, given the largely inadequate reporting and discussion of the case in the UK. Gary Ramona, the client's father, claimed to have been completely exonerated by the court's decision. However, Thomas Dudum, the jury foreman, stated after the verdict: 'we knew the case did not prove that he did not do it. I want to make it clear that we did not believe, as Gary indicates, that these therapists gave Holly a wonder drug and implanted these memories. It was an uneasy decision and there were a lot of unanswered questions' (Butler, 1994: 7).

The view of Justice Scott Snowden in the case that therapists necessarily held a liability for damages incurred by third parties represented a somewhat controversial extension of US case-law on this issue (Johnston, 1997). Failure to appeal on the case has resulted in a significant rise in the cost of malpractice insurance premiums for US therapists.

There have also been increased numbers of similar third-party claims against therapists, albeit at the lower levels of the US judicial system. These claims have been based on the liability principles observed in the *Ramona* case (Bowman & Mertz, 1996). The new phenomenon of so-called 'retractor action' has also grown since this case. One survey describes 20 abuse survivors known to the US False Memory Syndrome Foundation (Nelson & Simpson, 1994). Of this group, 19 reported that their visualisation of abuse (the term used instead of recovery of repressed or false memories) was influenced by their therapists. 8 former clients had filed lawsuits against their therapists; 3 of these lawsuits were settled, and 5 were pending (1994: 124). The therapists' techniques had included hypnosis (85%), regression (30%), trance writing (15%), sodium amytal (15%), relaxation/imagery work (5%) and dream work (5%) (1994: 125). Regression, imagery and dream work would all be considered as standard techniques by many therapists in the USA and the UK.

The USA has a much more extensive case law on third party actions for negligence (*Tarasoff v Regents of University of California* (1976); *Peck v Counseling Service of Addison County, Inc.* (1985)). Other action against therapists in the USA has taken the form of picketing, or making co-ordinated complaints to professional licensing authorities (Doehr, 1994). Under US law, in some states, legal action against therapists' supervisors is a further possibility (Harrar et al., 1990).

Using the law

In effect, in the USA the courtroom has become the chosen terrain for resolution of the wider social issues concerning the validity of retrieved memories of early childhood sexual abuse. The FMSF has allied itself with lawyers in an aggressive and largely successful campaign to overturn the initial legal inroads made by the survivor movement. This has taken the form of challenging the status of expert testimony sympathetic to the concept of recovered memories, the overturning of convictions based upon recovered memories, and litigation against therapists and agencies specialising in this area of work (Brown et al., 1999). The involvement of lawyers and of research psychologists as expert witnesses has been a crucial factor in the relative success of this approach (Barden, 1997; Perry and Gold, 1995).

One related development in the USA concerns the proposed model legislation in the form of the Mental Health Consumer Protection Act, being promoted in 21 states (Quirk & DePrince, 1995). This includes a raft of restrictive measures, which would tightly constrain the professional autonomy of therapists. The measures include:

- A requirement for evidence of informed consent by clients for therapy (on the tighter US standard, which is patient-rather than doctor-friendly)
- A ban on funding practice carried out using therapeutic techniques which are alleged to be non-proven
- Third party actions against Recovered Memory Techniques
- The criminalising of false accusations
- Psychotherapy to be subject to endorsement by the wider scientific community
- A Model Licensing Act for Therapists

In the UK, the British False Memory Society has also taken a keen interest in legal aspects of the issue, with regular coverage of court cases in its *Newsletter*, the appointment of a Legal Adviser and the provision of legal information on its website. There has been extensive networking and exchange of experience with their counterparts in the USA, evident via regular presentations at annual meetings by forensic experts from the USA and the UK. Unlike the situation in the USA, the legal system in England and Wales has so far proved resistant to the concept of litigation by a third party for therapeutic negligence. However, the evidential value of recovered memories has been successfully challenged in a number of cases, both civil and criminal (Lewis and Mullis, 1999; Mullis, 1997). Access to current or past records of therapy, or psychiatric treatment, via the legal process of discovery, can play a crucial role in undermining the validity of a plaintiff as a credible witness. The courts have also been used to prevent publication of material on false memory which was alleged to be defamatory towards key individuals (BFMS, 2000: 13).

Implications for therapeutic practice

It is unclear whether therapeutic recovery of memories which are later alleged to be false is a rare or a common occurrence (Poole et al., 1995: 434–435). The British Psychological Society's report clearly states that there is no evidence of psychologists routinely influencing clients to retrieve unfounded memories of abuse (BPS, 1995a; Weiskrantz, 1995). Further broad-based research into the beliefs and practices of therapists working with discontinuous memories of childhood sexual abuse would form a useful contribution to this discussion.

There are a number of implications of the debate about false memory for therapists. First, they need to be fully aware of the boundaries of responsible practice, for themselves and for the profession as a whole (BPS, 1995a; Mollon, 1996; Royal College of Psychiatrists, 1997). The use of hypnotic techniques, in the broadest sense, needs to be weighed against the potential consequences of action that might be taken by aggrieved parties (Yapko, 1993). There is a need for better education of therapists into the nature of memory, particularly traumatic memory in early childhood and its limitations as an accurate recording of events (Enns et al., 1995; Terr, 1988; 1994; Williams, 1992). The potential for suggestion to play some part in shaping retrieved memories also needs to be better understood by practitioners (Ceci & Bruck, 1993; Yapko, 1994). At a conceptual level, notions central to psychotherapy such as repression and dissociation have been challenged (Crews, 1997; Pope & Hudson, 1995; Scharff & Scharff, 1994; Singer, 1990). Established diagnostic categories within psychotherapy and psychiatry, such as Post Traumatic Stress Disorder and Multiple Personality Disorder (now Dissociative Identity Disorder), have also been subject to criticism (Aldridge-Morris, 1994; Merskey, 1995).

One consequence of this debate may be the emergence of 'defensive therapy' to parallel the development of defensive medical practice in obstetrics, where the risk of medical litigation is at its highest. Therapists may become reluctant to explore repressed material, and may be advised to protect themselves against future legal action by tape-recording sessions, or by making substantial contemporaneous notes. Therapists clearly need to be aware of the dangers in assuming automatically that abuse has occurred. One model worth exploring further in this context would be the model of the cognitive interview approach (Fisher & Geiselman, 1988; Lindsay & Read, 1994; Saywitz, 1992). This has parallels with the approach developed for the joint police interviewing of child victims of alleged sexual abuse, which stresses the need to avoid the use of leading questions (Home Office/Department of Health, 1992; Ryan & Wilson, 1995). The danger here, as in the case of work with children making allegations of abuse, is that the dynamics of therapy will be eclipsed by considerations of potential court action (HO, CPS, DoH, 2001).

One outcome may be to increase the pressure for statutory or more comprehensive self-regulation of therapy, in order for bad practice to be more closely monitored and controlled. As part of the process of establishing statutory regulation of therapists in the UK, the movement for voluntary and, ultimately, statutory registration has gathered pace, with registers of practitioners being set up by the leading organisations in the field, the United Kingdom Council for Psychotherapy, the British Confederation of Psychotherapists and the British Association for Counselling and Psychotherapy. One response has also been for therapists to recognise the wider social and political agendas being fought over, and to respond overtly to these with the setting up of groups such as Accuracy About Abuse. This has attempted to meet the criticisms being offered by the False Memory Society in the UK, thus mirroring the parallel groups operating in the USA. Another development has been the establishment of the Psychotherapists and Counsellors for Social Responsibility, which has an agenda for establishing a wider presence for the therapeutic community in current social and political debates.

Conclusion

The process of working with discontinuous memories of childhood sexual abuse has increased the therapist's vulnerability to legal challenge by third parties in the USA. Such an increase may be somewhat less likely under the legal system in the UK. Nevertheless, there are instances such as the disclosure of confidential records of therapy, where therapists in the UK may become involved in legal processes concerning clients alleging early childhood sexual abuse. The limited case-law from the USA and UK suggests that there are a number of difficult legal and ethical dilemmas which therapists can encounter while working in this complex and demanding area of practice.

References

Aldridge-Morris, R. (1994) 'Nightmare visions', British False Memory Society Newsletter, 2(2), pp. 4–5.

Aldridge-Morris, R. (1995) 'Memories of abuse or the abuse of memories?' British False Memory Society Newsletter, 3(2), pp. 12–18.

Anderson, J., Martin, J. Mullen, P., Romans, S. and Herbison, P. (1993) 'Prevalence of childhood sexual abuse in a community sample of women', Journal of the American Academy of Child and Adolescent Psychiatry, 32(5), pp. 911–919.

Andrews, B., Brewin, C., Ochera, J., Morton, J., Bekerian, D., Davies, G. and Mollon, P. (1999) 'Characteristics, context and consequences of memory recovery among adults in therapy' British Journal of Psychiatry, 175, 141–6.

Asquith, S. (ed), (1993) Protecting Children: Cleveland to Orkney: More Lessons to Learn? London: HMSO.

Barden, R. (1997) Law, Science and Mental Health: Protecting Liberty and Reforming the Mental Health System. Paper for the British False Memory Society Annual General Meeting, 8th May.

Bass, E. & Davis, L. (1991) The Courage to Heal (2nd edn) London: Cedar.

Bond, T. (2000) Standards and Ethics for Counselling in Action. (2nd edn) London: Sage.

Bowman, C.G. & Mertz, E. (1996) 'A dangerous direction: Legal intervention in abuse survivor therapy' Harvard Law Review, 109(3), pp. 551–639.

Brandon, S., Boakes, J., Glaser, D. and Green, R. (1997) 'Recovered memories of childhood sexual abuse: Implications for clinical practice', British Journal of Psychiatry, 172, pp. 296–307.

British False Memory Society (2000) 'Smear campaign book withdrawn', *Newsletter*, 8(1): 13.

British Psychological Society (1995a) *Recovered Memories*. Leicester: BPS.

British Psychological Society (1995b) 'The recovery of memories in clinical practice', *The Psychologist*, May, pp. 209–214.

Brown, D., Scheflin, A. and Whitfield, C. (1999) 'Recovered memories: The current weight of the evidence in science and the courts', *Journal of Psychiatry and Law*, 27, pp. 5–156.

Butler-Sloss, E. (1988) *Report of the Inquiry into Child Abuse in Cleveland 1987*. London: HMSO.

Butler, K. (1994) 'You must remember this', *Guardian*, 23 July.

Cameron, C. (1994) 'Women survivors confronting their abusers: issues, decisions and outcomes', *Journal of Child Sexual Abuse*, 3(1), pp. 7–36.

Campbell, B. (1989) *Unofficial Secrets: Child Sexual Abuse: The Cleveland Case*. London: Virago.

Ceci, S.J. & Bruck, M. (1993) 'Suggestibility of the child witness: A historical review and synthesis', *Psychological Bulletin*, 113(3) pp. 403–439.

Cohen, K. (1992) 'Some legal issues in counselling and psychotherapy', *British Journal of Guidance and Counselling*, 20(1), pp. 10–26.

Crews, F. (1997) *The Memory Wars: Freud's Legacy in Dispute*. London: Granta.

Daniluk, J.C. and Haverkamp, B.E. (1993) 'Ethical issues in counseling adult survivors of incest', *Journal of Counseling and Development*, 72, pp. 16–22.

De Tocqueville, A. (1840/1956), *Democracy in America*. London: Mentor.

Doehr, E. (1994) 'Inside the false memory movement', *Treating Abuse Today*, 4(6), pp. 5–13.

Dryden, W. (1997) *Therapists' Dilemmas*. (2nd edn) London: Harper and Row.

Enns, C.Z., McNeilly, C.L., Corkery, J.M. and Gilbert, M.S. (1995) 'The debate about delayed memories of child sexual abuse: A feminist perspective', *Counseling Psychologist*, 23(2), pp. 181–279.

Fisher, R.P. and Geiselman, R.E. (1988) 'Enhancing eyewitness' memory with the cognitive interview', pp. 34–39 in: Morris, P.E. & Sykes, R.N. (eds) *Practical Aspects of Memory: Current Research & Issues*. New York: Wiley.

Freud, S. and Breuer, J. (1895/1991) *Studies on Hysteria*, *Vol. 3, Penguin Freud Library*, Harmondsworth: Penguin.

Gardner, R. (1992) 'Belated realization of child sex abuse by an adult', *Issues in Child Abuse Accusations*, 4(4), pp. 177–195.

Golston, J.C. (1995) 'Current topics in the law and mental health: False memory syndrome, multiple personality, and ritual sexual abuse: the growing controversy', *Treating Abuse Today*, 5(1), pp. 24–30.

Gomez, J. (1995) 'Satanic abuse', *Counselling*, 6(2), pp. 116–120.

Harrar, W.R., VandeCreek, L. and Knapp, S. (1990) 'Ethical and legal aspects of clinical supervision', *Professional Psychology*, 21(1), pp. 37–41.

Home Office/Department of Health (1992) *Memorandum of Good Practice on Video Recorded Interviews with Child Witnesses for Criminal Proceedings*. London: HMSO.

Home Office, Crown Prosecution Service and Department of Health (2001) *Provision of Therapy for Child Witnesses Prior to a Criminal Trial*. London: Crown Prosecution Service.

Jenkins, P. (1997) *Counselling, Psychotherapy and the Law*. London: Sage.

Johnston, M. (1997) *Spectral Evidence: The Ramona Case: Incest, Memory and Truth on Trial in Napa Valley*. Oxford: Westview.

Jones, C., Shillito-Clark, C., Syme, G., Hill, D., Casemore, R. and Murdin, L. (2000) *Questions of Ethics in Counselling and Therapy*. Buckingham: Open University Press.

Karpman, S. (1968) 'Fairy tales and script drama analysis', *Transactional Analysis Bulletin*, 7(26), pp. 39–43.

Kermani, E.J. (1989) *Handbook of Psychiatry and the Law*. London: Year Book Medical Publishers.

LaFontaine, J.S. (1994) *The Extent and Nature of Organised Abuse*. London: HMSO.

Levine, M., Doueck, H.J., with Anderson, E.M., Chavez, F.T., Deisz, R.L., George, N.A., Sharma, A., Steinberg, L. and Wallach L. (1995) *The Impact of Mandated Reporting on the Therapeutic Process: Picking up the Pieces*. London: Sage.

Lewis, P. and Mullis, A. (1999) 'Delayed Criminal Prosecutions for childhood sexual abuse: Ensuring a fair trial', *Law Quarterly Review*, 115, April, pp. 265–295.

Lindsay, D.S. and Read, J.D. (1994) 'Psychotherapy and memories of childhood sexual abuse: a cognitive perspective', *Applied Cognitive Psychology*, 8, pp. 281–338.

Loftus, E. and Ketcham, K. (1994) *The Myth of Repressed Memory: False Memories and Allegations of Sexual Abuse*. New York: St Martin's Press.

Magner, E. and Parkinson, P. (2001) 'Recovered memories: The legal dilemmas', in Davies, G. and Dalgleish, T. (eds) *Recovered Memories: Seeking the Middle Ground*. London: Wiley, pp. 51–68.

Masson, J. (1985) *The Assault on Truth*. Harmondsworth: Penguin.

McGuire, A. (1997) *False Memory Syndrome: A Statement formally adopted by the Management Committee*. Rugby: BACP.

Memon, A. (1998) 'Recovered memories: psychological issues and legal questions', in Memon, A., Vrij, A. and Bull, R. (eds) *Psychology and Law: Truthfulness, Accuracy and Credibility*. Maidenhead: McGraw-Hill. pp. 147–69.

Merskey, H. (1995) 'Multiple personality disorder and the false memory syndrome', *British Journal of Psychiatry*, 166, pp. 281–283.

Mollon, P. (1996) 'Guidelines for psychoanalytically oriented psychotherapists for the avoidance of generating or colluding with false memories', *British Journal of Psychotherapy*, 13(2), pp. 193–203.

Mullis, A. (1997) 'Compounding the abuse? The House of Lords, childhood sexual abuse and limitation periods', *Medical Law Review*, 5, Spring, pp. 22–62.

Murdin, L. (1997) 'Recovered memories', *The Psychotherapist*, No 8, (Spring), p.1.

Nelson, E.L. and Simpson, P. (1994) 'First glimpses: An initial examination of subjects who have rejected their recovered visualisations as false memories', *Issues in Child Abuse Accusations*, 6(3), pp. 123–133.

Nelson, K. (1990) 'Remembering, forgetting and childhood amnesia' pp. 301–16 in: Fivush, R. & Hudson, J.A. (eds) *Knowing and Remembering in Young Children*. New York: Cambridge University Press.

Olafson, E. & Corwin, D. (1993) 'Modern history of child sexual abuse: Awareness, cycles of discovery and suppression', *Child Abuse and Neglect*, 17, pp. 7–24.

Orr, M. (1995) 'Accuracy about abuse: The 'false memory syndrome' debate in the United Kingdom', *Treating Abuse Today*, May/June, pp. 9–28.

Parton, N. (1985) *The Politics of Child Abuse*. London: Macmillan.

Perry, C. and Gold, A. (1995) 'Hypnosis and the elicitation of true and false memories of childhood sexual abuse', *Psychiatry, Psychology and Law*, 2(2), pp. 127–38.

Poole, D.A., Lindsay, D.S., Memon, A. and Bull, R. (1995) 'Psychotherapy and the recovery of memories of child sexual abuse: US & British practitioners' opinions, practices and experiences', *Journal of Consulting and Clinical Psychology*, 63(3), pp.426–437.

Pope, H.G. and Hudson, J.I. (1995) 'Can memories of childhood sexual abuse be repressed?' *Psychological Medicine*, 25, pp. 121–126.

Prendergast, M. (1995) *Victims of Memory: Incest Accusations and Shattered Lives*. Hinesburg, Vermont: Upper Access.

Quirk, S. and DePrince, A.P. (1995) 'Backlash legislation targetting psychotherapists', *Journal of Psychohistory*, 22(3), pp. 258–264.

Roesler, T.A and Wind, T.W. (1994) 'Telling the secret: adult women describe their disclosures of incest', *Journal of Interpersonal Violence*, 9(3), pp. 327–338.

Rose, S. (1993) *The Making of Memory*. New York: Bantam.

Royal College of Psychiatrists (1997) 'Reported recovered memories of child sexual abuse: Recommendations for good practice and implications for training, continuing professional development and research', *Psychiatric Bulletin*, 21, pp. 663–5.

Ryan, V. and Wilson, K. (1995) 'Child therapy and evidence in court proceedings: Tensions and some solutions', *British Journal of Social Work*, 25, pp. 157–172.

Sanderson, C. (1995) 'Fact or fantasy: making sense of false memory syndrome', in: *Counselling Adult Survivors of Child Sexual Abuse*. (2nd edn) London: Jessica Kingsley.

Saywitz, K.J. (1992) 'Enhancing children's memory with the cognitive interview', *Adviser: American Professional Society on Childhood Abuse*, 5, pp. 9–10.

Scharff, J.S. and Scharff, P.E. (1994) *Object Relations Therapy of Physical and Sexual Trauma*. London: Aronson.

Sinason, V. (ed.) (1994) *Treating Survivors of Satanist Abuse*. London: Routledge.

Singer, J. (ed.) (1990) *Repression and Dissociation: Implications for Personality Theory, Psychopathology and Health*. Chicago: University of Chicago.

Slovenko, R. (1994) 'Blaming a book', *Journal of Psychiatry and Law*, 22(3), pp. 437–451.

Terr, L. (1988) 'What happens to early memories of trauma? A study of twenty children under age five at the time of documented traumatic events' *Journal of the American Academy of Child and Adolescent Psychiatry*, 27(1), pp. 96–104.

Terr, L. (1994) *Unchained Memories: True Stories of Traumatic Memories, Lost and Found*. New York: Basic Books.

Tjelveit, A. (1999) *Ethics and Values in Psychotherapy*. London: Routledge.

Webster, R. (1995) *Why Freud was Wrong: Sin, Science and Psychoanalysis*. London: Harper Collins.

Weiskrantz, L. (1995) 'Comments on the report of the working party of the BPS on "recovered memories"', *The Therapist* 2(4), pp. 5–8.

White, S.H. and Pilemmer, D.B. (1979) 'Childhood amnesia and the development of a socially accessible memory system', pp. 29–74 in: Kihlstrom, J.F & Evans, F.J. (eds) *Functional Disorders of Memory*. London: Erlbaum.

Williams, L.M. (1992) 'Adult memories of childhood abuse: Preliminary findings from a longitudinal study', *Adviser: American Professional Society on Childhood Abuse*, 5, pp. 19–21.

Worden, W. (1991) *Grief Counselling and Grief Therapy*. (2nd edn) London: Routledge.

Wright, L. (1994) *Remembering Satan: Recovered Memory and the Shattering of a Family*. London: Serpent's Tail.

Yapko, M. (1993) 'The seductions of memory', *Networker*, September/October, pp. 31–37.

Yapko, M. (1994) *Suggestions of Abuse*. London: Simon and Schuster.

Legal references (UK)

Bolam v Friern HMC [1957] 1 WLR 835
Maynard v West Midlands RHA [1984] 1 WLR 634
Phelps v Hillingdon LBC [1997] 3 FCR 621
Werner v Landau (1961) *The Times*, 8/3/61; 23/11/61

Legal references (USA)

Ramona v Isabella, Rose, M.D., and Western Medical Center, Anaheim, (1994) C61898 Cal. Super Ct., 13 May

Tarasoff v Regents of University of California, (Cal. 1976) 113 Cal. Rptr 14, 551 P.2d 334

Peck v Counseling Service of Addison County, Inc., (Vt. 1985) 499 A.2d 422

12

The Implications of the Human Rights Act 1998 for Counsellors and Psychotherapists

Vincent Keter

If anything the Human Rights Act will strengthen the position of counsellors more than their clients. The Act, which came into force in October 2000, is very much law for lawyers. Its biggest impact is on how cases are argued and it redraws the map which lawyers use in both court and in negotiations. Certainly, this will have an effect on the interests of the lawyer's clients, but it is often difficult to explain what these might be without resorting to boggling legal technicality. Having said that, I will in this chapter attempt to predict what the impact of the new Act might be for counsellors and psychotherapists, based largely on my own experience as a lawyer specialising in these fields.

There are two main thrusts to the Act. First, there is interpretation. The traditional position is that courts do not make the law (that is for Parliament), they interpret. In every case the court must interpret the meaning of Parliament-made law (statute law) and the judgments of previous cases which are deemed to be authoritative (common law). These days there is also a body of law emanating from the European Union. The new Act prevents interpretations which do not conform to the European Convention on Human Rights and allows lawyers to refer to European human rights cases whereas before the court was not obliged to take any account of such cases.

Second, the acts of public authorities must conform to the Convention. If they don't then the person affected can sue under the Act or rely on Convention rights in other legal proceedings against the public authority. A public authority is defined as including 'any person certain of whose functions are functions of a public nature'. It is not so much who, as what kind of function the person (or organisation) is performing in any particular case.

What does all this mean for counsellors? Most of the rights enshrined in the Act do not have any obvious application in counselling. The right to a fair trial, however, is clearly relevant to the counsellor and a number of the other rights, as set out below, would probably be relevant in some circumstances.

Articles adopted by the Act and the rights they protect:

Article 2:   Right to life
Article 3:   Prohibition of torture or inhuman or degrading treatment or punishment
Article 4:   Prohibition of slavery and forced labour
Article 5:   Liberty and security of person
Article 6:   Right to a fair trial
Article 7:   Freedom from retrospective criminal offences and punishment
Article 8:   Right to respect for private and family life
Article 9:   Freedom of religion
Article 10: Freedom of expression
Article 11: Freedom of assembly and association
Article 12: Right to marry and found a family
Article 14: Prohibition of discrimination in enjoyment of Convention rights

---

Article 6: Right to a fair trial

Psychotherapy and counselling have been going through an extended period of professionalisation and developing self-regulation. National voluntary registers have been set up, some providing registration direct to individuals, some via member organisations who control their own criteria. At the heart of this movement lie various codes of ethics and professional practices which tend to follow similar principles with some variation on interpretation. Together with published codes of ethics are complaints procedures for disciplining practitioners. Along with a fax machine, photocopier and website, most organisations of whatever size now have a code of ethics and a procedure for receiving complaints.

That is all well and good until a complaint is actually received. I have yet to encounter a procedure that ran to the satisfaction of all its users. This is perhaps not surprising since the outcome is bound to displease at least one of the parties to the complaint. Nevertheless, there is often a serious concern about the fairness of the procedure. Clearly, here is an issue which could engage Article 6 of the Convention concerning the right to a fair trial.

However, simply because there is a trial of some kind does not automatically mean that Article 6 applies. It is necessary to look at the wording of Article 6:

In the determination of his civil rights and obligations or of any criminal charge against him, everyone is entitled to a fair and impartial tribunal established by law. Judgement shall be pronounced publicly but the press and public may be excluded from all or part of the trial in the interests of morals, public order, or national security in a democratic society, where the interests of juveniles or the protection of the private life of the parties so require, or to the extent strictly necessary in the opinion of the court in special circumstances where publicity would prejudice the interests of justice.

Clearly, the hearing of a complaint would not amount to a 'criminal charge' for the purposes of Article 6. The next question is whether a 'civil right' or 'obligation' is involved. This needs to be examined from the perspective of both the complainant and the practitioner.

Taking the complainant first, it is clear that a complainant has an interest in receiving ethical services from the practitioner. That, however, is a part of the contract between the client and the practitioner – whether or not there is anything in writing, a contract in law exists between the practitioner and the client. I should make clear that in law a 'contract' is not only a written document, but any kind of agreement (e.g. oral) which is legally binding. The court will probably find an implied term in such a contract that the services provided will meet accepted ethical standards. If they do not then this might mean that the complainant would be able to sue on the basis of the contract.

However, when a complainant lays a complaint within the organisation's procedures there is likely to be no legal contract between the organisation and the complainant and so the complainant could not sue the organisation if the practitioner is wrongly or unfairly exonerated. Their only option would be to appeal the decision to a superior organisation. Sometimes there is no superior organisation capable of accepting an appeal or a fresh complaint. Aside from taking the matter to court, I do not see, on the part of the complainant, a civil right or obligation founded in law that a complaints hearing would have jurisdiction to determine. Thus, I do not imagine that a complainant could rely on Article 6 in matters concerning the complaint hearing.

Judicial Review

If a complainant appealed to a national or superior organisation, then that organisation must process the appeal fairly and properly. If they do not, then there is a possibility that the complainant could take them to court under the process of Judicial Review. This is a special kind of civil action which can only be taken in the High Court. It is a process which allows the High Court to review a decision taken by a public body to ensure that it was reasonable, fairly processed and legal. If the decision is flawed then the court can overturn it and/or order that matters be put right.

In 1999 I successfully took the United Kingdom Council for Psychotherapy (UKCP) to Judicial Review. They argued that they were not a public body, but the court rejected this submission. The Judicial Review was against a decision of the UKCP Governing Board to drop complaints against two of their member organisations, GPTI and Metanoia, by Petruska Clarkson, on whose behalf, as her husband, I took the proceedings. The complaints had been accepted by UKCP and had been in process for many months when the Governing Board, without warning, took the decision to drop them. I applied to the court for permission to have this decision judicially reviewed which was granted by Mr Justice Collins in October 1999 (Clarkson v Gilbert and Others (2001)).

I then initiated a Judicial Review application after the UKCP refused to back down. Soon after that, a member of the Governing Board wrote to Petruska to inform her that he would be pursuing ethical charges against her on the basis that his name was mentioned in the affidavit in support of the application for permission for Judicial Review. The reason that his name was mentioned, was that he had taken part in the decision to drop complaints against Metanoia, whilst being an organisational member of Metanoia, a member of the training staff at Metanoia and a member of the Metanoia ethics committee whose actions were the subject of complaint. The submission was that this had the appearance of bias.

This appeared to me to constitute a 'criminal' contempt of court in that it was 'calculated to interfere with the due administration of justice'. This is not a criminal charge in the normal sense. I applied to the Divisional Court of Queen's Bench to take committal proceedings against the UKCP member. This was granted by Lord Justice Rose sitting with Mr Justice Mitchell, who consolidated the contempt proceedings with the Judicial Review.

The final outcome was that there was a full hearing of the Judicial Review and Contempt applications before Mr Justice Collins. During this hearing the UKCP argued that I could not bring the proceedings on behalf of Petruska for technical legal reasons and that the UKCP were not a public body which the courts could judicially review. Both of these arguments failed, at which point the UKCP backed down. The UKCP member gave an apology in open court to Petruska and I, which was accepted. In light of this, I agreed not to press for his committal to prison.

The rights of a complainant, however, are limited. From 1999 to 2000 I attempted to take the British Psychological Society to Judicial Review on behalf of a former client of Dr Peter Slade with whom he had admitted having an inappropriate sexual relationship. The decision of the BPS to allow him to retain his membership and fellowship provoked outrage among psychologists and in the national press. The Prevention of Professional Abuse Network (POPAN) invited me to make an application for permission for Judicial Review. I argued that the decision was perverse. The court decided that it could not intervene on behalf of the complainant.

Position of Practitioners

The position of the practitioner is quite different. The European case law reveals that the right to practice any profession is a 'civil right' within the meaning of the convention. Thus, any trial which might affect such a civil right would engage the Article 6 right 'to a fair and impartial tribunal'.

If the complaint is not fairly or impartially handled by the organisation, then the practitioner could probably sue on the contract between themselves and the organisation. This is usually the contract whereby the practitioner agrees to abide by the codes of ethics, submit to the complaints procedure and pay their subscription in return for being a member of that organisation, thereby having the opportunity of attracting clients. In a claim against the organisation in contract, the practitioner could probably rely on an implied term in the contract that the procedure should conform to natural justice as well as Article 6.

Furthermore, if the practitioner is found guilty and then appeals, Article 6, in my view, would also apply to the appeal. Depending on the nature and status of the organisation receiving the appeal, it is possible that the practitioner could also take legal action against the appeal organisation under the Act. This would depend on whether the appeal organisation were held to be performing functions of a public nature.

Legal Representation in Disciplinary Proceedings

There is no general principle which says that practitioners have a right to be represented in disciplinary proceedings. It is up to the organisation to decide if they will allow this. If they refuse, there is often little that can be done. However, if representation is refused in certain circumstances this may amount to a breach of Article 6 or principles of natural justice.

Often representation is allowed. This has its pros and cons. The benefits are that the opposing cases are often put with greater clarity by representatives. The emotional proximity of the parties to the case can often lead to an inability to let go of weak or irrelevant facts or argument. Disciplinary proceedings can be astonishingly stressful to both sides and this can have obvious effects on how individuals present their case. On the other side, the process can become overly legalistic when too many lawyers are present. Disciplinary hearings convened by the British Psychological Society are usually attended by lawyers on all sides. If this were to happen in counselling or psychotherapy hearings, I could well imagine that basic issues and realities might become lost amid a tangle of definitions, interpretations and evidential sword-play.

In my view, representation can often be a good idea if the representative has a confident grasp of the field and experience in such proceedings. As to covering the costs of representation, I know that many members of the British Psychological Society have professional indemnity insurance which covers disciplinary proceedings. I would be surprised to find this in the case of counsellors or psychotherapists. Most policies are limited to legal costs in court. Lawyers with an understanding of the field are few, and there is no advertised specialisation in the current directories for solicitors and barristers.

Article 7: Freedom from retrospective criminal offences and punishment

While Article 7 applies mainly to criminal offences, the European authority suggests that it might also apply to disciplinary proceedings. In any event, the normal principles of natural justice would require that a practitioner should not be retrospectively charged under a code of ethics, or particular item in that code, which did not exist at the time of the alleged offence. Most ethics codes I have read include this idea, although, in my experience, complaints panels sometimes do not adhere to this principle.

Article 8: Right to respect for private and family life

The intimate and private nature of counselling and psychotherapy immediately suggests the Article 8 right to respect for private and family life. However, this right probably adds little to the existing ethical, legal and contractual obligations of confidentiality. Disciplinary proceedings probably need to take account of this right on questions such as the confidentiality of the proceedings. Furthermore, any practitioner charged with a breach of confidentiality affecting the private life of the client should now have a tougher time excusing themselves where this is proved.

Article 9: Freedom of religion

If a practitioner were refused professional membership of an organisation because of their religious beliefs, this would probably infringe Article 9.

It is difficult to imagine anyone being barred from a psychotherapy or counselling organisation because they are, for example, Buddhist. However, I have heard of a 'born again' Christian who was not allowed membership allegedly due to his religious beliefs, as well as a Catholic priest who felt discriminated against on a therapy training course.

Article 10: Freedom of expression

This right would almost certainly apply to any complainant or respondent in complaints proceedings. Sometimes complainants are accused of being 'defamatory' in bringing their complaint. In defamation law this is allowed as long there is no malice. Given the nature of therapy and counselling, the existence of the right to freedom of expression would probably mean that the expression of personal feelings, however extreme, by complainants would be protected. A different standard might apply to respondents, given their position as providers of services and possibly the vulnerability of clients who complain.

Article 11: Freedom of assembly and association

The politics of psychotherapy regulation and the competing interests of organisations could engage the right to freedom of assembly and association. A few years ago the British Confederation of Psychotherapists (BCP) announced a single membership policy which ignited a dispute with the United Kingdom Council for Psychotherapy. The BCP's policy was aimed at preventing individuals from being members of both organisations at the same time. Since there were BCP members who wanted to be members of both organisations some complained that their right to freedom of assembly was being infringed. The history of psychotherapy from the beginning to the present day is littered with splits between and among individuals and organisations. Unless this pattern has somehow miraculously been resolved, there may still be recourse to Article 11.

Conclusion

Those are some of the ways I can predict the Human Rights Act could be relevant to counsellors and psychotherapists. As with any new law a great deal remains to be seen. Much of what I have written may also not hold out in individual cases. Often these things turn on the facts of the given case. Aside from the strictly legal implications, I hope that the spirit and wisdom of the human rights movement might also have a positive effect on the human potential movement. It may be that the greatest impact of human rights on the sphere of counselling and psychotherapy or indeed society at large will be at this level.

Legal reference

Clarkson v Gilbert and Others (2000) CA TLR 4/7/00

Appendix 1: The Academy of Experts: Model Form of Expert's Report

Introductory Note

1. Why a model form?

1.1 Some senior judges have expressed concern at the length of many experts' reports and at the tendency to mix matters of fact and opinion.

1.2 The Judicial Committee of the Academy has commented that the hallmarks of a good report include:

    a) A stand-alone, concise, user-friendly format, expressed in the first person singular by the person whose opinion has been given or who adopts as his own the opinion of others.

    b) Text which is arranged in short sentences and paragraphs.

    c) Judicious use of appendices.

    d) Matters of fact being kept separate from matters of opinion.

Conclusions should be given in the final section of the report before appendices. They should be cross referenced to the text which supports the Conclusions.

1.3 Each opinion expressed in the report must be the opinion of the writer whether it was formed by the writer or formed by others and adopted by the writer as his own.

1.4 The following must be identified separately and distinguished:

    a) facts which the writer is asked to assume;

    b) facts which the writer observed for himself, e.g., the results of experiments, investigations, etc., carried out by the writer himself;

    c) facts which others, acting on behalf of the writer, observed, identifying the persons concerned;

    d) opinions of others upon which the writer relies in forming his own opinion.

1.5   The model form of report has been developed with these comments in mind and with the aim of assisting both experts and those instructing to address the relevant issues in the most direct way. The model is intended as a guideline only. There may be valid reasons for departing from it and/or introducing additional sections.

2. The Scheme of the Model Form of Report

The Model Form is written in 5 distinct sections with suggested headings: notes are given.

The Front Sheet – *the first visible sheet* should contain the items of key-point information indicated by the model and should not be obscured by a cover. The first report prepared for disclosure should be entitled 'Report' and not First Report.

The Contents Page – may be omitted altogether in the case of a short report of say seven pages or less.

Section 1 Introduction – deals with all the formal matters and chronology. The text is largely standard. Most of the material is transferred to appendices.

Section 2 The Background to the Dispute and the Issues – this section of the report will normally include:

a)   A list of the people who will be referred to in the report with a short uncontroversial description of their role.
b)   The assumed or given factual background of the case.
c)   The issues, set out clearly and numbered, which the expert will address. *No opinion* is expressed in this section.

Section 3 Description of the Technical Investigation or Enquiry – this section is, again, factual only. The description should be given in itemised paragraphs with sub-headings.

Section 4 The Facts on which the Expert's Opinion is based – distinguishing those facts which he was told from those he observed for himself.

Section 5 The Expert's Conclusions – with opinion and reasons in full on each issue in turn, set out clearly and numbered. In this section, there should only be such repetition of fact as is necessary for the exposition of the opinion.

Signing Block – the report must be signed by the writer and dated at the end of the Conclusions.

Appendices – each Appendix should be provided with a front sheet of the type indicated in the model.

Headers – each continuation page of a section should be provided with a header on the left hand side showing the number and short title of the section and a header at the right hand side with the information suggested by the model.

Presentation – the practice is growing of the Court directing that a copy of experts' reports be made available on disc to the judge or official referee. Where practicable, therefore, reports should be typed in double spacing and prepared on or readily transferable to Wordperfect 5.1. The report should be presented on A4 paper, already hole punched for use in a standard lever arch binder and in a format that can be copied readily on a photocopier with automatic feed.

3. Evaluation of the Expert Witness

The following passage taken from the dicta of Stuart-Smith 1.1 in *Loveday v Renton* [1990] 1 Med LR 177 at 125 provides a clear description of the processes which the Court has to undertake in order to evaluate the Expert witness, the soundness of his opinion and the weight to be attached to it.

This involves an examination of the reasons given for his opinions and the extent to which they are supported by the evidence. The Judge also has to decide what weight to attach to a witness's opinion by examining the internal consistency and logic of his evidence; the care with which he has considered the subject and presented his evidence; his precision and accuracy of thought as demonstrated by his answers; how he responds to searching and informed cross-examination and in particular the extent to which a witness faces up to and accepts the logic of a proposition put in cross-examination or is prepared to concede points that are seen to be correct; the extent to which a witness has conceived an opinion and is reluctant to re-examine it in the light of later evidence, or demonstrates a flexibility of mind which may involve changing or modifying opinions previously held; whether or not a witness is biased or lacks independence.

Copyright: The Academy of Experts

Appendix 2: Therapy Notes and the Law

Stephen Jakobi and Duncan Pratt

This article first appeared in *The Psychologist* (1992: 219–21), at an interesting stage in the development of the law, and no longer represents the current law, or practice. In particular, readers should be aware of the introduction of the *Civil Procedure Rules*, and the European Convention on Human Rights, together with significant case law development in disclosure of confidential documents.

The background to the case we describe was that the client had given birth to a handicapped child, and subsequently issued proceedings for medical negligence concerning the birth. The practitioner was consulted some two years after the commencement of these legal proceedings and the presenting problem concerned the client's feelings towards the child. Medical negligence cases frequently last several years, and some three years after the commencement of the course of therapy the client's lawyers requested the practitioner to provide an expert report dealing with the client's mental condition. The practitioner prepared a report using the session notes compiled over the course of therapy for the use of the Court and the report was disclosed in the normal way to the lawyers for the Defendants. These lawyers sought access to the full session notes taken over the years of consultation and it was in these circumstances that the practitioner sought legal advice.

As far as we could discover, there was no case dealing with psychotherapists' notes. However, there is a wealth of authority dealing with the extent to which the records of doctors and hospitals must be disclosed and although we have considered various particular features of the notes which might differ from ordinary doctors' records, the conclusion we have reached and the advice given was that psychotherapy records will not be treated any differently from other medical records. In any civil action where either party has documents in their possession or control or within their power, the basic rule is that if they are 'relevant' they must be disclosed to the other side and are useable in Court. This rule is subject to exceptions, discussed later. We consider that a psychotherapist's notes of sessions may be relevant if there is an issue in the case concerning the client's mental condition either at the time of trial or as it was in the past. Therefore, as in the present case, because the notes were relied upon by the practitioner who prepared her report, they are relevant.

Distinguishing from medical notes

There are a number of specific points of distinction from normal medical records which we now examine. There may be other specific points of distinction that occur to the reader.

A.—*The notes do not consist of clinical observations at the time of the interview but a record of historical events in the eyes of the patient.*

We considered them not distinguishable from conventional medical records in dealing with the history of the patient.

B.—*They are entirely hearsay.*

The hearsay rule in law is that an assertion made by someone other than the person who is giving evidence is not admissible. In evidence about events and words uttered, it should be evidence by persons present at those events and the person uttering the words should give the evidence. Insofar as the session notes describe events of which the compiler was not present, they may be hearsay, but Parliament has provided machinery to enable them to be admitted in evidence nevertheless. It must also be observed that the client's observations are not being used to show the truth of what she said, but to show what she believed at the time the record was being made.

C.—*That since these notes are records of transitory states of mind, different sessions may conflict in relating to the same historical event and that the records were feelings about historical events rather than descriptions of them.*

Again it is the client's state of mind with which the record is concerned and not the accuracy of the description of events. We note that there may be great differences in clinical approach and the methodology of individual psychotherapists and psychiatrists, but the records of interviews made by psychiatrists, which to some extent contain similarly subjective accounts of the patient and reflect transitory states of mind are nevertheless liable in principle to be disclosed to the other side and used in litigation.

Privilege

There are a number of reasons for not disclosing relevant evidence. This is known to lawyers as privilege. Communications between a patient and medical adviser are not privileged, although they are always treated as documents of the most confidential type. By contrast, in the United States there is privilege for such documents in civil actions and some Commonwealth jurisdictions have also created a privilege for medical communications in civil proceedings. Unfortunately it is too late to change the English law by case decision and the Law Reform Committee has rejected statutory reform in this country.

There is of course another ground of privilege with which people are more familiar, being that relating to communications between lawyers and a third party, after litigation is contemplated or commenced and made with a view to the litigation or for the purpose of giving advice on it. It is also established law that this is so even when the document comes into existence for more than one purpose, e.g. the psychotherapist giving expert advice to a solicitor with regard to litigation, makes notes of a session for giving advice to the solicitor. Therefore communication between a psychotherapist and a solicitor to a party in actual contemplated litigation is likely to be privileged. Of course, once the report is prepared and relied upon in the litigation and served, the opposing parties are normally entitled not only to examination of the report, but to see the material – including records of consultation – on which it is based. We realised that the psychotherapist's session notes were not prepared in contemplation of the litigation and that was not its dominant purpose: they were prepared for therapeutic purposes and therefore were not privileged.

Unfortunately, English law does not regard confidentiality in itself as a head of privilege. Confidentiality of communication may however be relevant to a form of privilege called 'public interest privilege'.

Relevant evidence will be excluded on the grounds of public policy when it is available only in claims for personal injury (including psychiatric injury) and must be supported by an Affidavit describing the documents and showing that considered the inter-play of confidentiality and open justice: it was said 'the private promise of confidentiality must yield to the general public interest ... truth will out unless a more important public interest is served by protecting the information or identity of the informant from its disclosure in a court of law'. It is made in the context of extending public interest from matters affecting central government to matters affecting the conduct of effective investigations by agencies. The burden of establishing the justification for excluding evidence is on the person seeking to do so; in practice it is difficult. The argument that candour in compiling reports might be inhibited has been forcefully rejected by the Courts on several occasions and the nature of the confidential relationship relied upon in the 'candour' cases has parallels with the relationship between practitioner and client.

Compelling disclosure

The practical procedure for compelling the practitioner to disclose, even though the practitioner is not a party to the action, is to make the practitioner subject to a Court Order in one of two ways:

1. By a *Subpoena Duces Tecum*: this is a witness summons forcing the witness to turn up to Court on a specified date and bring the documents set out in the summons. If it is considered by the practitioner that there is no relevant evidence to give or the summons is oppressive, fishing or speculative, Court application may be made to set aside the summons.
2. An application to the High Court ordering disclosure of documents by a non party. This application is available only in claims for personal injury (including psychiatric injury) and must be supported by an Affidavit describing the documents and showing that they are relevant. It is important to note that an Order may be made on such other terms, if any, as the Court thinks just. The appropriate Act expressly says that the production may be confined to the applicant's legal advisers, or to those advisers and any medical or other professional adviser.

It is also important to note that whatever type of disclosure is being considered, the Court will not order disclosure if satisfied that disclosure is not necessary or not necessary at that stage. So there is a significant protection against abuse. Some examples of this are:

1. The party seeking disclosure can obtain equivalent information for its purposes elsewhere without obtaining access to the documents.
2. The party seeking disclosure cannot sufficiently identify the issues to which the documents are said to be relevant.
3. The party seeking discovery against a practitioner is not proposing to obtain an expert opinion of its own (using those materials), but appears to want to have them in order to make the best use that they can of them in cross examination perhaps as to credit.
4. Bearing no relevance to an issue, the records cannot really affect the determination of the issue.

It is also sometimes said that a Judge has the discretion to exclude otherwise relevant and admissible evidence as part of his/her function to control the proper conduct of the trial. There is doubt that this power even exists. However, a former Chief Justice gave the following guidance:

'If a doctor giving evidence in court is asked a question which he finds embarrassing because it involves him talking about things which he would normally regard as confidential, he can seek the protection of the Judge and ask the Judge if it is necessary for him to answer. The Judge ... can ... tell the doctor he need not answer the question. Whether or not the Judge would take that line, of course depends on the importance of the potential answer to the issues being tried.' (Assumption of male doctor in the original.)

Another possible factor in the Judge's decision would be likely to be the degree of harm done to the patient (over and above the mere breach of confidence) in relation to the importance of the answer to an issue. Thus if the answer to a question would involve revealing that the patient had experienced intense feelings of hatred towards his mother, of which she was unaware, present in court, and the feeling had no real connection with the matters being investigated in the trial, a psychotherapist might wish to seek the Judge's assistance.

The conclusion is perfectly clear: whenever a patient is involved in litigation in which his or her mental condition, whatever the causes of that condition, are in issue, the psychotherapist's notes and records are liable to be ordered to be disclosed to the opposite party.

Taking precautions

There may be a number of safeguards which can be adopted.

1. A psychotherapist is entitled to regard the request of the client's lawyer for a report to be prepared as sufficient authority from the client to do so. But whenever there is a request for a report to be prepared for use at a trial, it would be wise for practitioners to satisfy themselves not only that their patients consent to the disclosure of the report (which may include sensitive information) to the opposite party, but also that their patients understand that may lead to a requirement to disclose the practitioners' records, including notes of therapy sessions.
2. If practitioners who have prepared reports for use in litigation are subsequently met with a request for disclosure of their notes, they should be refused unless (a) the patient consents or (b) the Court orders disclosure.
3. Since any arguable privilege and right to confidentiality is, in law, that of the patient, a consent from the patient is not only an authority to disclose, but a Defence to subsequent allegations of breach of confidence.
4. Exceptionally, there may be cases where the practitioner is of the view that disclosure would be likely to cause serious harm to the patient: a reasonably robust approach to this is necessary since in one sense any disclosure is likely to prove something of a trial to the patient, which is why we consider this to be an exceptional circumstance. If so: (a) The practitioner should inform the client's solicitor in terms which enable adequate explanation to be made to the party requesting disclosure. (b) The requesting party should be asked, through

the client's solicitor, to identify the issue to which the disclosure is relevant and to state what arrangements have been made for the notes to be examined by a suitably qualified expert, or if not, for what purpose disclosure is required and/or (if it is thought that the feared harm might be avoided or minimised in this way) to invite the requesting party to agree to limit disclosure to the relevant expert, or the expert and legal advisers. Then the requesting party should be asked to consider whether the information can be obtained in some other way or to consider whether disclosure is necessary at this stage or could be deferred until after that party's expert has examined the patient and decided whether the expert really needs to see the notes and lastly, in any event, to undertake that the documents will be shown or referred to only by the parties and their legal and professional advisers and for the purpose only of the present proceedings.

The above suggestions are designed with an eye to the power of the Court to make Orders already referred to and it should be stressed that not all these enquiries will be appropriate in every case. The practitioner must look carefully at the facts of the particular case and in cases of doubt will be well advised to consult his/her professional defence society.

5. In a case of feared harm to the patient, if the requesting party shows a bona fide issue to which the information in the notes is potentially relevant, but does not propose to instruct its own expert, consideration should be given to asking the Court to impose such a limitation.
6. If harm is reasonably anticipated even with the limitation on disclosure, then consideration should be given to resisting disclosure on the grounds that disclosure is not necessary. If limitations on disclosure have been agreed or ordered by the Court, these limitations will cease to have effect once the documents are read out or referred to in open Court. This should be borne in mind in discussing matters with a patient's lawyers.

Once again the experience of Courts in dealing with disclosure of medical records is now so long established and commonplace that practitioners will find that limitations will be only imposed for good reason and in a small minority of cases. It therefore follows that privilege could only be argued on very exceptional facts which have application beyond the interests of the particular patient to the interests of the public at large. What we have said so far governs the situation where your patient is in a dispute with another person, or where your patient's mental condition is at issue. But as between you and your patient, the law has always recognised a duty of confidentiality, and there are two recent cases in which respectively a patient and a health authority brought actions for breach of confidence and they illustrate the balance between confidentiality and conflicting public interest. In one case a health authority sought to restrain a newspaper from using or publishing confidential information, which was the property of the health authority and had been supplied to the newspaper by its employee in breach of confidence, concerning two practising doctors who were being treated by the authority for Aids. It was held that the public interest in preserving the confidentiality of hospital records identifying actual or potential Aids sufferers outweighed the public interest in the freedom of the press to publish, and that disclosure of names was not necessary in support of any public interest in discussion of the issue.

The other case was that of a patient detained at a secure mental hospital as a potential danger to public safety who sought damages against a psychiatrist who had disclosed a report on him to his treating hospital and to the Home Secretary. The defendant here was not a treating psychiatrist and had examined the patient for the purpose of preparing a report in support of his application to the Mental Health Review Tribunal with a view to release. The report was so adverse that the application was withdrawn. Nevertheless the psychiatrist took the view that those charged with his management and the Home Secretary should see copies. It was held that the balance between public interest and disclosure and the public interest in the duty of confidentiality came down decisively in favour of disclosure.

We can only repeat that where your patient is engaged in litigation, a psychotherapist's session notes can be protected from disclosure and use in the proceedings only in the most exceptional of circumstances.

Legal references

W v Egdell and Others (1989) *The Independent*, 10 November
X *v* Y [1988] 3 WLR 776, [1988] All ER 648

This article was originally published in *The Psychologist* (1992) pp. 219–21.
Copyright: British Psychological Society, reprinted with permission.

Appendix 3: Relevant Organisations

Insurance for therapists

H & L Balen & Co
33 Graham Road
Great Malvern
Worcestershire
WR14 2HU
01684 893 006
01684 893 416 (Fax)

Psychologists' Protection
  Society
Standalane House
Kincardine
Alloa
Clackmannanshire
FK10 4NX
01259 730 785

Smithson Mason Ltd
SMG House
31 Clarendon Road
Leeds
LS2 9PA
0113 294 4000
0113 294 4100 (Fax)

Official organisations

Criminal Injuries
  Compensation Authority
North of UK:
Tay House
300 Bath Street
Glasgow
G2 4LN
0141 331 2287

South of UK:
Morley House
26–30 Holborn Viaduct
London
EC1A 2JQ
020 7482 6800
www.cica.gov.uk

Crown Prosecution
  Service
50 Ludgate Hill
London
EC4M 7EX
020 7796 8000
www.cps.gov.uk

Data Protection Registrar
Wycliffe House
Water Lane
Wilmslow
Cheshire
SK9 5AF
01625 545 745 (Enquiries)
01625 535 711 (Admin)
www.dataprotection.gov.uk

Home Office
50 Queen Anne's Gate
London
SW1H 9AT
020 7273 4000
www.homeoffice.gov.uk

Health Service Ombudsman
Church House
Great Smith Street
London
SW1P 3BW
020 7276 3000

Law Commission
Conquest House
37–38 John Street
Theobalds Road
London
WC1N 2BQ
020 7453 1220
www.open.gov.uk/lawcomm

Law Society
113 Chancery Lane
London
WC2A 1PL
020 7242 1222
www.lawsociety.org.uk

Legal Aid Board
85 Grays Inn Road
London
WC1X 8TX
020 7813 1000
www.legalservices.gov.uk

Lord Chancellor's Department
Selbourne House
54–60 Victoria Street
London
SW1E 6QW
020 7210 0618
020 7210 0725 (Fax)
www.lcd.gov.uk

Mental Health Act
  Commission
Floor 3
Maid Marian House
56 Houndsgate
Nottingham
NG1 6BG
0115 943 7100
www.mhac.trent.nhs.uk

Secretary, European
  Court of Human Rights
Council of Europe
F-67075
Strasbourg-Cedex
FRANCE
www.echr.coe.int

Therapists' organisations

British Association for
  Counselling and
  Psychotherapy
1 Regent Place
Rugby
Warwickshire
CV21 2PJ
0870 443 5252
www.bacp.co.uk

British Confederation of
  Psychotherapists
37a Mapesbury Road
London
NW2 4HJ
020 8830 5173
www.bcp.org.uk

British Psychological Society
St Andrew's House
48 Princess Road East
Leicester
LE1 7DR
01162 549 568
www.bps.org.uk

General Medical Council
44 Hallam Street
London
W1N 6AE
020 7580 7642
www.gmc-uk.org

Independent Practitioners'
  Network (IPNOSIS)
The Alexander Group
PO Box 19
Llandysul
Ceredigion
SA44 4YE
01545 560 402
ipnosis@aol.com

Royal College of Psychiatrists
17 Belgrave Square
London
SW1X 8PG

020 7235 2351
020 7245 1231 (Fax)
www.rcpsych.ac.uk

United Kingdom Council for
  Psychotherapy
167–169 Great Portland Street
London
W1W 5PF
020 7436 3002
www.ukcp.org.uk
www.psychotherapy.org.uk

Advocacy or consumer support organisations

Academy of Experts
2 South Square
Grays Inn
London
WC1R 5HP
020 7637 0333
020 7637 1893 (Fax)
www.academy-experts.org

Association of Child
  Abuse Lawyers
PO Box 466
Chorleywood
Rickmansworth
Hertfordshire
WD3 5LG
01923 286 888
www.childabuselawyers.com

British False Memory Society
Bradford-on-Avon
Wiltshire
BA15 1NF
01225 868 682
01225 862 251 (Fax)
www.bfms.org.uk

Children's Legal Centre
University of Essex
Wivenhoe Park
Colchester
Essex
CO4 3SQ

01206 874 416 (Office)
01206 873 820 (Advice Line)
www2.essex.ac.uk/clc

Citizen Advocacy Alliance
Douglas House
26 Sutton Court Road
Sutton
Surrey
SM1 4SY
020 8643 7111

Consumers' Association
(Publishers of *Which?*)
2 Marylebone Road
London
NW1 4DF
020 7830 6000

Freedom to Care
(Whistleblowers)
PO Box 125
West Molesey
Surrey
KT8 1YE
020 8224 1022

Immunity Legal Centre
(HIV+/AIDS)
1st Floor
32–38 Osnaburgh Street
London
NW1 3ND
020 7388 6776

Inquest (Campaign on
Coroners' Courts)
Ground Floor
Alexandra National House
330 Seven Sisters Road
Finsbury Park
London
N4 2PJ
020 8802 7430
www.inquest.org.uk

Institute of Mental Health
  Law (Training)
Murrayfield House
The King's Gap
Hoylake
Wirral

L47 1HE
0151 632 4115
0151 632 0090 (Fax)

Law Centres Federation
Duchess House
Warren Street
London
W1P 5LR
020 7387 8570
www.lawcentres.org.uk

Legal Action Group
242–244 Pentonville Road
London
N1 9UN
020 7833 2931

MIND (National Association
for Mental Health)
Granta House
15/19 Broadway
Stratford
London
E15 4BQ
020 8519 2122 (Office)
020 8522 1725 (Fax)
www.mind.org.uk

National Consumer Council
20 Grosvenor Gardens
London
SW1W 0DH
020 7730 3469
020 7730 0191 (Fax)
www.ncc.org.uk

National Youth Advisory
Service
1 Downham Road South
Heswall
Wirrall
LT 60 5RG
0151 342 7852

POPAN (Prevention of
Professional Abuse Network)
1 Wyvil Court
Wyvil Road
London
SW8 2TG
020 7622 6334

020 7622 9788 (Fax)
www.popan.org.uk

Public Law Project (Support for
Judicial Review procedures)
Birkbeck College
14 Bloomsbury Square
London
WC1A 2LP
020 7269 0570
www.publiclawproject.org.uk

Refugee Legal Centre
Sussex House
39–45 Bermondsey Street
London
SE1 3XF
020 7827 9090

Rights of Women (Legal
advice on domestic violence)
52–54 Featherstone Street
London
EC1Y 8RT
020 7251 6577

Survivors Speak Out (Mental
Health Survivors)
34 Osnaburgh Street
London
NW1 3ND
020 7916 5472
020 7916 5473 (Fax)

United Kingdom Advocacy
Network (Mental health
survivors)
Suite 417
Premier House
14 Cross Burgess Street
Sheffield
S1 2HG
01142 753 131

VOICE-UK (Support to carers
of victims with learning
disabilities)
Room B.11
College Business Centre
Uttoxeter New Road
Derby

DE22 3WZ
01332 202 555
www.voiceuk.clara.net

Witness Support Programme
  Victim Support
Cranmer House
39 Brixton Road
London
SW9 6DZ
020 7735 9166
020 7582 5712 (Fax)
www.victimsupport.org.uk

**Complaints concerning
legal representation**

General Council of the Bar
  (Barristers)
3 Bedford Row
London
W1CR 4DB
020 7242 0082

Legal Services Ombudsman
3rd floor
Sunlight House
Quay Street
Manchester
M3 3JZ
0161 839 7262
www.olso.org

Office for the Supervision of
  Solicitors
Victoria Court
8 Dormer Place
Royal Leamington Spa
Warwickshire
CV32 5AE
01926 820 082

Mediation

Advisory, Conciliation and
  Arbitration Service
Brandon House
180 Borough High Street

London
SE1 1LW
020 7210 3613
www.acas.org.uk

Centre for Effective Dispute
  Resolution
Exchange Tower
1 Harbour Exchange Square
London
E14 9GB
020 7536 6000
www.cedr.co.uk

Divorce Conciliation and
  Advisory Service
38 Ebury Street
London
SW1 0LU
020 7730 2422

Mediation UK (Alternative
  dispute resolution)
82a Gloucester Road
Bishopston
Bristol
BS7 8BN
011 7904 6661

National Family Mediation
  Charity Base
50 Westminster Bridge Road
London
SE1 7QY
020 7721 7658

Family Mediators'
  Association
  The Old House
Rectory Gardens
Henbury
Bristol
BS10 7AQ
011 7950 0140

The Cambridge Family and
  Divorce Centre
162 Tenison Road
Cambridge
CB1 2DP
01233 460 136

Legal References

Table of Cases (UK)

AG v Guardian Newspapers No.2 [1988] 2 All ER 545 .... 97, 125
Bolam v Friern HMC [1957] 1 WLR 835, 2 All ER 118 ....
.... 28, 61–2, 95, 155
Bolitho v City and Hackney HA [1997] 3 WLR 1151, 4 All ER 771 ....
.... 62
Clarkson v Gilbert and Others (2000) CA TLR 4/7/00 167
Compagnie Financière du Pacifique v Peruvian Guano Co. (1882) 11 QBD 55
.... 8
Gillick v West Norfolk and Wisbech Area Health Authority [1986] AC.112
.... 3, 97
Leach v Chief Constable of Gloucestershire Constabulary [1999] 1 All ER 215
.... 117
Lord Advocate v The Scotsman Publications Ltd [1989] SLT 705, HL ....
.... 123
Loveday v Renton [1990] 1 Med LR 177 174
Maynard v West Midlands RHA [1984] 1 WLR 634 155
Phelps v Hillingdon LBC [1997] 3 FCR 621 .... 61, 155
Prince Albert v Strange (1849) 2 De Gex & Sm. 652 (on appeal) 1 Mac r
  G 25 124
R v Liaqat Hussain (1996) Reading Crown Court T960220 8
R v Turner [1975] AC QB 834 .... 59, 64
Re R (A Minor: Expert's Evidence (Note)) [1991] 1 FLR 291 64
Seyfang v GD Searle [1973] QB 148 68
The Ikarian Reefer [1993] 2 Lloyds Rep 68 62–3
W v Egdell and Others (1989) The Independent, 10 November; [1990]
  Ch 359; [1990] 1 All ER 835 .... 130, 181
Werner v Landau (1961) TLR 8/3/1961, 23/11/1961, Sol Jo (1961) 105, 1008
.... 43, 47, 61, 97, 155
X v Y [1988] 3 WLR 776, [1988] 2 All ER 648 .... 128, 181

Table of Cases (US)

Jaffee v Redmond, 116 S. Ct. 1923 (1996) 139
Peck v Counseling Service of Addison County Inc., (Vt 1985) 499 A. 2d 422
.... 156

Ramona v Isabella, Rose, M.D. and Western Medical Center, Anaheim (1994)
  C61898 California Supreme Court Napa County 98, 144, 154–6
Tarasoff v Regents of the University of California 118 Cal. Rptr. 129, 135 (Sup.
  Ct. Cal. 1974); 113 Cal. Rptr 14, 551 P. 2d 334 (Sup. Ct. Cal. 1976)
  .... 130, 156

Table of Cases (European Court)

MS v Sweden (1999) 28 EHRR 313 136
Z v Finland (1998) 25 EHRR 371 136

Table of Statutes (UK)

Access to Health Records Act 1990 .... 49, 99
Adoption Act 1976 45
Children Act 1989 .... 64–6, 132–3
Chiropractors Act 1994 86
Crime and Disorder Act 1998 119
Criminal Justice Act 1991 66
Data Protection Act 1984 .... 45, 48–9
Data Protection Act 1998 .... 45–55, 99, 134–5, 139
Drug Trafficking Act 1994 133
Freedom of Information Act 2000 47
Health Act 1999 .... 4, 84–5
Human Rights Act 1998 .... 5, 47, 100–1, 135–6, 164–71
Limitation Act 1980 98
Osteopaths Act 1993 86
Professions Supplementary to Medicine Act 1960 49
Protection from Harassment Act 1997 30
Sexual Offences Act 1956 94
Supply of Goods & Services Act 1982 27
Terrorism Act 2000 33–4
Youth Justice and Criminal Evidence Act 1999 .... 111, 118

Index

(For individual legal cases and Acts of
Parliament, refer to Table of Cases
and Statutes)

abuse, 9, 60, 83, 91, 113, 143–63
   abusive therapy, 4, 34–44, 78
   memories, 152
   see also survivors; victims
Academy of Experts, 66
   Model Report, 172–4
access to records, 7
   by clients, 45–55, 83, 99, 141
   by courts, 1, 6, 8, 16–19, 138,
      157–9, 175–81
   by police, 137
Accuracy About Abuse, 145, 158
AIDS, 181
Alderdice, Lord, 85
American Counseling Association, 139
American Trial Lawyers' Association, 154
assault, 30, 98
   indecent, 93
   sexual, 137
Association of Child Abuse Lawyers, 100
audiotapes, 16–8, 53
autonomy, 78, 82–3, 131, 150–7, 156

barrister, 2, 5, 16–18, 21, 68, 111,
   116, 167
battery, 30
Bean-Bayog, Margaret, 51
Bell-Boulé, Annabell, 9, 87–103
Bollas, Christopher, 2, 7
Bond, Tim, 5–6, 122–42
boundaries, 4–5, 10, 83, 122
Bourne, Ian, 49
British Acupuncture Council, 77
British Association for Counselling and
   Psychotherapy (BACP), 15–19, 46,
   76, 108, 123, 133, 145, 158; see also
   Codes of Ethics and Practice; Ethical
   Framework
British Confederation of Psychotherapists
   (BCP), 76, 158, 170

British False Memory Society, 145,
   157, 159
British Psycho-Analytical
   Society, 23
British Psychological Society (BPS),
   5, 8, 15–19, 145, 157, 167,
   169, 175, 181
Brooks, Duwayne, 113
Butler Sloss, L.J., 65

Care Assist, 17, 19
case law, 1, 4, 54, 155, 168, 175; see also
   Table of Cases for individual
   references
causation, 28
Centre for Stress Management, 15
child abuse, 97, 132–3, 147–8
   compensation, 151
   reporting, 150
   sexual abuse, 92, 146
   sexual abuse, definition of, 1, 6, 89,
      95–6, 143, 148
   see also child protection
child care proceedings, 63
child protection, 9, 132–3, 149; see also
   child abuse
children, 60, 63, 66, 92–4, 97, 110–12,
   116, 132, 137
   as witness, 110–12
civil law, 7
   action, 98
   court, 30
   justice system, 61, 88
   proceedings, 10, 57, 148
Civil Procedure Rules (The White Book), 8,
   61–2, 175
Clarkson, Petruska, 167
Cleveland Report, 65–6, 148
client, 1, 4–10, 15–17, 24–30, 46, 51–3,
   58, 66, 69, 79–80, 88–90, 95–103,
   115, 122–3, 126, 137–41, 150, 157,
   164; see also access to records;
   complaints

Codes of Ethics and Practice, 22, 77, 91, 95–6, 101, 165, 168–9
  BACP, 15, 47
  BPS, 15
  UKCP, 90
  see also Ethical Framework
common law *see* law
Community Mental Health Team, 42
compensation, 7, 28, 79, 105, 116, 151–2; *see also* damages
complaints, 53, 88, 105, 167–8
  procedures, 5, 26–8, 32, 165
  to professional association, 26, 46, 77
Complementary and Alternative Medicine (CAM), 4, 34, 37, 42, 74–86
confidence, 5, 31, 96, 123
  law of, 122–42
  see also confidentiality
confidentiality, 2, 3, 5, 16–19, 46, 58, 68, 75, 83, 96–7, 108, 117, 169, 177–80
  breach of, 3, 101, 128, 179
  law of, 122–42
  limits to, 16, 25, 32, 169
consent, 6, 29–30, 44, 51, 54–5, 75, 82, 127–31, 134–41, 179
  explicit, 51–2, 55, 100, 127, 135
  informed, 148, 157
  patient/client, 179
  see also contract
contract, 2–5, 16, 24, 30–1, 95, 101, 125–7, 134, 167
  breach of, 27
  terms, 24–7, 33
  see also consent
convictions, 104, 137
counselling *see* therapy
counsellor *see* therapist
court, 2, 5, 7, 9, 16–18, 23, 47, 57, 66, 79, 97, 104–7, 112, 122–5, 137, 147, 165, 177
  access to records, 8, 16–18, 21–3, 175–81
  appearing in, 57–60
  contempt of, 7, 17, 21
  order, 8, 177, 180
  report, 1–3, 10, 57–71, 181
Court
  County, 134
  Crown, 8
  Family, 60, 63, 68, 137–8
  High, 21, 63, 134, 167, 177

Court, *cont.*
  Magistrate's, 69
  Small Claims, 29
Cresswell, J., 62
crime, 92, 104–5, 131, 135–7
Criminal Injuries Compensation Authority, 67, 98, 152
criminal law, 30, 101
  legal system, 1, 3, 9, 104–19
  offence, 76, 92, 94, 98, 107, 112, 133, 138, 165, 169
  proceedings, 62, 64–5
  prosecution, 7, 106–7, 137
Cristofoli, Gideon, 4, 24–33
cross-examination, 7, 66, 105, 177
Crown Prosecution Service, 9, 98, 111–12, 116, 137, 154

damage, 43, 94
damages, 27, 29, 97, 128, 137, 154–5
  psychiatric illness, 28
  see also compensation
data protection, 1, 3, 5, 32, 134–5
  data subject, 45, 48, 134–5
  data user, 47
  law of, 45–56, 134–5
Data Protection Registrar, 135; *see also* Information Commissioner
De Tocqueville, Alexis, 155
defamation, 157, 169
Department of Health, 116
Diagnostic and Statistical Manual of Mental Disorders (DSM), 89
disability, 118
disclosure, 8, 53, 83, 96–100, 125, 136–40, 150, 159, 175, 177–81
  by therapist, 8, 75, 127–43, 140, 179
discovery, 32, 51, 53, 157
discrimination, 165
Dissociative Identity Disorder, 158
Drama Triangle, 144, 148–50, 154
drug trafficking, 133
dual relationships, 42–3
duty of care, 5, 9, 28, 31, 94–5, 117
  breach of, 28, 59, 94, 98

Eire *see* law and legal system, Eire
Elliott, Michelle, 92
Emergency Protection Order, 69
Employee Assistance Programme, 127

employment, 3, 95
self-employment, 4
Employment Tribunal, 61
Ethical Framework (BACP), 46, 90–1
ethics, 6, 23, 75, 81–2, 88–97, 116, 123,
133, 144, 148–51, 167; *see also* Codes
of Ethics and Practice; Ethical
Framework
ethnic minority, 47
European Convention on Human Rights,
100, 135, 164, 175
European Court of Human Rights, 45, 136
European Economic Area, 49
European Union, 164
Directive, 45, 51
evidence, 9–10, 17, 57–63, 67–8, 111,
115–16, 124, 137, 146, 177–8
examination-in-chief, 7, 69
expert witness, 10, 57–62, 69, 154–6, 180
definition, 59, 61
evidence, 60, 63–4, 156
opinion, 59, 65, 180
report, 175–7

false memories, 1, 3, 6, 143–63
False Memory Syndrome Foundation, 145,
154, 156
Freud, Sigmund, 143, 147
Freyd, Peter, 145

Gaskin, Graham, 45
General Medical Council (GMC), 52
Gillick principle, 3; *see also* Table of Cases
government, 4, 122, 177
group therapy, 36, 38

harassment, 30, 61, 113
Hayman, Dr Anne, 2, 7–8, 21–3,138
Health Authority, 132, 180
Health and Safety Executive, 117
Health Service Commissioner, 88
HIV, 128
Home Office, 94, 99, 109, 116
Home Secretary, 52, 181
hospital, 100
human rights, 1, 3, 5, 124
law, 135–6, 164–71

Information Commissioner, 47–53, 135;
see also Data Protection Registrar
informed consent *see* consent

injunction, 30, 97
injury, psychiatric, 28
insurance, 29, 32, 77, 84, 91, 101, 131,
155, 169
International Psychoanalytic
Association, 23
Ireland *see* law and legal system, Eire
Isabella, Marche, 155

jail sentence, 7
Jakobi, Stephen, 8, 175–81
Jenkins, Peter, 1–10, 45–56, 135, 143–63
judge, 4, 16, 21–2, 59, 70, 105, 111, 115,
138, 177–9
Judicial Review, 166–8
jurors, 9, 104, 113–14, 119
jury, 4, 104–19

Keter, Vincent, 5, 164–71
Kidscape, 92

Lancet, 7, 23
law
common law, 5, 75–6, 84, 124, 130, 164
outline, 2–3, 5, 9, 48, 122–3
private law, 66
public law, 57, 66
law and legal system
Eire, 122
England, 2, 94, 104, 122–3, 154, 177
Northern Ireland, 123, 132
Scotland, 3, 122–3
United Kingdom, 133, 136, 144
United States, 22, 50–1, 139–40, 144,
154–55, 176
Wales, 2, 94, 104, 122, 154
see also civil law; confidentiality;
consent; contract; criminal law;
data protection; human rights;
legislation; statute
Law Commission, 115, 128
Lawrence, Stephen, 113, 118
lawyer, 2, 9–10, 57, 87–8, 105, 116, 136–8,
156, 164, 167, 175–9
learning difficulties, 113
legal action, 79, 99
legal advice, 32, 90, 92, 134, 175, 177
Legal Aid, 99
legal opinion, 4
legal proceedings, 31, 148
process, 10

Legal Services Commission, 57
legislation, 5, 45, 47, 50, 94, 123, 132–3,
    136; see also Table of Statutes
liability
    employers, 31
    supervisor, 31
    therapist, 18, 25–6, 31, 51
    vicarious, 31, 95, 101
litigants, 8, 57, 87
litigation, 1–6, 33–3, 62, 79, 86–9, 101,
    137–9, 155–7, 176–81
    United States, 6, 87–8, 137, 151
Litton, Roger, 18–19
local authorities, 99–100, 132, 148
    social services department, 108

McMahon, Gladeana, 46, 50
Macpherson Inquiry, 118
malpractice, 3–4, 22 ,30, 51, 155; see also
    negligence
'Mary', 15–20
medicine, 5, 55, 74–5, 125
Medicine, Complementary and
    Alternative (CAM), 1, 74–86
Memorandum of Good Practice, 65–6
Mental Health Review Tribunal, 181
mental illness, 115
Metanoia, 167
Miller, Ian, 50
Multiple Personality Disorder see
    Dissociative Identity Disorder
Murray, Sandy, 101

National Health Service, 31, 54,
    88, 100, 136
natural justice, 169
negligence, 3–4, 7–9, 27–30, 94,
    98, 154–9
    medical, 10, 59–62, 87–8, 175
    see also malpractice
Northern Ireland see law and legal system,
    Northern Ireland
notes see records

offence, 104
offer into court, 44
Orr, Marjorie, 145

Palmer, Stephen, 8, 15–20
paradoxical injunction, 83
parent, 65, 92, 94, 148, 153

parental responsibility, 138
Parker, L.J., 59
Parliament, 118, 123, 134, 164, 176
patient, 7, 21–3, 34, 74–84, 168–9,
    179–80
Patient's Charter, 88
personal data, 5, 51–5, 134
    sensitive, 51
personal injury, 10, 26–30, 33, 59–66, 98,
    154, 177–80
police, 16, 104–19, 137, 158
Pollecoff, Philip, 9, 57–71
post-traumatic stress disorder, 63, 91,
    113–17, 158
Power, Inge, 3, 34–44
Pratt, Duncan, 8, 175–81
precedent, 7
Prevention of Professional Abuse Network
    (POPAN), 4, 42, 168
private practice, 3, 29, 31, 36, 88, 91, 101,
    126, 136
privilege, 6, 21, 51, 176, 179
    definition, 177
    public interest privilege, 177
    therapeutic, 7–8
prosecution, private, 154; see also
    criminal law
psychiatrist, 22, 34–6, 43, 51, 63, 65, 98,
    130, 176
    legal action, 43, 181
psychiatry, 52
psychoanalysis, 23
psychoanalyst, 7, 21
psychologist, 58, 61, 156
    counselling, 49
Psychologist, 175, 181
Psychologist's Protection Society, 101
psychotherapist see therapist
Psychotherapists for Social
    Responsibility, 159
psychotherapy see therapy
Psychotherapy Bill, 85, 88–9
public authority, 100, 135–6, 164
public interest, 7, 96–7, 128–30,
    135, 177, 180
    immunity, 17–18

race, 113
racial origin, 51
racism, 113, 118
Ramona, Gary, 155

Ramona, Holly, 155
Rape Crisis, 107–9
recording, 5, 53, 55
record keeping, 5, 33, 45–56
records, 7–8, 16–18, 31–2, 54, 117,
    137–9, 175–9
  accessible, 50, 54
  computerised, 45, 55
  manual, 46–52, 55
  medical, 50, 53–4, 99, 108, 136, 175–6,
    179–81
  see also access to records; disclosure
recovered memories, 1, 6, 96, 98, 143–63
register, 84, 86, 165
regulation, 74–86
  self-, 4, 76, 85–6, 158, 165
  statutory, 1–4, 74–86, 158
reports see court, report
Roche, Très, 9, 87–103
Rose, MD, Richard, 155
Royal College of Psychiatrists, 43, 145

Scoggins, Mark, 18
Scotford, Roger, 145
Scotland see law and legal system,
    Scotland
Sedley, Mr Justice, 8, 45, 54
serious harm, 45, 54
settlement, 69
  out of court, 4, 43, 51
sexual abuse, 67, 83, 88, 97, 100, 143–63
  adult survivors, 2–3, 9, 91, 95–7
  definition, 92
  offences, 92–3, 106, 108
sexual contact, 147
Sherwood Psychotherapy Training
    Institute, 89, 92
Slade, Peter, 167
Smithson Mason, 16, 18
Social Services Department see
    local authorities
social work, 5, 45, 50–5, 143, 150
social worker, 69, 75, 140, 148
sodium amytal, 98
solicitor, 2, 4, 8–9, 19, 24, 30, 43, 51, 58,
    62, 64, 67–8, 99–100, 137, 169,
    177–9
stalking, 30
statute, 1, 5, 123–4, 164; see also Table of
    Statutes
Statutory Instrument, 50, 54

Stone, Julie, 4, 74–86
subpoena, 16, 21–3, 178
suicide, 35, 38, 42, 51, 127, 131
Sundelson, David, 2
supervision, 16, 26, 30, 53–4, 90, 92, 97,
    108–9, 116, 139
supervisors, 1, 83, 96, 101
survivors, 9, 88, 95, 148, 152–3, 156
  definition, 119

Tarasoff, Tatiana see Table of Cases
terrorism, 133
therapeutic relationship, 24, 32, 43–4, 52,
    78–80, 138, 150
therapist
  comparison with CAM, 79–86
  contractual duties, 24–33
  as data holder, 45–56, 122–42
  definition, 1, 45, 145
  dual relationship with client, 34–44
  duty of care, 28–31
  lack of privilege, 175–81
  presenting court report, 57–71
  subject of client litigation, 34–44
    97–8, 155–6
  supporting client in court, 15–20,
    99–100
  as witness, 15–23, 57–71
  see also expert witness; liability;
    negligence; records; witness
therapy
  and human rights, 164–71
  legal context of, 2–6, 86–103, 122–42
  in legal settings, 104–21
  pre-trial, 99, 107, 111–12, 116
  relationship with law, 5–10
  and sexual abuse, 87–102, 143–63
  see also confidentiality; negligence;
    records; regulation
third party, 16, 54, 134,
    150, 153–9
time limits, 47, 54
touch, 4, 29–30
training, 9–10, 43, 51, 75–7, 81–3, 90,
    106–8, 111, 116–18, 139, 167
Transactional Analysis, 6, 144
transference, 4, 7, 22, 39, 42–3, 97
  counter-, 51, 83, 96
traumatisation, 96
trial, 57,165
Trowell, Judith, 9

Underwager, Ralph, 145
United Kingdom *see* law and legal system, United Kingdom
United Kingdom Council for Psychotherapy (UKCP), 5, 76, 89, 145, 158, 167, 170
United States *see* law and legal system, United States

Victim Support, 108–9, 112
victimisation, secondary, 9, 104–6
victims, 2, 9, 104–19, 137, 143, 152–4, 158
video recording, 16, 53, 65
voluntary organisations, 15, 47, 107–9, 116, 136
vulnerable adult, 2, 9, 112

Wales *see* law and legal system, Wales
website, 101, 157

West, Fred, 9, 117
West, Rosemary, 9
Williams, Brian, 9, 104–21
witness, 2, 6, 9, 68, 99, 104–19, 137, 157, 178
  appearing as, 21–3, 68–70
  of fact, 59–60, 68
  professional, 10, 59
  statement, 57, 60
  summons, 7, 75, 178
  vulnerable, 112–13
  see also expert witness; subpoena
Witness Protection Scheme, 106–7
Woolf, Lord, 61

young people, 3
  rights, 123
  see also children